Simon Weston
moving on

Simon Weston
moving on

PORTRAIT

Visit the Portrait website!

· ·

PORTRAIT

Portrait publishes a wide range of non-fiction, including biography, history, science, music, popular culture and sport.

Visit our website to:

- read descriptions of our popular titles
- buy our books over the internet
- take advantage of our special offers
- enter our monthly competition
- learn more about your favourite Portrait authors

VISIT OUR WEBSITE AT: www.portraitbooks.com

Copyright © 2003 by Simon Weston

First published in 2003 by **Portrait**
an imprint of
Judy Piatkus (Publishers) Limited
5 Windmill Street
London W1T 2JA
e-mail: info@piatkus.co.uk

This edition published 2004

The moral right of the author has been asserted

A catalogue record for this book is available from the British Library

ISBN 0 7499 5020 X

Leo Marks quotation on page 83 reproduced by kind permission, from
The Life That I Have, by Leo Marks & Elena Gaussen Marks, Souvenir Press 1999.

Picture credits

All pictures from the author's collection except:

p. 2 (bottom) Derek Tamea; p. 3 (bottom) the *News of the World*; p. 4 (top)
Kenneth Bryant ; p. 6 (top left) Mike Farenden; p. 8 (top) Charles Green;
p. 8 (bottom) Malcolm Brinkworth/BBC Photo Library

Every effort has been made to identify and acknowledge copyright-holders of
photographic material. Any errors or omissions will be rectified in future edi-
tions, provided that written notification is made to the publisher.

This book has been printed on paper manufactured with respect for the
environment using wood from managed sustainable resources

Data manipulation by Phoenix Photosetting, Chatham, Kent

Printed and bound in Great Britain by Mackays of Chatham, Kent

To everyone who's helped to make it possible
for me to be who I am.

Acknowledgements

I would like to thank Jennifer Potter, more than anyone, for her role in helping me to write this book – for her time, for her patience and, most of all, for her wonderful sense of humour.

(Oh, aye – and my wife, Lucy, for the sandwiches, tea and coffee.)

Contents

Prologue

I'VE DONE SOME STUPID THINGS in my life but this must surely count as one of the worst. To jump out of a perfectly serviceable aircraft at 12,000 feet, when you could be sitting safely on the ground, takes some beating. It has scared the holy hell out of me for a long, long time – the fear of falling over the edge, into that terrible void that draws you ever downwards, the hard sudden stop at the end. Unfortunately for me I also believe that in life you've got to approach and conquer every fear you have, so the more frightened I am, the more important it is that I knock each fear on the head.

This explains how I found myself with a stomach full of butterflies pulling in to the Red Devils' car park one bright late-summer's morning. Despite all my trepidation, I was doing my best to remain calm. According to the forecast, there was only going to be a short weather window before the clouds came in again, and it might be several days before we could make another attempt at jumping out of the sky.

I'm not sure that prospect bothered me as much as it did all the other free-fall fanatics who were crawling out of the woodwork at news of a free plane going up. In fact for me it was probably good news, because if I'd had any longer to brood on what we were about to do there was every chance I wouldn't do it, I am that frightened of heights. But I had promised my filmmaker friend Malcolm Brinkworth I would jump and as Malcolm knows, I stick to my word, even when it means throwing myself out of a perfectly good aeroplane and hurtling down towards the ground. At least you know that when you reach terminal velocity, you can't get any faster, though when you reach that speed, you also realise it's an awful lot harder to stop.

On the drive down from Wales I listened to the radio and thought of Lucy, my wife, who had chosen to stay away with the children. James and Stuart would be getting ready for school, and baby Caitlin running rings around her mother. In fact I did everything I possibly could to avoid thinking about the moment when I would have to shuffle forwards to the gaping mouth of the aeroplane. 'God's open window' they call it, or something ridiculous like that. It might scare the hell out of me, but until I have actually got something to worry about, I'd much rather think of something else.

I deliberately hadn't told my mother about the jump as I didn't want to worry her. Now that she's in her sixties, I never tell her in advance about the stupid things I might be planning.

Along the way I stopped by the side of the road for a coffee and a hot dog. I couldn't face eating back at the house. Then I drove on down. The day looked like it was opening up to be really gorgeous, just a few wispy clouds in a bright blue sky.

I remember the conversation with Malcolm that had got me into this. We were making *Simon's Journey*, the fifth in a series of BBC documentaries about me from the moment I first arrived back in Britain from the Falklands, charred by burns across almost half my body and swearing blindly at what I took to be a news camera crew sniffing around for a freak show. (*'Piss off'* was the first thing I said to them, determined to reclaim some dignity.)

Right now Malcolm wanted an opening sequence for the new film, something strong and brave. In a moment of weakness, I had already floated the idea of a parachute jump, never thinking that Malcolm would take me up on the idea, but as usual he timed his approach just right.

'We could do it for charity,' he said in that calm, head-masterly voice of his, 'for Weston Spirit. I'd organise it. If we're going to do it, we might as well do it properly.'

'What does that mean?'

'We'd get the Red Devils involved.'

'What, get on a bloody plane and jump out? I don't want to do that. How high?'

'Oh, about 12,000 feet or so.'

'Eff off.'

'Okay, so you don't want to do it?'

'No. Hang about. When would it be?'

'We'd do it some time nice and warm, in the summer. Imagine you up there, conquering all your fears—'

I took a good few deep breaths. 'Yeah, all right. If I really have to. You're a bastard, Brinkworth. I really hate you.'

Malcolm was already waiting when I parked my car by the edge of the airfield, which had a huge hangar to the left, a runway to the right. Together we walked towards the control tower where the Red Devils have their crew room – the Red Freds as the Paras call them. At this point I was still feeling reasonably calm and collected.

Inside we chatted to the crew and had another coffee, then the man in charge said, 'Look, because of the weather, we've only got a short window. If you want to free-fall by yourself, we'll have to take you through a day's training, and the weather might not hold till tomorrow. But if you don't mind jumping in tandem you'll only need an hour's training and we can make the window today.'

'Let's do it in tandem,' I said, secretly quite happy that the weather was taking the decision away from me. While I was perfectly willing to jump out of the aircraft, at least doing it in tandem would save me from having to take responsibility for myself. All I would have to do was listen and follow instructions and, believe me, that was enough for my first time. As luck would have it, the weather closed in soon after, and we wouldn't have been able to film the following day anyway.

First they had to get me kitted out in one of their red jumpsuits. Finding one big enough was the first problem, and a leather helmet to fit, because I've got a head like a 14lb loaf. The guy who was jumping with me was slim, tall and handsome, dressed in black trousers and sweat-shirt and those fancy boots the Red Devils wear. He looked a million dollars in his jumpsuit, like a Hollywood movie star who gets all the best lines. Next to him I looked hideous, absolutely ridiculous, 10lb of crap stuck in a 6lb bag. I had this helmet sitting on the top of my head like a pimple, goggles, a suit that didn't fit and a pair of old trainers. Little and Large we were, and no prizes for guessing which one was me, my big beer belly stuffed uncomfortably into my zip suit, looking more like a weevil.

Then we went into the hangar for my hour's training. As we were jumping in tandem, it was more of a rehearsal really. I was even asked if I wanted to pack my own parachute. 'No thanks,' I said hurriedly. 'I'll leave that to the experts.'

The guy showed me how to cross my legs and arms to keep them out of the way, and explained how I had to push forward to the front of the door once we were up in the aircraft. He helped me into the harness that would clip me to him.

'How does it feel?' he asked.

'Snug fit.'

'If it starts to cut off the circulation, let me know.'

'I think you'll notice when I pass out.'

When we were clipped together, I could have counted the stitches in his appendix scar and I wasn't sure I wanted to be that closely attached to another guy.

As we headed outside, all these other parachute jumpers appeared from nowhere. 'It seems a shame to waste an empty plane,' one of them said to me. Those guys are absolutely barking. It's the cost of the plane that stops them jumping more often. But as we were paying, everyone else piled in too.

I got to talking with one of them as we approached the holding area. He was wearing plastic heel braces that went under the foot and up the back of his leg. So I asked him what had happened – I'm a fool like that. He told me he had drop foot and couldn't stiffen his ankles because he'd smashed them both in a free-fall jump out in Hong Kong, which had put a stop to his service career and everything else as he couldn't run or do anything much after that. And I thought, that's all I blooming need, this lunatic walking flat-footed out to the aircraft with me, and he still wants to jump. Most of the other guys had suffered horrible accidents too, which they told me about with the greatest delight. Even the chap I jumped with claimed that he'd had one near-miss.

As soon as we got inside the plane, packed together like sardines on the floor, all the other clowns settled down straight away, smiling, chatting away to each other, joking and laughing, absolutely comfortable with the fact that they were about to throw themselves into the atmosphere. I'm sitting with my back to the pilot, looking down the fuselage and thinking, they do this for fun? I'm sure they could smell how nervous I was, not to be too blunt about it.

My Red Fred has me firmly wedged between his legs. He hooks himself on to my back then pulls me towards him as tight as he can. We are clipped together in three or four places. Basically, if I'd had a boil on my backside he'd have felt it, or even just a tattoo.

You're like a snail with a shell. On the ground, you're in control because you've got free movement out in front. But the second you get into the plane, he's in charge because he can see everything and he's got this extra weight hanging out in front – in my case, a very big weight, let's be honest.

At a nod from the pilot, the other guys are clambering all over the place, eager to get out. Some are hanging on to those little handrails on the outside of the plane, jump-suits flapping against their bodies, before they all fall off together.

Then it's my turn.

You shuffle towards the door, a bit like a dog dragging its bum, feeling fairly sick. I've got the same feeling now, just remembering: extreme butterflies and a tingling in my arms from the elbow to the tips of my fingers. Just imagine. Your stomach is churning and you're not feeling good about this at all. You get to the door, where you're looking down at the clouds and at all the other guys who have jumped before you. You watch them fall away, hurtling into tiny specks as they arrange themselves into free-fall formations or whatever it is that skydivers do.

There's one guy still hanging on to the outside of the aircraft with a camera strapped to his head – just an ordinary video camera literally stuck on with masking tape, very Heath Robinson but it works. He's getting ready to film me falling out. I'm sitting by the door with my feet crossed underneath the plane, arms across my chest. I've got to sit like that with my head held back, balancing on the cheeks of my bum. I'm so scared at this point that the wind outside doesn't matter. The only wind that counts is my own, and I'm terrified.

Then the guy behind me falls forward and I don't have any choice. I fall forwards too, hands across my chest, feeling totally disabled. There's thick ribbing down the sides of my jumpsuit. With my damaged fingers, I can't grip it but I can just about hold on. I've got to keep my legs tucked underneath me in the free-fall position; I remember seeing it on TV.

The free-fall bit must count as one of the scariest things I have ever accomplished. There's this guy at my back screaming, '*Yeeeehaaa*' because it's the seven-millionth jump he's done in his life, for the British Army and the Paras. Then there's this other guy with the camera coming down close, yelling and waving at me, saying, 'Give us a yahoo,' and I'm thinking, no way, just get me down. Deploy the canopy and let's get down to earth, slowly and safely.

It takes maybe 45 seconds to fall 7,000 feet. We're hurtling towards the ground at this horrendous speed and my eyes are literally filling with fluid, tears of fear, I'm sure, and bulging so much I'm getting glass burn from my goggles as we fall. Yet the ground doesn't seem to be getting any closer, it just seems to be there.

At about 5,000 feet the guy at my back checks the altimeter on his wrist and pulls the cord which pops the canopy. The next thing you know, *whoosh*, you get lifted back as everything tightens. My guy loosens off the straps on his legs.

'You can do the same,' he says, 'it's much more comfortable.'

Not on your Nelly. I am staying as tightly strapped to him as I possibly can.

To show me how it all works he pulls one toggle, which turns the chute this way, then pulls another, which turns it that way. Then he says, 'See what happens when I do this,' and he collapses the chute. That makes me go, 'Aaaaargghhh.'

There's a set of toggles I can play with too, but I hadn't realised how much strength you needed to pull them down.

So that's the way it was. I'm not going to say it was the most enjoyable thing I have ever done, but it was certainly exhilarating, unreal. Even after your chute has opened, it still takes quite a long time to come down. Only when you get closer to earth do you get any sense of depth or perspective, as buildings start to appear like a pop-up book. But the closer you get to the ground, the faster it comes up to meet you. Your backside is doing half a crown, sixpence, or it was with me.

We were gliding this way and that.

'Can you land into the wind?' he asked.

There were gusts coming from every which way. We found the wind and came into land.

'Remember to stand up when I tell you to.'

My grandfather always said it's not the fall that kills you, it's the sudden stop at the end. But actually, coming in to land is a lot easier than you think. The last couple of feet you come in at an angle. Then you go into a little walk, or a run if you have to. It's almost like gliding in, so the ground isn't breaking your fall. But I lost my footing as we touched the ground and the other guy went down on one knee. It was only a stumble really. It's not as if we landed in a heap.

'Look at that,' he said as he picked himself up. He was really miffed. 'There's bloody dirt on my trousers. I'll have to wash those now.'

'Oh, sorry,' I said. To my mind it was an excellent landing, one we could walk away from. I thought, I've just risked my life and landed safely and all you can think about is a bit of dirt on your trousers. It wasn't even ingrained dirt. He could easily brush it off.

But he soon got over it. 'Very good, easy,' he said. 'What d'you think?'

'Unreal,' was all I could say.

'Would you do it again?'

'I would, yeah,' I said, determined to show some bravado. 'I'm not sure how *soon* I would do it again, and someone would have to donate buckets of bunce to tempt me up there again, but yes, count me in. Shame the weather's no good,' I added, in case anyone thought to take me at my word.

Once we'd got unclipped from each other, we went back for the debrief, up some stairs to the crew room overlooking the runway.

Almost as soon as we had finished, the weather closed in and it started to rain. I felt fine chatting to the guys who had been up in the plane with us, the Paras and all the others. I climbed out of my fetching skin-tight jumpsuit. The television presenter Anneka Rice used to wear them too. Hers weren't always very flattering but my suit was a good deal worse. Does this suit make me look fat?

Well, no, not exactly, you look like a fat swine because that's how you are. I should have been in a *Carry On* sketch. We had a cup of coffee and watched some instant film footage on the telly in the crew room. Then Malcolm said, 'Right, that's it then. We're off.'

So we shook hands with everyone and went outside. For me, the end of each day's filming always comes as a bit of an anticlimax, partly because it's ages before you see the end product. What happens now, I wonder, where are the party poppers? It was only when I got back to the car that I had a little tremble. I'd done it. I'd survived. There are people who do far, far more dangerous things, but I had just faced up to one of my biggest fears. Heights terrify me and they always have. It's got even worse since my hands were damaged and I know that I can't hang on.

Making the jump in tandem had made it vastly easier for me. I had put my trust in my companion. That guy was skilled. He had brought us down just where he wanted. Of course, there's always an unknown element to any danger sport. That's what makes it what it is. But as we came down, I experienced this massive adrenalin rush. It was fantastic. It was exhilarating. I had faced my worst fears and they hadn't paralysed me.

And that, really, has been the story of my life these past 20 years. I almost died when my troop ship, the *Sir Galahad*, was bombed in the Falklands. I had to face up to being a different person, disfigured and disabled. Yet getting injured wasn't the worst thing that ever happened to me in my life. In some ways it was even the best, because look at all the good that's come from it. Look at all the positive aspects of my life that have grown from my injuries.

If I hadn't got injured, I would never have met Lucy, my wife. I love Lucy and I'm in love with her. When she smiles, she lights up the room for me; that's what love does. No matter what's going on, she never makes me feel bad. Of course, she makes me mad at times, but when you live with someone, you wouldn't be taking much notice of them if that never happened. We have three fine children who mean the world to us. And although we've had our share of family tragedies, we still have Lucy's parents and my sister and my Mam, who's been an absolute rock in my life. She and my regiment, the Welsh Guards, helped me through the early years of my injuries, when I hated myself and everything I had become. 'Abandon hope all ye who enter here' was Dante's inscription at the gates of hell, and that's just how it felt to me in those dark moments.

Getting injured changed my life, that's for sure. I've had my own radio show and featured in six television documentaries about my life. In the past decade I've run the New York marathon, met Paul Newman, been kissed by Shirley Bassey, donned my best suit for *Question Time,* lunched with Prince Andrew and others from Weston Spirit in the Chinese Room at the Palace, made my choice of *Desert Island Discs,* jumped out of the sky for heaven's sake and done 101 other daft things to raise money for the causes I believe in.

You'll read a lot in these pages about the two charities that mean the most to me. There's Weston Spirit, the charity I co-founded with Paul Oginsky and Ben Harrison back in the 1980s for disenfranchised young people from our inner cities. And there's the Royal Star & Garter Home at Richmond in Surrey, a fabulous place that cares for injured and disabled ex-service men and women, whatever the cause of their disability. People think veterans' homes are always for older people, but they forget that it's our young people who go to war. So both these charities are about turning the past into a good future – giving people independence, dignity and self-esteem, however young or old they are.

In the end, it's not what happens to you that counts, but what you do about it. What matters is where you are going to take your life and how you are going to make things better. The one big constant in life is change, and the challenge that each change brings. That's what this book is about, and that's why I wanted to write it. It's not really about me – I'm the one subject that bores me to tears – much more about the events and people who have helped shape my life. I know I can talk a glass eye to sleep and the way things have worked out, I talk about me all the time. I do it for a living because I had to find some way to support my wonderful family and kids are an expensive hobby, believe me. It's odd, though – no one ever dreamed I would turn into a public speaker. I suppose it's the Welsh in me coming out. But I get more than enough attention already. Other people's stories interest me much more than mine.

I've been back to the Falklands three times now and each time has brought something new. It's like unwrapping those Russian dolls, taking off layer after layer until you finally get down to the tiny heart. Meeting Carlos Cachón, the Argentinian pilot who dropped the bomb on our troop ship, was a hugely important step on my road to a fuller recovery. Forgiveness didn't come into it. The only person I ever had to learn to forgive was me, for failing to help anyone out of the fire, failing to go into action and all the rest. None of that was Carlos's fault and I was glad to welcome him and his lovely wife, Graciela, into my home.

Not everyone agrees with the friendship that has developed between me and Carlos, but you can't go through life forever worrying about other people's opinion. You have to do what you think is right. Carlos and I met as strangers in peacetime, linked only by the bomb. Though we had first encountered each other as adversaries, we became friends. I think most people would like him. He's a man of standards and very courageous. I'm not going to apologise for meeting or liking him, though I will say sorry if I caused offence.

Unless I'm given a very good reason, I don't plan to go back to the Falklands again. Been there. Done that. Bought the T-shirt. Sent the postcard. Made the video (well, three actually). I even came home with the little statuettes – two Royal Marines, they were. I would have bought Paras as well but there were none on sale. Yes, I hope I can truthfully say I have laid my ghosts to rest. Though much of the background to the war is only now beginning to emerge, you'll not find me harping on too much about who was right and who was wrong, either. It just doesn't interest me.

Not all of my friends have been so lucky. Forty-eight men who were with me on the *Sir Galahad* lost their lives and 97 were badly burnt and injured. I will always remember that. When I went back to the Falklands at the beginning of 2002, to film the stories of some of the conflict's real heroes, I hadn't realised how much sadness was still locked up inside me – sadness for those who died, for those whose lives were turned upside down, and sadness for their families. I shall carry them with me, always.

As in any traumatic event, some people suffer injuries that remain hidden for a long time, and this book is for them too. At least my physical injuries are there for all to see, and they gave me a focus to overcome. But more soldiers who served in the Falklands have since committed suicide than were ever killed in the conflict. That's unbearably sad and it illustrates the terrible lack of support we give to the boys and girls who go out and fight for our country, giving of their very best, yet who receive so little in return. Never let accountants rule the military, they will sell our people short. But the politicians too have let standards slip to the point where we lay ourselves open not just to criticism but to ridicule as well.

I hope this book might alter the way we view war and its aftermath. There's nothing glorious or glorifying about conflict. When we go to war, there are no winners. We all lose, some more than others. Yet I still describe myself as a passionate supporter of Britain and of the military. I really do believe we can make a difference, as long as the wars we choose to fight are just and right.

'What will you say to your boys,' Sue Lawley asked me on *Desert Island Discs*, 'if they grow up and say they want to join the army?'

'Be the general's driver,' I replied. 'You never see too many generals at the front line now, do you?'

But don't let's forget the good times, either. This book is full of the people who have helped me keep my sense of humour. As well as the documentaries and the books about my life, I have co-written two military thrillers. If I ever write another work of fiction, I promise you it will be full of the natural comedy of life. For instance, a woman I met recently in Aberystwyth was telling me about her mother, who was taken on as a film extra, playing a corpse in a coffin. After filming had finished, they offered to give her a lift home. 'It's all right,' she said, 'I'll just pop down the road as I've got some shopping to do.' The trouble was, she forgot to take off her make-up. Everyone she met took one look at her and said, 'Oh dear, you don't look too well at all, love.' I'll put her in the novel, and all the other people who make me laugh. In this day and age we need them more than ever.

1

First Return to
the Falklands

SO MUCH HAS HAPPENED in my world these past ten years, it's hard to put events in some sort of order. It's more than 20 years now since the Argentine bomb exploded aboard the *Sir Galahad* as we were anchored off Fitzroy, waiting to go ashore. I'm 42 now, which means I've spent more of life injured than I ever knew as the old Simon Weston, Welsh Guardsman and one-time tearaway from the Welsh valleys.

Life was very simple then. I remember that part of my life so very well because it was one of my happiest times – certainly the easiest. As soldiers, we had no real responsibility, apart from responsibility towards each other: no mortgage, no bills to pay, enough money to phone my girlfriend from a callbox, get a taxi or a train. I was a soldier and then I was a soldier off duty. I played a lot of rugby and I just loved that.

I have told the story of my early life in *Walking Tall* and don't wish to bore you by going back over the same ground – childhood as a service brat, growing up in Nelson, Mid-Glamorgan, then joining the Welsh Guards, which gave me the only status I'd ever had in my life; more than that, it was the first time I had ever really belonged to anything, either. I joined the army at 16 and after a year's training at Pirbright in Surrey, I served in Berlin, Northern Ireland and Kenya before we set sail for the South Atlantic on the *QE2* to join the Falklands conflict.

Some things remain with you for ever, but I'm not trying to drag the past back into the future. It's weird, though, how selective your memory becomes. I can no longer hear the sounds of the explosion as the bomb went off. Perhaps I never heard it in the first place. I remember the sound of the aircraft going over, yet I can't recall even the vibration of the bomb tearing through the ship. Maybe getting injured stopped me hearing it. I do remember this great grey streak coming straight across in front of me like a shark, and the colours as the fireball came back at us – burnished dirty oranges from the sixties and seventies, the same colour people used for curtains and clothes, and dirty bright yellows. I once described it as 'the dance with orange' – when you saw the flames licking around, and people on fire, they seemed like they were dancing, poor buggers. I was getting pretty deep-fried myself. It was only when I tried to grab hold of someone to help them out that I realised the palms of my hands had gone.

In my first book I dealt with the immediate aftermath of the explosion – sadness at the loss of so many friends, guilt that I had survived, and the slow process of physical recovery. The 46 per cent burns I received meant the surgeons had to harvest fresh skin from my body, so by the time they had finished with me, I had scarring over 80 per cent of my body. I've lost count of the exact number of operations and surgical procedures I've had – more than 70, at least.

Lucy has heard this story so many times I'm not allowed to repeat it at home any more, but they used skin from my backside to rebuild my nose. So whenever I kiss someone, they don't realise how close they are to kissing my arse. I told it to the Duke of Edinburgh at the opening of the refurbished Imperial War Museum when I'd wandered away from the official party and came across him unexpectedly. He was trailing some way behind the Queen with Prince Andrew, patron of Weston Spirit, who introduced us. The Duke clearly hadn't heard the joke before because he howled with laughter.

But if my body was slowly getting back together, the deeper psychological wounds remained. As everyone who has been through trauma will tell you, you have to find the key that will unlock the ills and grief that take you spiralling down. I must have a big combination lock, the sort you see on bank vaults in old cowboy films, because for me, several things helped. People kept me on an even keel – my mother and stepfather especially – but it was events that did it for me mostly, stepping out of the comfort zone into different environments. Going back to visit my regiment in Germany helped to kick off the process, watching my friends play rugby and being treated like anyone else, not the victim I had begun to feel.

Seeing *Simon's Peace*, the second BBC documentary about my recovery, was another. It helped to turn me around through sheer embarrassment at the pathetic drunk I had become. I went up to London for a special screening and stormed out twice – once watching my Mam in tears talking to my grandmother, and then again when Malcolm had filmed me drinking from a sherry bottle at a New Year's Eve party.

'You bastard,' I said to him as I left the room, 'how could you do that to me?'

I went back in, watched it to the end and said my grumpy goodbyes.

About a week later I phoned Malcolm. 'Hiya,' I said.

'Hello, Simon, how are you?'

'I've stopped drinking. Hated that bloody thing. Is that how I am?'

'Well, it's not quite a mirror, but it's not far from it. If it was a mirror, it would be worse.'

'Worse?'

'Have you ever counted how much Strongbow you drink when you go out to the pub?'

'It's not that much.'

'How many times do you go to the Social Club a week, and to the pub? Add it all up.'

'All right, all right. When are you next coming down?'

'I'll be down in three or four days.'

'Okay. See you.'

Life slowly turned around. For a year I stopped drinking, apart from the occasional pint on Sundays. I spent most of the time trying to get fit through exercise and training in the gym which the council had helped to build on the side of my mother's house. Much of the equipment was purchased through the incredible generosity and warmth of one or two people, as I didn't have any money at the time. From using the gym three times a week I went up to five or six, and I was also running a lot and training with my friend Keith Cullen.

Because of the film, offers of work started to come in. A security company offered me a job guarding its vaults, where at least I would be kept warm and dry and well out of sight. I believe the offer was made with the very best of intentions and the kindest of hearts, but it wasn't for me.

It was simply a job, offering neither prospects nor future. I thought I still had enough left within myself to carve out a bigger role in life than locking myself away in a vault. I thanked them for their kindness and support but turned it down. There were other job offers too. The Post Office asked me down to Cardiff for an interview and again I said 'thanks but no thanks'. Charities for physically and mentally disabled people started approaching me for help, which made me feel better about myself even if I resisted the idea of being typecast.

Someone I owe a special debt to is the late Dame Felicity Peake, founding director of the Women's Royal Air Force, who was not just incredibly kind to me but also saw the potential in me to do things and gave me tremendous support in whatever I wanted to do. She was Weston Spirit's first trustee and without her support we probably wouldn't have got a number of other notable people on board, either. She was a wonderful lady, sharp as a tack, and a lady in every sense of the word. I think of her as being very strong and determined, not easily flustered, and incredibly humble. She hated fuss. 'Yes, yes, enough of that,' she'd say if you tried to pay her too many compliments. I liked and respected her hugely, and took my Mam to her memorial service just this year.

Doris Collins was another lady who was incredibly good and kind. Driving up to see her, you had to pass through a village called Cold Christmas. Once her husband Basil snuck me aside and took me into an anteroom where he showed me a Gurkha knife, a kukri, that had been carried in the Falklands. He'd bought it at a charity auction for a phenomenal amount of money, far more than it was actually worth. 'Doris doesn't know I've got it,' he said in a whisper, and I bet he never told her.

Another thing that helped was learning to drive, which I did shortly before going off to Australia with the Guards Association of Australia. Driving gave me back a taste of independence. I was just training, stuck at home and doing little else with my life. Unless you take a bus to catch the train and spend 73 days getting anywhere, you are pretty much marooned in the Welsh valleys. Your car becomes your new life. I bought a Ford Fiesta XR2, petrol blue, and never looked back. By now I had my military pension, some money from the South Atlantic Fund and other funds that people had raised for me. There is no way that I can ever thank the good people of this country enough for all that they have given me. If I had one desire it would be that people were so accepting of everybody in the same way, for all their faults and foibles.

After Australia I came back home for three weeks, then went out to New Zealand with Operation Raleigh as a member of staff. That's where I met Paul Oginsky, who had joined as a venturer, and the idea for what became Weston Spirit was born.

By the time I came back to Wales I knew it was time to leave home because although I owe my recovery most of all to my Mam, I was drowning in her kindness. I went to Liverpool, where Paul Oginsky and Ben Harrison and I set about getting our young people's charity off the ground. For a time I lodged with Ben's mum in Birkenhead, near the Tranmere Rovers ground. It was a case of 'watch the man, watch his dog', there were so few people in the ground. The pasties were great, though. You could use them as sporting rattles because there was a little bit of meat inside you could shake around to make a noise.

It was Paul who dreamed up the name Weston Spirit. I was a bit diffident at first as I didn't think my name carried that sort of credibility, but Paul identified it as a kind of shorthand for my spirit of determination and tenacity, of never saying die. First we called it Operation Weston Spirit (an echo of Operation Raleigh) and when that began to sound a little too military, we changed it to The Weston Spirit and finally just Weston Spirit.

In those early days I wasn't taking any money for all the time I spent on Weston Spirit, not even petrol money. There just wasn't any. Ben carried on working at his other job for a year or two, but Paul spent all his time on Weston Spirit and had no other income. He obviously needed to earn something, as did Ben when he took the plunge and began to work for the charity full-time, even if it did mean a big drop in salary. It was three years or more before I even saw any money back to cover my expenses, so unlike Ben and Paul, I would always need to find other ways of earning a living.

At last my life was taking on some sort of shape, and meeting Lucy gave me back a taste of happiness. But the start of my real healing came with my first return to the Falklands in 1991, nine and a half years after the *Sir Galahad* was bombed. Malcolm had organised it all for the fourth of his BBC documentaries, *Simon's Return*, and he had also found Carlos Cachón, the Argentine pilot who had led the squadron that dropped the *Sir Galahad* bomb and whom I had long wanted to meet. Lucy had spotted Carlos's name in a book about the Falklands and passed the information on to Malcolm, who then tracked him down. We were joined by two other soldiers who had fought in the Falklands, Gary Tytler of the Scots Guards and John Meredith, a former sergeant in 2 Para. The plan was to fly to Argentina, meet Carlos and a handful of Argentine veterans who had fought against Gary and John, then continue on to the Falklands.

Those two guys were brilliant, funny and witty, absolutely magnificent, and I can't thank them enough for the help and support they gave me. We'd sit in a café across from our hotel in Buenos Aires, drinking and talking till three or four o' clock in the morning – not getting hammered, but it was such an emotional time for all of us. Poor John had the trots the whole time we were away, and lost so much weight. For me, the opposite happened. Just the idea of returning to the Falklands had set off the nightmares again, in which I relived the bombing and woke up sweating. To compensate, I was eating and drinking hugely, so by the time we left for the Falklands I'd hit 18 stone; that's at least two stone overweight on an already large frame.

In my second book, *Going Back*, I tell the day-to-day story of that rollercoaster of a journey. To give you a flavour of its ups and downs, I remember our driver, Oskar, taking us to a café right on the docks in the colourful La Boca district of Buenos Aires, where the houses are put together with scavenged corrugated iron and painted amazing colours – pink, green, yellow, purple, blue and red. The café owner found out who we were and asked us to sign the wall. Then he told us he had lost his cousin in the Falklands. 'Hey, they're our islands,' he said. 'Geographically, they're only 200 miles away from our shores.'

We thought, here we go, we're heading for one almighty punch-up. But he just shrugged and said, 'In all reality, gentlemen, if you want to fight about it, keep them. They aren't that important.'

John, Gary and I looked at each other in amazement. Bloody hell, we thought, this is surreal.

For me, the highpoint of Argentina was undoubtedly my meeting with Carlos, which freed up so much inside me. It was like that game of marbles – Kerplunk, I think it's called – where you fill a tube with marbles and have to pull out straws sticking into the sides. There comes a point when you pull out one last straw and the whole lot comes crashing down. That's how it felt, meeting Carlos for the first time. In the evening I went out with the crew and the others and got absolutely verschnickered.

The next morning I said to Malcolm, 'I feel like I've put something to bed I thought I would never get rid of.' I could just as well go home now. I had achieved what I set out to do.

In fact going back to the Falklands was also hugely important and anyway I was doing the journey with Malcolm for the film we were making together, and you can't just walk away.

There was one time I put my foot down, though. Malcolm had fixed up a meeting between Gary and John and some Argentine veterans who had fought in the same battles, at Goose Green and Tumbledown Mountain. Carlos would be there too, I knew, but I felt I couldn't risk seeing him again, in case we lost what we'd gained. I had at long last cast off the Charlie I had been carrying all these years on my back. What if we said or did something that alienated each other? I had no wish to sit down with a map and get all tribal. The way I was feeling was new and very fragile. It's like making a beautiful vase which you're about to put in the kiln, terrified in case it should crack in the firing.

So while the others went off to their meeting, I stayed behind in the van. Gary and John had both fought in the conflict. I hadn't. This was their meeting, not mine. Malcolm must have been pulling his hair out, but at that point I couldn't get my head around seeing Carlos one more time.

After a while Carlos came out to find me. He sat with me in the van and we carried on talking as best we could, without the aid of an interpreter. Then Malcolm (who speaks Spanish) came over and joined us in the van, helping us to understand each other. By this time I felt fine being filmed, but I had been trying to protect my own emotional journey and needed Carlos to come and find me.

Malcolm will say that I behaved badly on the trip but it was a hugely complicated operation. As well as my own journey, we were taking two other soldiers who had fought there. And we weren't alone. On top of the camera crew, we had the writer who was working with me on the book, John Man, and my journalist friend Pat Hill, who was serialising the as-yet-unwritten book for the *News of the World*. Everyone had their own deadlines and their own agendas, so it's hardly surprising that relations got a bit explosive at times. I like Pat and I like Malcolm, but if there's one thing that journey taught me it's that when you are working on the same job, print and television don't mix.

Of course, Malcolm kept a very clear idea in his head of the film he was trying to make. I went along with the flow as best I could but my emotions were deeply involved and Malcolm couldn't always guess how I would react. For both of us it was uncharted territory. I had never before met anyone who had blown me up – but there's a first time for everything.

After a little more filming in Argentina, we flew on to the Falklands via Santiago in Chile, stopping briefly in a café where moments before the police had shot dead a couple of failed bank robbers out in the street. Our taxi driver then took us up to the high peak above the city where he pointed out landmarks like the football stadium

General Pinochet had used to imprison and execute his people. The driver's neighbour had been taken away and never returned. A young girl cousin had been 'disappeared' for several weeks before she was found raped and dead in a ditch, 70 miles from Santiago. It made you realise how lucky we are in this country.

After Santiago we had a brief stopover in Punta de Arenas, a Chilean naval and air force base down in Tierra del Fuego. Go any further and you fall off the map.

One of my strongest memories of Chile is hunting for a late-night drinking establishment in the fog, a real pea-souper, thick as your auntie's hat. 'Look for the red light above the door,' they had said. We stepped into the night and headed blindly towards a faint red light some way in front. When the fog suddenly lifted, we discovered we had been doggedly pursuing a car with one tail light.

The journey on to the Falklands was scarcely any better. The plane that flew us there was a small Otter. To get to the cockpit, you had to jiggle a piece of wooden planking that had a square hole cut into it. Behind that was a large aluminium tank used to store spare fuel, because the distance to the Falklands was so great.

What they didn't tell us at the time – and I'm only thinking about it now – was that if you flew all the way out to the Falklands and the weather was too bad to land, tough. You couldn't fly back because the plane didn't carry enough fuel to get you all the way home again.

You can smell aviation fuel in the cabin and there is the loadmaster smoking away. John Man is sitting right at the front by himself. We can none of us breathe properly because we're flying so high and the cabin isn't pressurised. I'm getting quite distressed. Then John kicks a little tap on a piece of piping close to the floor. We're maybe 10,000 feet up and he's only managed to turn off the bloody fuel with his foot. When the engine started to splutter, the pilot knew something was wrong and the loadmaster switched it back on. Then I'm looking out at the ice forming on the wings when all of a sudden the ice breaks off and whacks into my window. It was all pretty scary.

The Falklands must count as one of the weirdest places in the world. The weather in summer is on-and-off rain, which turns to constant in winter, like horizontal stair rods. As we flew into Port Stanley airport, the aircraft ran into wires slung between two radio masts. It snapped the two poles off the top, which then wrapped around the plane's undercarriage, so we landed with all this wire and gubbins hanging out the back. I swear to God I got down and kissed the ground when we finally got out.

Though this was technically my first return to the Falklands, I was really seeing the place for the first time. During the conflict I had spent about five days on the islands, much of it dug down in a watery trench near San Carlos Bay, where we had first disembarked. So although I had been on land, I hadn't really seen anything, and after I was carried off from the *Sir Galahad* I wasn't in any sort of state to appreciate the scenery.

The Falklands are beautiful in a very stark and rustic way. You've got these wonderful hills and dramatic landscapes – very craggy and rocky and a fragile peat environment. In many ways the people still lead a pioneering existence. But the stress I had experienced in Argentina had in no way subsided. I was going back with writers and a camera crew to a very emotional place. All sorts of emotions were whirling about inside me, while at the same time I was having to perform in front of the camera.

* * *

The Union Jack was fluttering in the wind as Gary, John and I went into the war graves cemetery at Ajax Bay. After we had been driving across peat bogs for eight hours or so, Malcolm got quite upset that we hadn't waited for the camera crew, who were still unloading their equipment from the van, and so he missed our first sighting of the graves, but none of us had anticipated how emotional and beautiful it would be. In a country of wild beauty, you don't expect to see this well-manicured lawn or the bank of gorse bushes at the back, all budding with their lovely yellow flowers.

There are no Welsh Guards buried in the cemetery. Those who died on the *Sir Galahad* were towed a mile out to sea, where the ship itself was sunk as a war grave. At Ajax Bay the graves we saw were mostly those of Paratroopers and a few Marines. I'll always remember John Meredith saluting the grave of Lieutenant Colonel 'H' Jones, Commanding Officer of the 2nd Battalion Parachute Regiment. He walked up to the grave, stood to attention, saluted, put his hands back in his pockets and walked away. Other Paras who came back with us on a later journey did exactly the same, an instinctive mark of loyalty and *esprit de corps*.

At the back of the cemetery is a huge plaque inscribed with all the names of the war dead. My eye was drawn to the place where my name would have gone, between Weaver and Wigley, if I had been a foot or maybe even an inch closer to the explosion. At that moment I experienced a whole surge of emotions – guilt at having survived, sadness because a lot of the lads were still left there and huge relief because my name wasn't on the wall.

It was another fine day when I visited the Welsh Guards memorial at Fitzroy, and nowhere near as windy as it might have been. 'Please can you not come down with me,' I had said to Malcolm beforehand. So much of my life has been made public, like the operations and surgery on my injuries, but this was a very private moment and I didn't want the cameras anywhere near. Malcolm understood how I felt. 'That's okay, Squeaky.' He always calls me by my squaddie nickname when we talk about things like that.

We arrived at Fitzroy, where I changed out in the open, putting on the blazer and slacks I had brought all the way to the Falklands especially for this moment. The rest of the time I went around in jeans, tracksuit trousers, baggy jumpers and saggy shirts, but now I wanted to dress the part in shirt and tie.

It felt like one hell of a long lonely walk down to the memorial overlooking the bay as there were no real tracks then. It was the first time I had been back since that fateful day and even then I had never put my feet on land as after the bombing I had been carried everywhere on a stretcher.

The memorial is a large Celtic cross in Welsh granite from Gelligaer quarry, just a mile and a half away from my home town of Nelson. I used to play there as a boy, and now have a large lump of granite from the same quarry on my front lawn. I stayed there some time, reading the names and looking out over the water. Damn, I remember thinking, how close we were to safety and yet how far away. Forty-eight men were alive then who weren't any more. It was hugely tragic yet for me bitter-sweet because I was alive and standing there. Afterwards I walked around the little horseshoe of other memorials. The Engineers have a broken pick and shovel that struck me as powerful beyond belief.

It was right to keep the cameras away. If I had broken down, the cameras would still have caught it from a distance, but I didn't want anyone to see the tear in my eye.

2
Rebuilding a Life

Relief was uppermost in my mind as we flew home from the Falklands at the end of filming. It was all very different from 1982, the time of the conflict, when it was touch and go whether I would make it back alive. That journey had taken several days as we had first sailed to Montevideo in Uruguay and flown on from there, after a 24-hour delay when the first plane lost an engine on take-off, scattering pieces all over the runway.

This time I was free of pain, sitting in the cockpit with the pilots as we made a night landing at Ascension Island, which was scary enough, because the runway is literally carved out of the hills.

After refuelling at Ascension, we flew straight home to RAF Brize Norton, where Lucy was waiting for me with our baby son James, then four months old. I'd been phoning Lucy every day and couldn't wait to be back. Mam was there too. It must have been good for her that this time she could recognise me as I walked off the plane. I was just so relieved at putting all that behind me so that now I could get on with the business of living.

By going back to the place where I'd got injured, I knew that I had done something that was worthwhile for me. As I said at the end of the film, 'It's time for the living now, time to enjoy our lives. There's no point trying to live with the destruction of the war. I've settled something in my mind and that'll do for me.'

Looking back now, I realise that I hadn't got everything out that I needed to. Just as Gary Tytler said in the film, I thought I could go back to the Falklands, then put my experiences in a box and leave it on the shelf. I'm not the brightest bulb on the Christmas tree and I didn't fully appreciate how badly my life had fallen apart. What I took to be the end of healing was really only the beginning.

I still had to decide what to do with the rest of my life. There was my charity, Weston Spirit, but my role there wasn't enough to keep me occupied completely. I'm a doer, not a desk jockey. The army had suited me perfectly in that respect. You spend most of your time doing things and although you might be working things out, it's always connected to something physical.

Weston Spirit is something I got involved in because I didn't want to be pigeonholed for ever afterwards as 'Falklands veteran Simon Weston', as if my only achievement was going off to war and getting injured before I even got involved in any fighting. Imagine being an actor who has made hundreds of movies and the only one people ever talk about is one you made before you even turned 21. Whatever else you do, and however much you change, that's the only one people remember.

Lots of things about Weston Spirit make me feel proud, not least the fact that we three ordinary guys got it off the ground: Paul Oginsky, whom I'd met through Operation Raleigh in New Zealand in 1986; another Merseysider, Ben Harrison; and myself. Our first office was in a broom cupboard at the Merseyside Council for Voluntary Service. Yet over the years we've come through two recessions, experienced massive stock-market crashes and seen the organisation grow into what it is today – a recognised leader in the youth-work field, promoting self-esteem and confidence in young people from our inner cities. When I was growing up in Nelson, I got into all sorts of trouble because there wasn't much else to do. The army offered me a way out and we wanted to give youngsters today more of a choice.

Although we had got the original idea in New Zealand, Paul traces the charity's core philosophy back to a beer mat in a Liverpool pub on which one of us had written the words 'peer pressure'. Young people influencing each other, that's what we wanted to tap into, helping young people develop a sense of their own self-worth and confidence in their own abilities. As we see it now, all people are of equal value as human beings, although shyness makes some people feel inferior and arrogance makes others feel superior. Having confidence means developing an awareness of what you can and cannot do.

Our role at Weston Spirit is to inspire young people to go out and find their own journey. Many young people lack the confidence to set an ambition and a goal for themselves. If you don't do that, you'll never know what you might have done. And the danger is that you might end up on someone else's journey or lose your way and plod about in a big minefield of negativity, mired in apathy. Weston Spirit, by contrast, encourages young people to explore the world and themselves, to find out what really sets them alight.

I'll always remember in the early days going to see a youth worker at a government training scheme to talk over our ideas. I suppose we were getting a bit passionate and at the end, she said, 'Okay, let me get this clear this in my own mind. What you want, you say, is to get young people to believe they can do anything they want – get them really excited about the future and what's out there. Get them enthusiastic about their potential, so that they believe anything is possible, as long as they work hard. Is that it?'

'Yeah, yeah,' we said, 'that's exactly what we're trying to do. We want them to believe that they can be something and do something if they really believe in it.'

'Oh no, no, no,' she said, shaking her head. 'It takes us at least three months to knock ideas like that out of their heads.'

Where on earth do you go from there?

But over the years we have proved her pessimism to be badly misplaced. To our very first residential course came a young man called John who had already spent time on a government training scheme where he'd been just another bum on the seat, a statistic to prove that young people were being successfully kept off the streets. John hadn't been in trouble or anything, as far as we knew, but until he came to us he was just marking time. After Weston Spirit he went on to work in films and even took one of his productions to the Cannes film festival. He came back to see us at our 10th-anniversary reunion and he said to me then, 'Weston Spirit gave me the chance to look at my life and evaluate it in a different way.'

Also on one of those early courses was a lad everyone said would be in prison within six months. Well, he stayed out of trouble, got himself some training and he's now an accredited chef in the Midlands.

Finding a job or a direction in life are not the only outcomes. For some young people, getting them to make a phone call or take part in a circle discussion is a real measure of achievement. Paul remembers one lad at a course in Newcastle who hardly spoke all week. Staff and the other young people there wondered if he was engaging at all with what was going on. Towards the end the youth worker asked for a volunteer to chair a discussion circle at which participants could raise any topic they wanted. To everyone's surprise, the young lad put his hand up. Well, his way of chairing the discussion was simply to point at the people sitting round in a circle, but in the feedback that followed, one girl paid tribute to the chair.

'I was really pleased he put up his hand,' she said. 'I was wondering when he would get involved.'

Another one said, 'I think that was really brave of him, because he's obviously not comfy in a circle.'

At this, the lad started to grow in stature. You could see a physical change come over him and for the rest of the course he was so full of energy you couldn't put him back in the box. It turned out that his sister had committed suicide and he had been the one to find her. He'd been carrying all this locked away inside him and we had given him the chance to start opening the lid.

It's incredible the things that come out of these young people on their strange, cathartic journeys. Many really do discover themselves in the space of a short, sharp week. They have to retrace the first decade or two of their lives and then try to bring the lessons from that forward, while leaving the baggage behind. They are not the ones who are responsible for all that's gone wrong with their lives, least of all in the early part. We try to encourage them to unhitch themselves from the baggage that is holding them back, preventing them from moving on; and to get them to realise that they do have something to contribute.

There's no doubt that without Ben and Paul, Weston Spirit wouldn't be half the organisation it is today. When he finally took over the helm, Ben proved himself to be a fantastic leader who has steered the ship superbly. Paul's imagination has given the charity its heart. He's the one who has developed all the courses and created all the different ideas that make it what it is. I took part in planning the first courses and helped in practical ways, driving the bus that ferried the kids to the different courses, cooking the food and doing all that stuff. Even at the beginning, I was best able to help at fund-raising, using my name to show we knew something about pulling yourself up by your bootstraps. But soon after Lucy and I got married, we moved away from Liverpool to a new home in the Welsh valleys near Nelson, so playing a more active role became impossible as I had anyway to concentrate on earning some money. For two or three years I took a bit of a back seat, getting more heavily involved again as we expanded and I could draw on my own strengths in publicity and promotion, convincing potential backers that we have the best product, a bit like the monkeys in the PG Tips advertisements. In those early days especially, I had a better chance than Paul or Ben of getting my foot through the door. And the way the organisation has developed, it's extraordinary how our three strengths continue to complement each other.

Just before the time of my first return to the Falklands, I also became involved with another charity, the Royal Star & Garter Home on Richmond Hill in Surrey, a residential home for ex-service men and women who need the care facilities it can provide, and they're the best in the country bar none. I have my friend and adviser, Geoffrey Hamilton-Fairley, to thank for making the connection.

Geoff is someone Malcolm introduced me to at my lowest point, around the time we were filming *Simon's Peace*. Malcolm was also working on a film about the sportsman Daley Thompson, who was then a client of Geoff's. Malcolm thought that maybe Geoff could take me under his wing too. I had been approached to write a book about my life and clearly wasn't yet equipped to handle all the attention I was getting.

I suppose at first I looked on Geoff as my commanding officer, though I've outgrown the need for that now. He's a very nice guy, very direct, and as blunt as the flat end of a spade; he'll tell you straight out what he thinks. Over the years we have become friends as our trust in each other has grown.

I told Geoff I was amazed that people still seemed to hold me in some affection. 'Don't pin your hopes on it,' was Geoff's characteristically blunt reply. 'You'll probably have another year or two of shelf life but start looking for something else.'

It was Geoff's idea that I should concentrate my efforts on two or three main charities where I might be able to achieve something, rather than running off in all directions and getting nowhere for anyone.

Geoff had had a call from Ian Lashbrooke, then in charge of fund-raising for the Royal Star & Garter Home, who set out their problem very exactly. Running the home costs several million a year and as they were prudent, they had enough money in the reserves to carry on for another couple of years. But because they had money in the reserves, they couldn't get funding from all the usual official charitable sources and raising that sort of money through their own efforts was proving a real problem. Geoff went to visit them and when he came back he said, 'It's a wonderful place – we've got to do something with them.'

'Fine,' I said, 'what do they want?'

'They want you to help with their 75th-birthday celebrations, put your face to a poster or something, but I've got a better idea. I think you could really do something here – there's a long-term future if you want to get involved.'

Geoff set out his plan for a full-blown campaign over the year that would help establish a database of potential donors, seeking donations and then legacies for the longer term. 'It's a gamble,' he said, 'because they'll have to invest a lot of money in the campaign itself. I think it could work. Of course, even if Ian agrees he'll still have to convince his board, but the governors are military people, they're not stupid. They'll realise you have to take risks at times like this.'

It was a gamble for me too, as I had never put my name to that sort of campaign, so we had no track record to suggest how much money we might raise. But Geoff had come back really fired up by the place. He'd seen some of the older residents wandering about and asked Ian what would happen if one of them had a heart attack. 'We walk, we don't run,' was Ian's reply, which impressed the hell out of Geoff – it's such a caring place, yet realistic with it.

'I've trusted you up to now,' I said to Geoff. 'If I like it, let's go with it.'

So we went along and as soon as I walked in, it took my breath away. The home had opened in 1916 to care for severely disabled soldiers returning from the battlefields of World War I. Though it started life in the old Star & Garter Hotel in Richmond, a new home had been purpose-built with money raised by the British Women's Hospital Committee. Queen Mary opened the new building in 1924, dedicating it as the Women's Memorial of the Great War. Absolutely gorgeous it is – marble everywhere, marble stairs, marble floors, it wouldn't surprise you to find marble in the loos. It may be wasteful of space but it's so opulent, and everywhere you turn there are colonnades and pillars and verandas. You'd never build a place like that today, you couldn't, and the amazing thing is that it doesn't smell of pee and cabbage.

But even better than that is what it gives the people who live there – independence, dignity and self-esteem, all the things that are imperative for you to feel good about yourself. Just walking in there and sensing the wonderful atmosphere, I realised that these people needed someone to support them and help create something good for them. And that somebody was me.

So you can say I got hooked on the place from the moment I stepped inside. It's a home in the greatest sense of the word, a place where people live. Even the food has always been great, provided by an ex-army chef called John. He must be the only army cook who has ever passed the course. Army cooking is usually appalling and being a 'cabbage mechanic' can only be described as a no-win situation as everybody complains non-stop. John is now leaving the Home, though he's going to continue to help out on a voluntary basis for fund-raising events. It seems that all good things must end sometime.

But back in the early 1990s, I knew I had to get involved, and the results of our first mailshot campaign exceeded all our hopes. An unfortunate coincidence undoubtedly helped. The Home had opened on 14 January 1916, so the main thrust of the campaign was planned for mid-January 1991, just as the first Gulf War was breaking out. We mailed over 28,000 potentially supportive donors. A little over 27 per cent responded – hugely successful for a mailshot – giving a total of more than £350,000 and winning the Direct Marketing Silver Echo award for cost-effectiveness.

At the end of the day, it's not the money raised that counts but the difference it makes to the lives of the people who live there. Each one has a story to tell, like one old chap – sadly no longer with us – who made the Star & Garter his home for more than 40 years. A soldier in World War II, he had been taken prisoner in Poland by the Germans, who marched him for over 100 miles. He developed frostbite from the cold, and got gangrene in his lower legs. The German officer said to him, 'I'm going to treat my boys first and if I've got time, I might do something for you.' The Swiss Red Cross found him by chance, amputated both his legs and repatriated him. He was a very pleasant man, such a lovely fellow, like so many of the other residents, men and women who have come to us from Northern Ireland, from the Gulf, from the Balkans, from the Falklands, and all the other conflicts in which this country plays a part.

Since getting involved with all the good people at the home, I have helped them raise some of the millions they need to keep the place going. A lot of the money now comes from legacies as people see it as a worthwhile cause. As well as helping with mailshots, videos, cassettes and brochures, I've given speeches to schools, cadets, apprentices, medical staff and regular army units up and down the country. I've spoken in town halls, churches, cathedrals, military bases, at band concerts and social clubs. There have been a lot of fun events too, like walking across Finland and cycling 900 miles across the US from Moab in Utah to the Boulder City Dam.

The buzz I get is seeing somebody new come into the home, able to make the most of its brilliant facilities, or somebody reaching the end of their time, knowing they've had as good and as long and as decent a life as they possibly could, no matter what they might have suffered previously.

I hope to remain involved with the Star & Garter for as long as they want me, and for as long as it remains in place, providing the highest-quality care to military people so that residents lead lives that are full, contented and as happy as they can be. That's what makes the place what it is and that's why I give a damn.

3
Love and Family

AFTER I GOT INJURED, one of the greatest fears
of my life was that I would never find another girlfriend,
never find a girl I would want to settle down with and
enjoy the life that most people take for granted – marriage, home, kids, work, just the ordinary things people
do. All my life I've set out to be Mr Joe Average but
circumstances have worked against me on that one.

When I went off to the Falklands I was engaged to be
married to a nice girl called Sue who used to come and
visit me in the military hospital at Woolwich after they'd
got me home. It was a testing time for both of us and after
a while it became clear that it wasn't working any more.
She had fallen in love with the guy I was when I left and
I had come home a completely different person. It wasn't
just the outside that was different, either. So we decided it
was wrong to carry on, and looking back, that was
absolutely the right decision. Anyway, if we hadn't split I
would never have met Lucy.

First, though, I had to get my confidence back with
girls. Whenever there's a problem in my life – especially

something as major as this – I have no option but to throw myself in feet first. In fact you could probably say that I jumped in with lead-lined boots and broke a lot of toes, including my own, but that's just the way I am. If something scares me, I have to confront it. And I was that intimidated by my looks, by my future and just about everything else that the only thing I could possibly do was dive straight in.

I didn't have gallons of girlfriends before I met Lucy, but there were quite a few, and they were all great girls. Maybe they were daft as brushes to be with me but there were one or two lovely relationships. Though I wasn't afraid of how I looked, I was frightened of how people saw me until I got to the point where I didn't give a sod. If girls didn't want to go out with me because I wasn't six foot two inches tall, slim and extremely handsome, that was their loss. If they didn't like me because I was drunk or a fool, that was perfectly fine, but if they weren't going to give me a chance just because of the way I looked, that only showed how shallow they were.

For about three or four years I suppose there were several girls in my life. Some I liked, some I didn't know terribly well, the same as everybody else. Some of them may have felt sympathy towards me, fame may have been a factor for others, and I know one or two genuinely loved me. But they weren't relationships set to last for ever, and by the time I met Lucy I was ready to settle down.

We met through Weston Spirit, where Lucy was working as a volunteer. She also worked part-time for Merseysport, giving Keep Fit classes and things like that, and was studying Leisure Management at college. I remember seeing her in a leotard and thinking, wow, that's a good advertisement. I liked her when I first met her, she was always very pleasant and helpful, but I didn't think much more about it. We had an unwritten rule that you didn't go out with anyone from the organisation. She went off to Camp America for the summer, while I was busy learning to fly and getting into all kinds of other things, and we didn't keep in touch. Lucy says we could have gone out together sooner but I didn't notice. I'm very slow on the uptake.

The story of how we got together I told in my last book. When Lucy came home to Liverpool, she heard I'd been poorly and knocked on my door one afternoon to see how I was. It could have been embarrassing because there was another girl staying in the house for the weekend, a lassie whose husband had been killed in the Falklands and who wanted help in laying her ghosts to rest. There wasn't anything going on between us and, to prove it, the three of us went out together for a Chinese meal. I thought it took a lot of courage on Lucy's part, coming out with me and the other girl. Things between us just started from there. I never did find out if the other lassie discovered what she was looking for in life. I certainly hope so.

My Mam took to Lucy from the moment she came bounding down her steps dressed in tracksuit bottoms and a top. Mam said there was a youthfulness about her that was so energetic, so vibrant and clean, full of life and spirit. I found out later my Mam also had a word of advice for her that worked for us as it might for others. 'He's got to be free to fly,' she told Lucy. 'You let him fly and he'll come back twice as quick.'

I asked Lucy to marry me after she crashed my car, a Ford Sierra Cosworth, a street version of the one I used to race. It happened on a wet and greasy day, as Lucy was pulling away from some traffic lights. She gave it too much throttle, the car fishtailed and Lucy lost control, crashing into a large stone gatepost and a gate that hadn't been opened in years until Lucy crashed through it. The police took her to her mother's and she phoned me from there. Once I knew she was okay, I rushed over to caress my car; the crash did more damage to my wallet than to the car itself. When I had calmed down, I reckoned it was time we thought about marriage: as my girlfriend she was difficult to insure and if she continued to crash my cars, she was going to cost me too much money. Besides, if I still loved her after she'd done that, I was fairly certain it was for real.

We were married in the Guards Chapel at Wellington Barracks, in London's Birdcage Walk, on 12 May 1990, exactly eight years after I had sailed for the Falklands on the *QE2*. The choice of date was deliberate. At least it would help me remember our anniversary. Lucy's maid of honour, Suzy, fainted – *whack* – in the aisle, the press were out in force and I was shot so full of nerves the day passed in a blur.

As Lucy soon discovered, being married to me is no honeymoon. In fact I never got around to booking one, I suppose because I'm not a great holiday person. I don't find it that riveting to sit beside a pool in another person's country, just because the sunshine is guaranteed. We went to the racetrack instead, getting up at 5 a.m. the day after our wedding to go to Donington Park in Derbyshire, where I was entered in a race. First we had to pick up my car from the barracks and on the way we stopped at a roadside van, where I bought Lucy a hot dog – that's how romantic I am.

The race was a wash-out, I'm afraid. After we'd been driving for about an hour I braked really hard. The car started to slow, then released its grip on the wheels. By then I don't think I had any brake pads left because the car was jiggling about and going out of shape. I just managed to put into a gravel trap and that was it. The brake pads were completely shattered when they took them off. We stayed till the end of the race and then came home.

Gren, one of my favourite cartoonists, produced a cartoon about the day for the *South Wales Echo*. My stepfather got me the original, which now hangs in my bedroom. A golfer is teeing off golf balls from his Spanish hotel bed overlooking the bay. 'Oh come on, fair play,' he says to his busty bride. 'Simon Weston's bride let him play his sport on his honeymoon.'

Lucy was always very supportive of my racing. She claimed I was safer on a racetrack than driving on motorways and ordinary roads – at least all the cars are going in the same direction. Well, you hope they are, anyway. While I was still racing, she helped with the pit boards and cleaning the car, though since I stopped she has never cleaned a car again.

Ours is a very balanced partnership. I tell people she's such a well-balanced person because she has a chip on both shoulders but really it's a case of 'She who must be obeyed' and 'He who must be ignored'. I can put my foot down anywhere I want as long as she tells me where that is.

There's no doubt that meeting Lucy started to punch pegs into holes for me. It's like when you're sitting in front of a great big jigsaw puzzle and you have to put the pieces together. It'll only work if you put this piece there and that piece there and she just did it for me. It's a wonderful feeling to be with her. She never makes me feel bad, no matter what is going on. She can make me feel annoyed and cross, but never bad. And she's so funny, we laugh constantly. We don't argue a huge amount, either. She says she was looking for Mr Right. She just didn't realise my first name was 'Always'. Apart from occasional fallings out, she completed an awful lot for me.

Love will do that for you every time. Between two people it is probably the most powerful emotion there is, but in people themselves, the greatest power in the world is hope. Without hope you have nothing. Even love on its own isn't enough. Hope is what keeps people going: hope that things will work out right; that you'll meet the right person; that things will resolve themselves; hope that war doesn't happen. Hope is truly the most wonderful emotion you can possibly imagine.

How I look has never been an issue between us. In fact Lucy says she loves my bald head because she can spot me easily in the supermarket. It only seems to bother other people but that's their problem really, not ours.

Years ago, about the time we got married, we were invited out to dinner, in Swansea, I think it was, and as we came down the stairs Lucy got taken away by the women. The first thing they said to her was, 'Oh, hello, we didn't expect you to be quite so pretty.'

'What did they mean by that?' she asked me later. 'Just because you're scarred, does that mean they thought you wouldn't find anyone attractive to marry?'

'Maybe they thought you'd have spots and blackheads and warts coming out of the top of your head, I don't know.'

We still sometimes get jibes like that, but on the whole most people are lovely.

After Lucy and I got married, we moved back to live with my mother in Nelson while they finished the house we were having built not far away. For some months now I'd been driving down every week from Liverpool to Cardiff, where I was recording a weekly radio show for BBC Radio Wales, and the strain of a 500-odd-mile round trip was getting too much.

I loved doing that show: a bit of music, a bit of chat and usually a good interview somewhere in the middle. Jimmy

Nail came on the show about the time he recorded 'Crocodile Shoes', which was such a coup as he wasn't doing many interviews; and Cilla Black, who cried when she talked about her baby who had died. That was incredibly sad. We went up to London to interview her and she really opened up, so we ended up doing two shows around her. She was really, really good with us. We were also able to get some great sporting legends, people like Welsh rugby international Jonathan Davies, one of the finest rugby players of all time, and fly half Phil Bennett, another of my sporting heroes.

Not all the guests behaved quite so well – I remember one actress I shan't name eating her way through an entire interview. I thought, how rude can you get? But most of the time I liked my guests and enjoyed their company. Instead of trotting out my questions, I always tried to listen to what they had to say so that our talk could turn into a conversation.

During the show I would also talk about Nelson and local things, where I'd been, the letters that came flooding in, about three or four at a time – a post pocket rather than a post bag, but never mind. Yes, doing a radio show was a lot of fun and I had a great time. I liked the fact that on radio it doesn't matter what you look like, it's what you do with yourself that counts – how you talk, how you ask questions, how you listen and what you have to say. You can sit in the studio dressed in jeans and flip-flops if you like (though not in BBC Radio Wales because it was always so cold) and nobody knows.

At first the show, which was pre-recorded, went out early on Saturday afternoons – a brilliant slot, just before the sport. A lot of the referees and people travelling to the game would listen to the show and they'd turn up at the rugby match or whatever and see me standing there.

'I've just finished listening to you on the radio,' they'd say. 'How the hell have you got here so quick?'

'I've got a fast hang-glider, that's how.'

But while I loved doing the radio show, moving back to the Welsh valleys was more of a problem. Quaker's Yard, where we were having our house built, is the next village along from Nelson, the place where I grew up. I loved the new house but not its situation at the top of a big nasty hill reached only by a single-track road used by drivers as a handy cut-through down to the main road, though it's so narrow and dangerous it should be for access only. There aren't any shops up there and you have to be bloody fit to reach the shops in Nelson on foot. Even then, you wouldn't want to struggle up the hill with all your shopping.

Being back in Wales was nice because I'm a Welshman and it meant my kids could grow up Welsh too. Unlike our later move to Cardiff, though, moving close to my original home was a big mistake. People say you should never go back and now I know what they mean. It wasn't the people of Nelson who were the problem – they're great – but the going back itself. Nothing stays the same – or if it does, you don't, and memories are very misleading. You've got to be sure that what you're going back to is what you expect.

When I went back, I found a lot of people had moved on. Although many of my friends now are the same ones I had at school, people like Carl Dicks and Bobby Brain, others had married and moved away. Jobs and careers had changed, relationships fallen apart and one or two people I thought were my friends subsequently let me down. It was good to be of use to my mother and sister, who were both living close by, but really, as long as Lucy and the kids are with me, I'd be happy wherever I am.

Before we could move into our new house, we had to endure a couple of months of living back at home with my mother. I found it very hard, though Mam says she enjoyed having us, apart from all the chocolates she and Lucy used to eat. By the time we moved back to Wales, I was independent of my mother and having two women in the house just doesn't work. It's not that my mother was a problem. She and Lucy have got on famously ever since. In fact they get on better than I do with my mother. But she's allowed to irritate the hell out of me; that's what mothers do.

I love my mother desperately; she's one of the best people I have ever known. And I admire the way she's coped with everything she's had to. For me, the greatest strength she gives me is to know that she's there. While I was injured, she gave me 101 per cent of her care, then as I got better, I upped and left home. For my first nine months in Liverpool, she never visited me once. I think she was worried that I was striking out on my own and would no longer have her as a go-between. But she must also have known that I had to get free.

There was a time when I thought my mother's word was absolute. It was brilliant, and everything she said was right. Then as you move through life you realise that other people's advice is only what they would do for themselves, their guidelines. You have to take the bits that are right for you. I think the way I dress has been her biggest disappointment about me. She has a very fixed idea of what is proper and right. If Mam had her way, I'd be wearing a suit every day and maybe golfing jumpers and slip-ons when I come home. My late step-dad wore a jacket and tie every time he went down the road. You'd never see him outside the house in an open-necked shirt.

But I owe my mother everything. Love is the one emotion the devil can't fight against. And that's it. I suppose the devil tried to take me in his way and my mother kept me alive by loving me so much.

When we moved in with my Mam, my stepdad, Loft, was still alive. She loved him too, beyond distraction. The only other two men in her life at that time were me and her grandson Richard, my sister's boy.

We called my stepdad Loft or Lofty because he was six foot five, though his real name was Harold. He worked as an engineer at Whitchurch Hospital in Cardiff, where Mam was a psychiatric nurse before doing her district-nurse training. Mam started seeing him when I was about 14 and they married a couple of years later. I adored Loft, he was everything a father should be to me, unlike my real father, who had left home when I was ten. When Mam and Loft came to visit me in Woolwich after I'd been injured, I could feel myself relax from the top of my head down to my toes. In my choice of records for *Desert Island Discs* I chose the theme tune to *Match of the Day* to remember Lofty and all the Saturday afternoons we'd spent watching sport on television.

Even if the move to Quaker's Yard was less than perfect, Lucy and I were very happy. We obviously realised that we were right for each other because we went for children straight away and never looked back. We were married in May and James came along in July the following year. Life would never be the same again.

I remember phoning Lucy from the rugby club and saying to one of the boys, Steve Jones it was, 'Hey, I've only got to pick up the phone and Lucy'll come and pick me up. No problem. She always comes whenever I call.'

We hadn't long had James. When I came back from the phone I said, 'Has anyone got any taxi numbers?' Steve has never let me forget it.

But more than that, having children changes your thought processes; it certainly changed mine. I didn't realise just how much difference James could make. I remember talking about it to my mother. I said, 'I can't get over the fact that this little bundle is so totally dependent on me.' It was unconditional, the love, the joy – totally unconditional – and I couldn't get over that. You just try your best not to let any of them down.

Having James meant that other things had to go too. It curtailed a lot of my Saturday-night boozing at the rugby club and I gave up motor sport. That was largely because the sponsorship ran out, but I wouldn't have been able to continue it with a young family. The death of a friend during the European Touring Car Championship made me realise how dangerous the sport is. I was watching the race live on telly at the time, it was absolutely tragic. He had his name on the door so I knew who it was. I pretty much lost a shine on motor sport for quite a while after that.

I miss the thrill of it now but I wasn't the greatest racer and was never going to be world champion. There were far quicker drivers than me who could lever off that extra second going into a corner and find speed where I couldn't. Maybe if I had practised longer and worked harder I might have got somewhere. I never won a race. The best I managed was third in some celebrity charity race. No excuses. You wear gloves and with power steering my hands weren't really a problem. It's just that the other guys were better than me.

When James was only two weeks old, Terry Wogan invited us as a family on to his show – me, Lucy and the lad. I've always found Terry such a pleasant guy, entertaining and very straightforward. He told me he doesn't ask many of his Irish friends round for dinner because they stay too late and drink you dry. But he and I get along fine.

This time, to much cooing from the audience, he went misty-eyed over James's little knees and fingers. We talked about changing nappies and whether I was shaping up to be a good dad. Lucy gave me limited approval.

'It's hard doing an interview with you,' said Terry. 'You keep looking at the baby.'

He asked if I'd ever thought I'd become a father.

'There were times when I had my doubts, certainly. And there were times when I looked at myself in the mirror and I thought I'd never have a girlfriend, let alone a wife and a child, so it's a very special time for me. If I'd known I'd be this happy, I'd probably have gone out and got one somewhere else. I don't know where I'd have bought one, though.'

Even in James's first two weeks I had discovered the one thing that could really tear me apart. 'Emotionally,' I told Terry, 'it upsets me terribly when he cries. I didn't know anything would affect me that much, but he cries terribly when he has his nappy changed and when he has a bath, and I can't cope. Now, I can cope with anything else but I can't cope with his crying.'

Throughout his first television interview, James lay snug in Lucy's arms and behaved like the perfect gentleman he is and always has been.

4

Earning a Crust

I PUT A HELL of a lot of effort into life, because the life we have is so important. To be honest, if I didn't have Lucy and the kids to worry about, I probably wouldn't work half as hard as I do. I'd do just enough to get by, but they deserve everything you can give them.

Money is nice to have but it's a means to an end, that's all. I've always been somebody who could go out and earn a crust. I may not end up being the richest guy in the world, not financially, but I've got a lot of other riches and the one person I can always rely on is me. If I fell in a bucket of dung, I'd come out smelling of roses. It just happens that way, but if you think yourself lucky, then you generally are. If you think positive about everything, then you generally do get to see the better side of life.

That doesn't mean things come easily. If I hadn't been put in the public eye, I would never have had the opportunities that have come my way. But the opportunities didn't stay around because I relied on the publicity of being injured. I didn't just take from life and say, 'Woe is me, I'm a victim.' I put things back into life. I put things

—— 51 ——

back into this country for all the help I've had from the people who owe me absolutely nothing, zip, zilch, nada, nowt.

It's something that my Mam and Lofty drummed into me right from the start, when I was still lying on my back in hospital. The world doesn't owe you a living. You have to get up and make your own way in the world. You're lying there, flat on your back in intensive care, and they're saying, 'Pick yourself up and start all over again.'

If you want to be part of life, you have to accept yourself as you are and then look around to see who you might aspire to be in the future. You're not going to become a different person, but you can make yourself more successful, make yourself luckier by working harder, putting more effort into your preparation for life, reading up more, studying harder.

There was a golfer – I can't remember who it was – who was always winning tournaments but the press kept on criticising him, putting his achievements down to luck. Then he won a major tournament and when everyone gathered round he said to the press, 'I just want to tell you guys something. You've been saying I've been lucky to win this tournament and that tournament. You know, it's amazing that the harder I practise, the luckier I get.'

Even Tiger Woods has to practise endlessly. It's hard work that gets you to be that lucky. Look at David Beckham and Alan Shearer, look at how hard they have trained and worked to overcome injuries and personal problems, how diligently they've put the practice in on the training field. That's why they're the world's best. That's what's got them to the top of the tree. It's not just a matter of turning up and kicking a football around for 90 minutes, then going off home. I can't afford to do that either, nor can I afford to play football or I'd never earn a bloody penny. I play football like I'm wearing two shoe-boxes on my feet.

Muhammad Ali was the best boxer that ever was, and voted the best sportsman of all time. I loved him when he said, 'Yeah, if I'd been a trash man, I would have been the best trash man in the world.' And that's what it's all about. It's not so much what you do but how you do it. Remember all those little old adages your mother always hit you with when you were a kid, and she wanted you to tidy up or make your bed? 'If a job's worth doing, it's worth doing well.' Or as the rich say, 'If a job's worth doing, it's worth paying somebody else to do it for you.'

But ultimately, that's what my life is all about too: try-ing to continue to be as good as I possibly can be, dipping in and out of so many different areas. I'm no angel at all but at least all my skeletons are out of the closet, thank God, unless there are one or two I can't remember. I go to work and I go home. I like to have a drink, I really do enjoy drinking. But I enjoy waking up not having had a drink. I sleep better if I don't drink, so I'm trying to catch up on lots of sleep.

One of the things I found I could do was motivational speaking. I get an adrenalin pump from speaking in pub-lic as I do from going on the telly. I still get nerves and butterflies beforehand, because I don't want to make myself look stupid. I don't want to let people down. The instant you get up to speak, the nerves get left behind like the tail of a meteor. Once I'm up there, I love trying to get involved with people. It makes me feel like an actor play-ing in front of a live audience and really that's what you're doing – giving a performance. You're projecting, you're emphasising and you're pausing, doing all the things that actors do. You're a player, that's what you are.

I remember the very first time I made a speech in public and it was bloody awful. I was with the guys from Weston Spirit and we were talking to a Rotary Club in Kirkby, Liverpool, trying to get all these businessmen to back us. Kirkby is renowned as being a tough kind of place but the hotel we chose on the edge of the East Lancashire Road was a nice little spot. I was using crib cards with bullet points on them. Paul Oginsky of Weston Spirit was there with me and he'd taken charge of the cards.

I started working through the cards. The first two went fine. Then I came to the third, on which Paul had written: 'The rest of the cards are blank. Now let's see what you can do.' He's a practical joker, Paul is, and he made me feel a complete git. I'd said a few words at other events, thanking people for different things, but this was my first proper speech. It was a boiling hot day, I remember, and I was soaked when I came out. It was like that scene inside the cockpit from the comedy film *Airplane*. The windscreen wipers are going like crazy and the pilot is sweating buckets as he tries to bring the plane down. I felt just like that, bringing out all these cloths to mop up my sweat. Because so much of my body was burnt, I don't sweat evenly, and I would have gone round the room getting underpants off people, I was that desperate.

In spite of that experience, I started to do motivational speaking as a way of earning a living, and because it gives me a chance to make sense of my experiences in a way other people can share. I'm not one of those book-taught motivators. I want people to listen to what I have to say and take away the bits that are relevant to them. I don't want them to swallow the whole thing and say, 'Wow, that guru was good.' I'd much rather they went away saying, 'That's a life story I can reflect on. I'll be able to walk away and take bits and pieces out of that for the rest of my life. Some of it I accept and some of it I disagree with, because it's not relevant to me.'

Basically, what I try to say to people is that whatever you're going through, I've been through something similar and come out the other side. We encounter stresses and strains all the time, isolation and loneliness from the pressures of the job or whatever. Maybe some of the things that have happened to me have been worse than most people have to suffer. The fact is, I've come out the other side. I've survived and been able to make it work for me. I've been able to lead a very positive life, earn enough money for my family, have a happy life, be a bit extravagant at times – not overly extravagant. I'm not an actor or an overrated pop star, for God's sake. I'm just an ordinary guy with a good story to tell, which I try to put across as best I can.

I might talk a little about the *Sir Galahad* and what happened in the Falklands, but I don't linger over it or hang on to it. I talk about facing up to challenges and accepting change. The only thing that ever stays constant in our lives is change. Every day changes. You won't have the same day tomorrow you had today. Even people who do repetitive work do it differently each time, otherwise it gets boring.

That's what it's all about. You have to meet the challenges that are thrown at you, and sometimes they can be very tough. What you have to do is to rise to those challenges and if you can't do it on your own, that's okay. It's not a sign of weakness if you can't do everything on your own. Have the courage to show your vulnerability and say, 'Hey, I can't do this by myself. Can you help?'

Sometimes it's like when you were a kid, and you're trying to work out a mathematical problem that just isn't clicking. Then somebody says, 'Well, have you tried doing it like this? Put this here and that there and off you go.'

'Oh, of course,' you say, 'it was there all the time.' Then the rest just falls into place.

It doesn't mean you have to rely on other people all the time. You can still remain an individual and be an independent thinker, but there will always be times when you are vulnerable. Even the best and toughest in the world are vulnerable, even that guy in jail, Charles Bronson, he's vulnerable. Everybody needs somebody else at some point.

Whenever I'm speaking at these motivational events, I work towards the same ending. If I can do it, anybody can. Because as much as I hope I'm special to my family, I don't see myself as being special. I don't see myself as being an exceptional guy or any better than anybody else. I don't see myself as being worse than they are, either. They may be better than me at certain things, like football or rugby or singing or whatever, but that doesn't mean they are better than me as a person, as a human being. They're not better than me because they've got more money or a title or a fortune from birth. That just makes them lucky, though not necessarily luckier than I am. It's the same philosophy that drives Weston Spirit: as human beings we are all of equal value, worth neither less nor more than anybody else.

The way I end my speeches is purely and simply this: you have to accept change in your life. Not all change is good but it isn't all bad, either. All those people who continually rail against change without good reason are simply wasting their breath. The ones who accept change and make it work for them have stolen a march on you. They're ten miles down the road while you're still trying to catch up. As you see in a marathon, anyone that drops a mile behind the leaders is never going to catch up. So while you're arguing and complaining, life is passing you by. It's like congestion charging in London, which people are moaning about at the moment. If it's going to be a problem for you, find a way to make it work. And if you don't like it, go and live somewhere else. You can sell your house in London and buy a county in Wales.

Over the years I've spoken to insurance salesmen, credit unions, banks, soldiers, the SAS, raw recruits, nurses, doctors, clinical psychologists and psychiatrists, farmers, gardeners, even golfing-greenkeepers at a worldwide conference up in Harrogate. I'll try to make it relevant and personal to each audience, and I try to entertain. I can tell funny anecdotes that will make you smile, they'll make you chuckle, but I'm no comedian. I can't give you belly laughs. I'm just an ordinary Joe doing what an ordinary Joe does.

I'll never forget the first big event I ever did. It was to an audience of financial managers at the Barbican in London. I hadn't been on the speaking circuit long and I watched this guy from South Africa go on first. He went out on stage with a pushbike, an old sit-up-and-beg sort of bike, and he was hilariously funny. He was bright, he was to the point, he was clever, he was sparkling. I remember being so terrified at the thought that I'd have to follow him on stage that I had to shut myself away in the toilet. I could still hear him, even in the loo. He was talking about different aspects of the job, and life and everything, using the bicycle as a prop. At some point he actually rode it on stage. And I had to follow that. I thought, hell, or something similar. I knew the power of adrenalin and it came in lumps. I had prepared a lot for my speech, but I wasn't prepared enough. That was something I regret because I didn't give them my best.

It's funny how the bad times stay with you. Also quite early on, I was asked to speak in London to an organisation called Families for Defence. I went along, not thinking it was going to be anything big. When I turned up I realised all of a sudden that the room was full of some of the most influential people in the country and ambassadors from all over the world. One of the other speakers was Tim Rice; I remember him because he was incredibly nice to me. I don't know whether he was nice to me because he could see the terror on my face, or whether he was just being pleasant. Either way he had a tremendously calming influence on me, but when I got up on that stage my lips stuck to my teeth. I was like a pub singer having a really bad time. It was terrible, unbelievably bad.

Afterwards they all went off to the Café Royal and I went to see a friend of mine who was having a few problems and wanted to chat about things going on in his mind. I thought talking to him was more important, and I couldn't cope with any more pressure. Now it doesn't bother me. I can mix with anybody and not feel threatened or inferior. Then I just wanted out of it.

I found that speech difficult because I was nervous and intimidated. But there are two speeches I found even harder to make. The first was at my own wedding. When you speak in front of your family and friends, anything you say, any *faux pas* you make, is going to revisit you for the rest of your life as these people don't just go away for ever afterwards.

For a guy, the next hardest speech to give is at someone else's wedding. Fortunately for me, I've only ever once performed as best man, for my friend David FitzGerald, better known as Fitz, who was marrying a lovely girl called Karen. It was a great wedding with so many nice people who genuinely cared about the two of them. As Fitz runs a radio station down in Devon, there were quite a few media people at the wedding breakfast, including a number of comedians and actors like Frank Kelly of Father Jack fame (in TV's *Father Ted*). I was trying to make people laugh because Fitz had asked me; and when it's that personal, you can't help but get more nervous still.

First on his feet was Karen's brother, who spoke lovingly about Karen and her mum, and about her dad, who isn't with us any more. Next came Karen herself, then comedian Richard Digance, another of Fitz's friends, who spoke hilariously for 15 minutes, leaving me as best man to bring up the rear. This threw everyone a curved ball because at the weddings I go to, a lot of people bet on how long the best man's speech will last – often 25 or 30 minutes, which is far too long. I always reckon the shorter the better, and thankfully at Fitz's wedding, 20 minutes or more had elapsed without my saying a word. So I got up and spoke for about seven or eight minutes, which is plenty long enough to say all the rude things I wanted about Fitz. We call him that because none of his clothes ever do. He has no fashion sense whatsoever and Karen has had to work on him like a torturer wielding a rubber truncheon to try to persuade him to upgrade his clothing.

As far as I know, my speech went down well, but whether the rest of the audience liked it is not really the point. You're doing it for two people you like very much, and that's what counts. As for speaking professionally, I hope I've got better over the years. I've certainly worked hard at it, because I believe that if I'm going to get the best out of me, I've got to give of my best to other people. No matter how tired I am, no matter how irritable or lousy I feel, once I'm there those people deserve the best I can give them. It may not be the very best I'm capable of, but it's the best I can give them at the time. That's all I want to do and that's no more than people deserve.

5

Bosnia: Back to a War Zone

THE IDEA OF GOING to Bosnia to raise money for the children there came about through fatherhood really. There were three of us involved at the start – myself, my agent Geoffrey Hamilton-Fairley and my journalist friend Pat Hill, who was then working with the *News of the World*. All three of us had recently become fathers. My son James was born in July 1991, Pat's eldest (another James) a couple of weeks later, while Geoff and Mouse had their son Gordon in December. Pictures started coming through of what the war was doing to the children in Bosnia and the former Yugoslavia – especially photographs of children blown up on a bus in Sarajevo – and we knew we had to do something.

I have always got on well with Pat. He's the happiest depressive I know, and he's probably the best drinker I know too. I'm not far off the top of my best drinkers' list but Pat is right there at the top. Yet even when he's had a drink, he can still remember everything. That's a journalist for you.

We first met when Pat was the *News of the World*'s television and show-business reporter. He had approached me to review a television series with Nigel Havers called *Perfect Hero*, about a burnt pilot in World War II. I trusted him because they printed more or less what I wrote, though Nigel Havers wasn't best pleased as I thought the programme was dreadful and had described it as his 'Bridge Too Far'. Pat and I had done several pieces together after that, including an interview when James was born which they printed under the headline 'Sir Galadad'. Pat had come down to Quaker's Yard with photographer David Thorpe and we'd gone out to wet the baby's head, conducting the interview around the pubs of Nelson. I remember tiptoeing home over the grass with a giant teddy bear they had brought for James, absolutely banjaxed: how stupid can you get?

Pat and David had both come out to the Falklands with me on my first journey back, as Pat was going to serialise my subsequent book for the *News of the World*. Having writers and journalists on board caused some difficulties to Malcolm, but for me it was good having Pat there as a buffer between me and all the other things that were going on. He's the one who took the photograph of Carlos hugging me at the war memorial in Buenos Aires. 'WORLD EXCLUSIVE: SIMON'S HUG FOR HIS ARGY BOMBER,' said the paper, when they ran the picture on the front page. Some of the families found this shocking as the caption suggested that I was the one doing the hugging when really it was Carlos who had grabbed hold of me. I'm a Welshman from the valleys, for God's sake. Hugging someone you don't know is something you just don't do – you don't even hug strange women.

Pat's life is full of cock-ups, and true to form, he nearly didn't make it to the Falklands at all. Not only had he failed to get a visa for Argentina but no one told him he was supposed to confirm his flight 24 hours before leaving, so when he turned up at the airport his name wasn't on the passenger list. We nearly had to leave him behind until a Mr Fix-It helped him approach the right person at the airport and he was slipped on to the plane masquerading as a Chilean rock star. There he was in first class, sipping pink champagne, while the rest of us were back in the cattle trucks, knees up around our noses, drinking warm beer.

But he never did make it to Bosnia, despite his help in setting up the trip. It was actually Geoff's suggestion that we should travel out there to try to raise funds for the children, after the three of us had got quite emotional about the photographs coming out of Sarajevo. Pat went along to his editor, Patsy Chapman, to see if she would support the idea of launching an appeal through the paper to support the children of Bosnia.

'I'll think about it,' she said. Then photographs started coming through of the concentration camps, and she called him up in the middle of the night. 'Right,' she said, 'we'll do that appeal. How about tomorrow?'

The impossible takes just a little bit longer than that, but the *News of the World* put £10,000 into our Children of Bosnia appeal, and Geoff did the rounds of the aid agencies.

The Red Cross were the ones we went with in the end. Our main concern was to make sure that any money we raised went directly into aid, not overheads. If school kids were going to be persuaded to part with their pocket money, we wanted to be able to tell them exactly what their money was buying. The purchasing power of organisations like the UNHCR (United Nations High Commission for Refugees) really is enormous. Twenty pounds would then buy a full set of winter clothing for a child and for £10 you really could feed four children for a month.

Geoff worked out a deal with the Red Cross that would allow all the money we raised to be inputted directly back into Bosnia. That way, we would be piggybacking on the aid infrastructure already in place and our money really would make a difference to the children and families whose lives were being torn apart. Red Cross officials were a little unsure about how the deal would work out in practice but to their credit they agreed, despite a few misgivings about taking us into a war zone. The appeal's initial aim – overtaken in just two or three weeks – was to raise £100,000, enough to buy basics like food and medicine for 40,000 people for a month.

Then Pat had a setback when the *News of the World* refused to let him go on the trip, sending Stuart White instead, their investigative journalist based in Sarajevo. But at least they let photographer David Thorpe come along, which gave me another familiar face.

In August Geoff and I flew out to Zagreb, where Stuart and David joined us from Sarajevo after filing harrowing reports of injured children in the city's Kosevo Hospital. Judging it too dangerous to take us into central Bosnia, the Red Cross took us three hours down the coast to the refugee camps of Croatia.

The girl who drove us was stunningly attractive but a bloody awful driver, I remember. Instead of braking before she hit a bend she let the bend slow us down, then accelerated as the vehicle was struggling round. Her driving got so bad there was no way I could relax. Geoff would be nodding off and I would sing to keep up my spirits. He said it was a horrible sound to wake up to – I am living proof that not every Welshman can sing. 'Whatever job you do in life,' he pleaded, 'please make sure it has nothing to do with singing.'

The camps, when we finally got there, were full of women and girls. The only males you saw were very young boys as all the men were off fighting or being killed. Starved of information, the women had no idea what had happened to their menfolk, which might have been a blessing in that they didn't know how terrible it was.

At Umag refugee camp, temperatures reached 35°C and more. Here the refugees were housed in the caravans and chalets of a former holiday camp. Though conditions in the heat were bad enough, we knew things could only get worse when the rains and cold of winter arrived.

These people had virtually nothing, yet in the camp's community hall they had laid out food for us as a way of saying 'thank you' – little bits of cheese and meat and beer. I was absolutely gobsmacked. I felt so small and insignificant in front of these people who were just desperate for any help they could get. I had never felt so impotent in my life, and so unimportant. What could we possibly achieve for them? Yet they appreciated the little we actually did and put on this modest buffet affair so that we were made to feel important. They provided all this for us and I felt overwhelmed.

Stuart's report of our visit to the camp appeared in the *News of the World* on 23 August 1992. Just one week later we were heartened to learn that our Children of Bosnia appeal had already reached over £177,000, and money was still pouring in.

Yet news coming out of Bosnia was getting worse all the time and we knew there was more we could do. Geoff and I talked about it, then he went back to the Red Cross and said, 'We can do better than this. If we go into Bosnia again – and we'll do it just one more time – we have to go into the front line, see the worst things possible and bring the pictures back. That's the only way we'll raise a serious amount of money.'

The Red Cross said okay and without knowing what kind of journey they had lined up for us, we set about organising another trip. This time we went with Lynda Lee-Potter of the *Daily Mail,* a very plucky woman who said she was game for it. I have known and trusted Lynda for a long time. She and I get on exceptionally well and I like her very much. Despite her fearsome reputation, she's hugely compassionate as a person and I found her great company.

Lynda brought along her son, a young journalist who was just starting out, and the *Mail* sent out their war photographer, Steve Back, a fascinating guy who had done it all a thousand times before. As well as Geoff, there was also a sound man, Martin Gifford, who was to record a radio diary I was doing for BBC Radio Wales.

In November, with winter fast approaching, we flew to Split with Colin McCallum of the Red Cross, spending the first night in a lovely little place where we ate on a veranda overlooking the picturesque Mediterranean countryside. I didn't sleep much that night; it must have been the nerves getting to me. Soon after 5 a.m. the next day we put on our flak jackets and joined a Red Cross convoy of lorries taking food parcels into central Bosnia over unmade mountain tracks along the only supply route still operating – the Ho Chi Minh trail, they called it. The road wasn't as bad as I had been expecting, but the journey took ten hours or more, so you ended up with a very numb bum.

All along the way we passed through roadblocks and checkpoints. The sight of an anti-aircraft gun at one of the checkpoints made me uneasy and we spotted the biggest Russian helicopter I have ever seen unloading supplies to a hut in the middle of nowhere. We had no idea which side the guards were on, or which nation was flying the helicopter. We had stopped for a pee on a high plateau and had spread out off the trail, each looking for a convenient bush. 'Come back, all of you,' shouted Steve Back in some alarm. 'You must stick to the trail – there could be mines all around.' That brought us in quickly. The men went round the front of the truck, leaving Lynda to have a pee on her own round the back. Some time later, on another short break, I went for a little jog up the road until I saw some menacing soldiers coming down towards me. At another of the checkpoints the Croatian guards got very irate when one of our guys took a photograph of a valley with nothing much in it except three Croatian guards, one Kalashnikov rifle and an awful lot of ego.

As we came off the mountain, the countryside reminded me of Wales, only the roads were different: in Bosnia they were just dirt tracks. In one place we passed a big school that had been turned into a refugee centre and a group of gypsies begging from a burnt-out Volkswagen minibus they had turned into a home. They were shunned by everyone: the Bosnian Muslims didn't like them, the Serbs hated them, the Croats didn't like them, they were just left in the middle with no food, no money, no nothing.

Eventually we reached Zenica, close to the front line and a completely lawless environment. It was about three weeks before the UN peacekeeping forces arrived under Colonel Bob Stewart of the Cheshires. Here we were booked into the International Hotel, which was still open for business, though much of the city had closed down. Shops were shut. Schools closed. The steelworks bombed and silent. The football stadium next to the hotel quite empty. There wasn't any real shelling, though terrorist bombs were going off all the time. You would go to bed in your flak jacket, hoping that you'd wake up in the morning. Everybody was blowing everything up, that was the trouble. They blew up a bridge about half a mile away from the hotel, and a couple of foreign journalists were murdered in the car park.

One night they tried to attack the hotel while we were in there. I wasn't overly concerned, to be honest, which shows how unimaginative I am. I might have been more concerned if the attack had been concentrated and sustained. But it wasn't – more small bursts of automatic gunfire, some of which hit the hotel, and a large explosion that fell well short. You might have been killed if your luck had run out that day, but none of our windows got broken, so it didn't bother me at all.

As far as we could tell, the battle lines were as much economic as ethnic. People were having to give up houses in some areas and gain them in others, so they were trying to work things out economically. As our interpreter explained to Lynda, 'I am a Croat married to a Serb and I cannot accept closed ethnic communities. But the more there is danger that you are killed, the harder it is. I am afraid that in one year's time we shall all have to stick to one side to survive.' We found it very distressing and none of us could work out the politics of it. All I could see was right and wrong, and most people were acting wrongly – Serbs, Croats, Muslims, they were all guilty of acts of barbarism.

Each day we went out with the Red Cross to see as much as we could. You would travel through this beautiful country, absolutely stunning, and you would feel at peace with everything, then you'd get these sharp little reminders that stabbed you in the sides – checkpoints manned by youngsters, some with hunting rifles, some with Russian AK47s, some with Magnums or sawn-off shotguns; young men being drilled in a field; howitzers; mines laid on roads; babes with rifles, honest to God. It was scary – they were only children, they shouldn't have been anywhere near them. There was a madness to the whole affair and it seemed to be getting worse. Hundreds of thousands of people, mainly Muslims, were being forced into areas that were already overladen with people, areas with no food and very little quality shelter or accommodation. It made you sit up and wonder how it was going to affect the younger children. Kids as young as four or five would either wave at you or give what I can only describe as a fascist salute. What was this whole conflict going to do to them?

The only thing that protected us from snipers and the rest of the lunatic fringe was the big red cross on the side of our trucks. I was glad to have it when we drove along 'Snipers' Alley'. It wasn't a real alley, just a road that was flat on either side, rising up into the hills where we were told the Serbs would sit and wait, drinking and taking pot-shots at the cars as they passed. We drove along there so fast we were almost taking off in the back of our Toyota Land Cruisers.

Even the painted red crosses nearly let us down one day, when we were driving out to a supply depot to see how aid was distributed – an operation that required speed and vigilance as the place suffered nightly attacks from all the different factions wanting to get their hands on the kit. It was a two-hour car journey away. The distance wasn't far but you travelled in convoy through constant checkpoints and many of the bridges had been blown up. Half the time you had no idea whose territory you were crossing.

Our Red Cross chaperone was an incredible young Frenchwoman called Claire, who later married Colonel Bob Stewart. She was able to make herself understood in most of the local languages and always arrived at our hotel wearing Chanel suits and high-heeled shoes amid all the grime and misery. That day we were travelling at the back of the convoy. Claire was driving the Toyota with me, Geoff, Steve Back and the interpreter. The others were travelling at the front. After a time we noticed a car weaving about the road behind us. When the convoy stopped, as it invariably did, these young guys with Kalashnikovs jumped out and started shouting and screaming at us, clearly drunk and out of their heads.

'Sit where you are,' was Steve's advice. 'Don't say a thing.'

One of the youngsters thrust his Kalashnikov through the window, right in Claire's face.

She wasn't having any of it. 'You get that effing rifle out my face,' she shouted back at him in whatever language it was. She was just a young thing but she gave him an absolute earful, bollocking him like a mother would her child. Without her, they would probably have hoicked us out of the Toyota and shot us, but the lad with the rifle did as he was told. It just shows how immature he was.

In Zenica itself, we visited a refugee holding centre that housed about 600 people, mainly Muslims, though some Croats and even some Serbs had been among the many more who had passed through. The first thing you noticed was the smell. There were just two lavatories – one for men, one for women. Through our interpreter, we gathered as many stories as we could. One family of six we talked to – parents, grandparents and two children – had been forced from their home, about 300 kilometres away, leaving everything behind.

'Whoever appeared on the streets was shot by a sniper,' they told us. 'In just two days a hundred people were killed. They were lying on the streets. Anyone still alive was forced to leave.'

'How did you get out and not be killed?' I asked.

'The order was given to all Muslims in the city to go to a certain place. There was a convoy of trucks and the former Yugoslav Army took us to the Bosnian border. Then we had to walk for maybe four kilometres, and while we were walking, they were shooting at us. About four or five people were killed and 15 wounded as we were coming down from the mountain. My nephew and his wife were killed. Now we really don't know what to expect. At the moment, we have no hope.'

'It was terrible,' one of the others told us. 'The soldiers came into the houses by force. They burnt some houses. We didn't have electricity for two months before we left, no water. They didn't give the Muslims any food, though the Serbian population got food regularly. The only chance of getting food was if you had a Serb friend who would sell you some wheat flour or whatever – that was your only possibility to survive.'

'I don't really know what happened,' added one of the women. 'We all lived together and got on quite well. They told us that we shouldn't be afraid, nothing would happen to us, but some extremist groups came in from outside and they did criminal acts. We were told our neighbours would protect us but every night there were people killed. We don't know who killed our people. They came and they killed and we couldn't stay any longer.'

I found listening to their stories surreal. Nothing made sense. I didn't think I could be easily shocked but their stories made all of us feel numb. We only had their word for the horrors they had experienced, but seeing that look of total honesty on their faces, you couldn't imagine they were telling you anything but the truth.

It was all very distressing. Every night we would return to our hotel, where they served some of the most floury pizzas I have ever tasted, and we'd get drunk at the *Mail*'s expense on the very good wine that was all they had left in the cellars. Alcohol was about the only thing you could get in any quantity. There was virtually no meat and the streets were tellingly empty of dogs.

Of all the sights we witnessed, one of the worst for me was after we had driven right up to the front line, near a place called Banja Luka. The Serbs were bombarding it and we couldn't get through. You could feel the ground shaking and pounding, just like in a disco. Though we didn't know it at the time, a terrible massacre was taking place. On the way back we came across some abandoned farm outbuildings where up to 20 children were living with their mothers. There were no men with them. Some of the children had no shoes and they didn't seem to have much food. They were just waiting, and no one knew what would happen to them.

The kids looked at me strangely, as if I was frightening them. Steve Back wanted to photograph me with them. It didn't feel right, but Steve and Geoff insisted. 'You've got to do it,' Geoff said to me. 'We haven't come all this way for you to say "no". We need your picture so that we can raise money for them.'

Leaving the group huddled together, cold, shoeless, on an exposed piece of land affected us all, even hard-nosed Steve Back. You wanted to pick them all up and take them away, but there was no room for them in the Land Cruisers. The Serbs were only hours away and we had to get out. I asked Claire what would happen to them. She would report the group to the Red Cross when we got back, she said, but in reality whatever would happen would happen before anybody could intervene.

Geoff said he learnt something about fear on that trip: you can't be frightened day in, day out, not all the time. Of course, we were all concerned to get back alive, but inside the hotel life could seem pretty normal, apart from the day the local Muslim warlords decided to hold a peace council in there. With the Serbs only a few miles up the road, it maybe wasn't the safest place to be. We were sitting at a couple of tables close to the stairs, having a few quiet beers, when a Muslim cleric in flowing robes and full Arab regalia swept into the hotel surrounded by several Arab bodyguards. It was really spooky, seeing the cleric in the middle of a war zone. Ignoring us completely, he headed for the lifts and disappeared. About a dozen local warlords also piled in, all bristling with weapons – shotguns sawn off to fit into holsters, masking tape wrapped around their grips, Uzis, Kalashnikovs, pistols, submachine guns, old guns, new guns, obsolete guns, and a whole bunch I didn't recognise.

It was clear to me that this was a ragtag militia rather than a real fighting army. They were learning as they went along, and they didn't seem to have a huge amount of discipline or organisation. Everybody was vying for power, everybody wanted to be a warlord, everybody wanted to be in charge. It was all so tribal and factionalised. One village would have Croats and Serbs fighting the Bosnians, the next would have Bosnians and Serbs fighting the Croats and sometimes you'd get Croats and Bosnians fighting the Serbs. All the villages had different parties and different agendas, that's what made the place so screwed up. They were picking who they wanted to fight with and against as a matter of personal choice. And everybody was drunk. All these armed youngsters in black shirts would go off drinking, then fire off their AK47s in the middle of the street.

* * *

We had flown out in November and already snow was threatening. There's an incredible wind in the Balkans that continues for about three months. It strips the ground and strips the trees, and the wind chill makes you feel colder still. According to the aid agencies, the snows would bring a halt to the killing, but the problem was keeping people alive through the winter, giving govern-ments and parliaments the chance to help them through the rest of their lives by stopping the war.

I came away with huge admiration for the unarmed aid workers who were risking everything to help these people. When you have large organisations like the Red Cross and Médecins Sans Frontières, there is bound to be a certain amount of chaos. It's different with the military, because they are given tramlines to walk down. You can't do that with civilians, who tend to walk a separate path to every-body else. Of course, we encountered some difficulties in the aid efforts but, on the whole, the dedication of the people we met impressed the hell out of me.

The drive back to Split seemed to take even longer than before. Again we passed the gypsies begging beside the burnt-out VW van. Here Lynda stripped off her coat and gave it to a girl who carried a little baby in her arms. Then she opened her bag and started dishing out cash and what little stuff she had with her. Steve Back was getting really concerned. 'We can't go on doing this,' he said to Geoff, 'because they'll think we have loads of cash and we'll end up getting killed.' There were hundreds of them in the area and only a few of us. Geoff persuaded Lynda to stop. 'You feel so impotent, so awful,' she said. The truth was, we all did.

Winter rains had turned the mountain track to mud. Lorries had simply slithered over the edge, and we saw cars full of families struggling to escape the conflict. There was barely room to pass other vehicles. On one side of the track was a sheer drop down, while on the other our Land Cruisers literally scraped against the trucks coming down in the opposite direction. As we tried to negotiate a particularly huge aid truck I thought, I'm not taking this any more. You can drive, I'll walk. I got out and walked for several hundred yards before I judged it safe to get back in. Several others agreed with me that discretion was the better part of valour, apart from the driver, who had no choice.

It's weird: I remember the journey back almost more than our time over there, perhaps because in Bosnia I was blanking out so many things. Our flight to Zagreb was truly horrible. Lightning filled the clouds and snow was driving against the aeroplane. From Zagreb we flew on to Germany and I remember chatting to Lynda's son, a very pleasant young man, and going through Duty Free, thinking how absolutely bizarre it was to be comfortable and warm. Then we arrived at Heathrow and went straight into a press conference. Again I was struck by how surreal it felt to be back in British normality after spending time in a place so horrendously affected by conflict, hoping that the aid we had delivered would make a difference, though I suspect that any aid would have helped, it was that desperately needed.

I never got to find out exactly how much money we raised, but people responded so generously after both journeys and I'm told it was well over half a million.

6

Family Fallouts

AFTER ALL THE UPSETS over Bosnia, 1993 ended brilliantly with the birth of our second son, Stuart, in October. Your life changes with each new child that comes along. When you have two, you discover that having one was none. It might be a bit inconvenient at times, but having two can become impossible as you have to learn to split yourself into different parts.

Even when he was a baby, you could tell that Stuart with his huge open eyes was completely different from his brother. They are both funny but in their very different ways. While James is always trying to crack a joke, Stuart is the jester who gets into all sorts of trouble. He's just a bundle and makes mistakes and gets told off all the time. When people ask me what he's best at, I say he's best at being confused. Whenever he sees a film, that's who he wants to be, until he sees the next film and he's on to being someone else.

We were still living in Quaker's Yard, close to my Mam and Loft and the rest of the family, and I tried to settle back into some sort of routine. Stuart was only nine days old when James had his first asthma attack. Mam looked after the baby while Lucy and I rushed James off to hospital. At the first hospital a nurse made him panic even more as she tried to force the oxygen mask over his face. I got so fed up at the way they were treating him that we signed him out and took him to another hospital where the nurses were brilliant.

Cycling across the Canyonlands and the Grand Canyon in the States for the Royal Star & Garter Home got me out of Lucy's hair for a bit. I was doing it with a team from the Royal Logistics Corps and we raised about £250,000. I flew first to Colorado and then drove through the Rockies, where we did some mountain biking to harden us up for the real thing. The Rockies were perishing cold while temperatures in the deserts of Utah, Arizona and Nevada reached 49°C or more, so I'm not sure how much good it did us. I remember calling Lucy from Vegas to tell her what a great time we were having, but strangely enough she didn't really want to know.

Then, in April 1994, our family was struck by a double tragedy that opened rifts which even time didn't heal. It started with the death of my grandfather, Percy.

I adored my grandfather and it made no difference that we weren't actual blood relations. My Mam's real father had been killed during World War II, six weeks before she was born. An ARP warden, he'd been hit by a truck while he was riding his motorbike. My grandmother, Nora, had married again when Mam was nine. As Mam says of Percy, 'If I had to choose a father, I couldn't have chosen a better one,' just as I couldn't have wished to choose a better grandfather. Percy was blunt and very funny, a little man in size but huge in stature, to me. My stepfather, Loft, used to tower over him. Loft was deaf and Percy very softly spoken, which made seeing the pair of them together even funnier.

My grandfather's life had been a hard one. Brought up in Merthyr Tydfil when it was still a really tough town, he'd been taken prisoner by the Italians during the war and because of what he experienced, he hated Italians with a passion. He used to tell me stories about how brutal the prison guards were and how they kept all his Red Cross rations for themselves. He rarely told his war stories to anyone else in the family, but Percy and I had a very strong bond. When I got injured he started smoking again, even though he hadn't smoked in years.

After he came back from the POW camp, he had a massive stroke and my grandmother basically bothered him back to health. He couldn't just lie in bed. Every 30 seconds she'd be puffing his pillows, dragging him around. 'That did it,' he said. 'I'd had enough and in the end I just got out of bed. She got on my bloody nerves. All she did was fuss and bother me. I couldn't stand it any longer.' That's the sort of woman my grandmother was. She never gave up on anybody. If you were a cause, she'd rally to it.

Looking back at Percy's life now, you wonder how he survived as long as he did, with all the stresses he had to put up with. He was a signwriter as well as a painter and decorator, painting the sides of wagons and vans, shops, anything that needed it – a hard-working, good man. He would have had his own business but my grandmother stopped him, or so he said. Anything for a quiet life was Percy's way, though he'd often ignore her and do his own thing behind her back. While he was working in a chemical factory down in Trefforest, he fell into a vat of caustic soda and almost turned into a bar of soap. What saved him was a bit of piping that allowed him to clamber back out, his skin badly burnt from the caustic soda. Once again, Nora didn't so much nurse him as bully him back to health.

I think, by the end, Percy just felt his time had come. He was losing strength and his heart gave out. He'd been ill for a while and my Auntie Judy, my Mam's half-sister, virtually lived up at the hospital.

On the night he died, my Mam went to visit him in the evening, then came back home. She got a call from the hospital just before two in the morning, asking her to come back straight away. They don't tell you over the phone what has happened in case you crash the car, but it was pretty obviously serious. She went with Judy, leaving Judy's husband Terence to bring Nora, who was in a state of shock. But by the time Mam reached the hospital, Percy was dead.

The sadness wouldn't end there, but we didn't know that then.

On the afternoon before Percy's funeral, my Mam was busy in her kitchen baking for all the people expected back at my grandmother's after the funeral. Loft was helping her with the dishes. A few months before, he'd had open-heart surgery and a triple-bypass operation in London because nothing was being done in Wales. When he came home he was getting stronger and fitter and his heart was beating properly for the first time in 20 years. But that day he wasn't feeling well. 'I don't know, Pauline,' he said, 'sometimes I feel I won't make Christmas.'

'Don't be so daft,' she replied as she rolled out the pastry. 'You go up and watch the sport and I'll make you a nice apple pie and custard.'

'All right,' he said. 'What shoes are you wearing to the funeral tomorrow?'

'My black patent ones.'

'Okay. Put them on the side downstairs and I'll clean them when I come down in the morning.'

Loft went up to bed first. Late in the night he woke up my Mam, saying he had terrible pains. She didn't bother with a doctor but dialled 999 straight away for an ambulance. They tried to save him but as soon as she saw his arm drop, she knew that was it. Basically, his aorta had ruptured in his abdomen because it couldn't take the pressure of the blood being pumped around, and he died from the haemorrhaging.

Two of Loft's sons from his first marriage, Paul and Christopher, lived close by. Mam tried and tried to call them, thinking they should be there with their father, but it was the early hours of the morning and she couldn't reach either of them. In the end she called me and said, 'I'm at the hospital, can you come up? Loft is dead.'

I put on my clothes and drove up to the hospital straight away.

I was devastated by Loft's death, which came as a complete shock. Because it was classed as a sudden death, the police had to be involved, and that really hurt my Mam. 'Loft was such a good man in his life,' she says, 'they should never have had a policeman there to look at him in death.' She feels this very strongly, even though Loft had been a policeman himself in his earlier years.

They asked me to identify him and though I was only with him for a short period, I remember it like yesterday. I loved my stepfather very, very much. He was very special to me and we got on exceptionally well. I would have done almost anything for him.

After we'd seen to everything, I drove Mam home. By now it was six in the morning and just getting light. Chris, Paul and his wife, Glynis, were waiting outside the door. When Mam went inside she saw the pie she'd cooked for Loft, with the one slice eaten, and her shoes still sitting on the side, waiting to be cleaned. In all their married life together, she'd never had to clean her own shoes; he had always done that for her.

Mam went upstairs to hunt for Loft's birth certificate, which was needed to register the death. He kept all his bits and pieces in an old tin box, his police uniform and mementoes from his sporting career. She remembers bargaining with him in her head, 'If you'll only come back to tell me where your birth certificate is, that's all I ask.'

We still had my grandfather's funeral to get through, despite the fact that Mam had barely slept all night and neither had I. We buried Percy at half past one that day in the small graveyard at the top of the mountain. I used to walk up there when I was growing up in Nelson, but I'd never been into the graveyard until the day of my grandfather's funeral. The weather was absolutely appalling – horizontal rain that turned the ground to a mudslide. Your socks got wet as the rain bounced up inside your trouser legs. Anybody with smooth soles was in danger of slipping into the open grave, but I remember thinking they had prepared for that with planks of wood to help lower the coffin into the grave.

There weren't many of us gathered there, just friends and people who knew him. We're not a huge family, and Percy's family from Merthyr Tydfil wasn't huge either. He had two brothers who came, each the spitting image of him and hard like Percy was. I don't mean that in a bad sense. Percy loved with all his heart, and he loved kids; he just wasn't the cuddling sort, especially as you grew older. Dry as a chip but funny. When he said something, it was worth waiting for.

Afterwards we went back to my grandmother's. My Mam left after a time and walked home as she needed to be alone. She and my grandmother had exchanged words before Percy's funeral, when Nora first heard about Lofty's death. Out of respect for my grandmother, my Mam doesn't want me to repeat what Nora said and out of respect for my Mam I won't, so let's just say that words were spoken that are best forgotten. My grandmother had never really liked Lofty, she just tolerated him because of my mother, and what she said was unfair, uncalled for and unnecessary. But it was the timing of her remarks that really hurt and that explains a lot about what happened afterwards.

The weather turned around for Loft's funeral, which took place at the end of that week. By then it was such a beautiful day that the sun was cracking the paving stones. Lofty never wore black to a funeral. He'd wear a dark suit brightened by a touch of colour in his outfit. I wore red or blue in my tie, and colourful socks. The service was held in St John's Church in Nelson. All the family came, and two of Loft's sons. Malcolm Brinkworth drove up from Dorset and Mam asked him to read their favourite poem, by Leo Marks:

The life that I have
Is all that I have
And the life that I have
Is yours
The love that I have
Of the life that I have
Is yours, and yours and yours . . .

True to character, Nora took issue with the hymns my mother had chosen – 'Jerusalem' and other hymns with a military theme. 'I don't care what you like,' said Mam, 'I'm having them.'

After the service we went to the crematorium and a few days later Paul and his wife drove my mother with Loft's ashes up to his home town of Northallerton in North Yorkshire, where he still had family. Lucy and I came across from Liverpool, where we'd left our two children with Lucy's mum and dad. After meeting up with Mam and the others, we stayed at a motel on the outskirts of Northallerton. Though he'd lived more than half his life in South Wales, Loft still considered himself a Yorkshireman. 'God's own county,' he called it. That's where his heart was and everybody loved him up there. They still called him 'Toot', the name he'd had as a baby when he couldn't say 'toothbrush'. He was always wanting to go back and my mother knew that's where he would want to be buried, so she got permission to bury his ashes in the grave of his mum and dad.

Lofty's death, so soon after my grandfather's, was the start of the rift that opened up with my grandmother. She changed when Percy died and wasn't the person I remembered. She said things in grief she quite possibly regretted. To cope with her own grief, my mother walked away and never really went back. I suppose I did the same.

She was fearsome, my grandmother. There was no better woman to have on your side but no better woman to rile you or to set one against the other. As she got older, I suspect my grandfather shielded us from an awful lot. She was such a strong character but very controlling, and she didn't like you to be too independent of her. If you stood up to her, she wouldn't speak to you. I went to see her once and she hardly said two words to me. She had decided not to like me that day, and that was that.

With my grandmother, you couldn't be adventurous, either. When I learned to fly, she said, 'You don't want to do that. Oh, no, no, no, oh God, you don't want to learn to fly.' It was the same with cars. 'Oh, don't race cars, oh, God alive, don't do that.' When I stood on the wings of an aircraft as it went up, 'Oh, my God,' she said, 'what are you trying to do? Do you want to kill yourself?' It was the same old story when I went back to the Falklands. 'Oh, you don't want to go back there.' Yet she herself had learnt to ride a motorbike, even if she never drove a car.

Some people become domineering in later life, as she did, which is tragic really, because she was a wonderful woman in many ways, just not so wonderful towards the end. I still love her for the strength she gave my family and the things she created when she was younger, even if we didn't like each other very much by the end.

Nora's divisiveness drove a wedge between all the members of the family. She would work her way in between people deliberately, or so it seems now, just to separate you. Of my three aunts, the only one I see now is my Auntie Judy, who pretty much brought me up when I was a young boy and my mother was working. Pamela, another of my aunts, helped to bring up my sister Helen, and Penny did the same for her kid brother, my Uncle Jeremy, who is actually the same age as me.

Judy is absolutely crackers – the best woman, so down to earth, and she says things that make you howl with laughter. Her life is like a comedy sketch. My two cousins would bring their boyfriends home early from the pub on a Friday night, and they'd all look forward to going home, just to hear Judy going at Terence, who used to go out and play darts on Friday, returning with armfuls of food to Judy's habitual harangue. It was very entertaining. Yet however much they argue, they've been married the longest out of everybody in our family – more than 30 years — and are still as much in love as they ever were.

In October of that same year there was more unrest in the family when our Siân, my Auntie Pamela's daughter, came to live with my mother. Siân was still at school, just finishing off her GCSEs and going on to A levels when my Mam took her under her wing. I was very pleased and still am.

She's such a gentle, caring and considerate person and they both needed each other – Mam gave Siân stability and routine, while Siân gave Mam a focus and help in getting over Loft's death.

'She was partly my salvation,' Mam says. After Loft's death she couldn't go into the sitting room or look at his chair for months. She couldn't move home either, because that would mean leaving him behind, and his wonderful garden. Loft had been a terrific gardener and passed on his knowledge to James, who got to know all the names of the plants he grew, like roses, sweet peas and arum lilies, and all the different parts, the petals, the stamens and all the rest. James cried terribly when I told him his grandfather wasn't coming back. Mam said Loft had gone to look after the flowers in heaven and James wanted to know when he'd be back to look after ours.

But for Mam, Siân coming into her life six months after Loft's death was the saving of her. Getting Siân to university was her goal, and when Siân got a place at Reading to read classics, the next goal was seeing she got a good degree, and then her teacher training and then a good job. Mam is proud of Siân for all she has achieved and I'm so proud of my mother for taking all that on. And then my sister Helen goes and gets a good degree as well, in humanities, and now she's studying for her Postgraduate Certificate in Education. The women in my family have truly made their mark and my life has been guided by these matriarchal women. Only Nora thought that Siân should go back to her own mother and in the family divisions that followed, Mam took Siân's side and I took my Mam's, naturally.

7

Thrillers with Pat Hill

ON MY OWN, I doubt if I would have dreamed up the idea of writing thrillers. I had enjoyed working with Martyn Forrester on my first autobiographical book, *Walking Tall*, and I started getting ideas for novels, scraps of stories that came out of the army life I had known. After I'd been boring Geoff with them for some time, he said, 'Why don't you write something down and I'll see if I can get a publisher interested.' I suspect he was trying to shut me up but I thought, okay, let's give this a try. Work had gone a bit quiet and I found I was getting bored.

They say there's a book in everybody and there probably is but not everybody can write it down. I spoke to a few people about possible collaboration but nobody got very enthused. I didn't immediately think of my journalist friend Pat Hill, who always seemed so busy at his day job as TV and show-business correspondent at the *News of the World*. Then Pat and the paper parted company in June 1994 and soon after I called him at home.

'How do you fancy writing a novel?' I asked.

He said, 'Yeah, okay, let's give it a go.' I think work was boring the holy heck out of him too, and like me he wanted a different departure.

I was then living in Quaker's Yard in Wales and Pat lives near Godalming in Surrey, so we weren't exactly on each other's doorstep. Nevertheless we quickly came up with the idea for our first book together: a plot to derail the peace process in Northern Ireland investigated by our undercover hero, ex-SAS Sergeant Jim Scala. Blown up on active service in Bosnia, Scala was left with a scar and a limp and – like me – the prospect of life outside his regiment. He had enough of a limp to make a service background seem unlikely, allowing him to go undercover without suspicion. Geoff got a publishing deal set up with Bloomsbury, who wanted to publish the thriller under a joint imprint with Little, Brown called 22 Books. All we had to do was get it written.

It's only natural to put a little of yourself and those you know into your characters, though they soon develop a life and a background of their own. Now I can see bits of my grandfather in Jim Scala, especially his hard, working-class upbringing in Merthyr Tydfil, but we made Scala Italian-Welsh. His name carries echoes of Welsh rugby player Jim Scarlet, whom I remember seeing on TV, virtually chasing a referee off the field because the game hadn't gone his way. 'Overenthusiastic' is probably the best way to sum him up – he used to stamp and thump on the field, but he was a fine rugby player for all that, when he put his mind to it. Our man's Italian-Welsh blood gave him dark hair, blue eyes and a slight air of romance that was miles away from your stereotypical Taffy, all flat forehead, broken teeth and no neck. But scarring and a limp brought our hero down to earth.

The Bosnian bombing that caused Scala's injuries draws on my own experiences but was actually based on an

Sky-diving with the Red Devils for charity.

Freefalling – one of the scariest things I have ever accomplished.

Lucy and me on our wedding day, 1990.

My grandparents Nora and Percy with baby James

Family portrait. Left to right: James, Caitlin, me, Lucy and Stuart.

t Kidlington Airfield. Left to right: Gary, me and Noel McConkey. Even if you'd strung us all gether, you wouldn't have had a complete working model!

leeting Bosnian refugees staying in what used to be a holiday caravan site; Umag refugee camp, roatia, 1992.

Pat Hill and me signing books on the publication of *Cause of Death*, 1995.

In front of an Apache Longbow helicopter. Left to right: James, our neighbour's son Gareth, me my nephew Jonathan, Stuart.

Meeting Carlos again, 1998. Left to right: Graciela, Caitlin, me, James, Carlos and Stuart, Lucy.

With Denise Welch (left) and Stephanie Powers at a Café Royal Weston Spirit event.

With Weston Spirit founders Paul (far left) and Ben (next to him), after the New York Marathon, 1998.

With young members of Weston Spirit on the rooftop of the charity's first home, outside Liverpool city centre.

On the Cresta Run, St Moritz, Switzerland … 80–90mph lying on your belly on a tea tray.

With Derek Traylen, a resident at the Royal Star & Garter Home (left), Peter Smith, who bred the 'Heroes' lily to raise money for the home, and Joan Kelland, also a resident; Chelsea Flower Show, 2002.

My first ever race in the Firestone Production Saloon Cars Race at Thruxton, Hampshire, 1989. I'm not leading – they're all about to lap me!

At the Grand Canyon, cycling for the Royal Star & Garter Home.

Enjoying the Freedom of the City in Liverpool. I was just thinking, 'I hope they don't shit on my jacket.'

With Lord Snowdon in London after receiving the Snowdon Award Scheme's Special Award, 1989.

Lucy and me meeting Princess Diana again, at a Welsh Guards event near Chelsea Hospital.

With Lucy and Mam, getting my honorary degree at Glamorgan University, Pontypridd, 1999.

With Mam, Lucy and Loft, after receiving my OBE at Buckingham Palace, 1992.

Last visit to the Welsh Guards memorial, Fitzroy, the Falklands, 2001. Closing the final chapter of this part of my life.

incident Pat remembered from World War II, when the Germans wiped out a village in the Vercors area of France by lobbing mortars over the cliff. As Pat says, we did a bit of poaching and plagiarising of reality and turned it into fiction.

To get the novels plotted, I would go and stay with Pat for a few days, and we once borrowed a cottage in Dorset belonging to a friend of his wife. We wanted somewhere quiet to think and drink, and the pub was only 50 yards up the road. Sometimes we'd go out for a drive and talk over the plot. Pat has this fantastic memory and he'd say, 'Yes, we could work this in here and that in there, and then maybe that would happen.'

Of the two of us, Pat was the more gung-ho. 'We're not writing a movie script for James Bond here,' I'd say, 'let's keep it real.' Pat would pass me bits of writing and I'd ask, 'What did the place smell like? What did it sound like when he opened the door? Were they living in absolute squalor in a filthy, dusty, cobweb-ridden room?' When you're writing a novel you need to know how a place smells before you can properly taste your characters' fear. Come to my house and you can't smell any fear, but in some places you can smell the dread the instant you step inside. We couldn't put all that into our novels, of course; that's for masterclass writing, which very few writers achieve. But it marks the road we were going along – we wanted to be honest.

We also wanted to keep the stories simple. Some people write great novels with convoluted plots but we didn't want that. We just set out to write a book that would be a good holiday read, something you could pick up and read over three or four days, or if you wanted to take longer over it, one where you wouldn't lose the plot. There are one or two twists, nothing too complicated, and a bit of

bodice-ripping that was largely Pat's. It was a collaboration that worked well – I was better at the military side
and Pat at the sexy bits, though we agreed there should be
no gratuitous sex or violence beyond the crunched noses
demanded by the plot.

For each of the books, we'd go off on research trips
together. The first took us to Belfast, where I had a friend
in the RUC who could put us up. His name is Noel
McConkey. My son Stuart is named after him, Stuart Noel
Weston – all my children are named after people I admire.

Noel met us at the airport. I hadn't thought to tell Pat
that Noel was the first man in Northern Ireland to be
blown up by a remote-control bomb. He has only one
arm, a hook and no legs, but he still carries a gun in his
back pocket. Pat told me later that standing between Noel
and me was the healthiest he has ever felt in his life. We
went out to Noel's car, where he put another attachment
on to his hook and drove us around. He had a 9mm pis-
tol on his lap, he was eating an ice cream and he didn't
have even his one good hand on the wheel. Pat was going
purple, unaware that Noel was steering with his knees.

Noel and his wife, Hilda, were fantastic to us all the
time we were over there. 'The name Hildegard means
"warrior maiden",' Noel used to say. 'Very apt.' Noel and
I had first met when we both learnt to fly on a scholarship
for disabled pilots with the International Air Tattoo, paid
for by King Hussein of Jordan. It has to be said that Noel
made a much better pilot that I did, despite my four working limbs to his one.

For the Belfast book, Pat and I seemed to do an awful
lot of our research in bars. One Sunday night we were
down in the bar in the village drinking our whiskeys
(which neither of us touches normally) when we met
someone who was to prove very helpful in making

connections: a policeman called Kevin who invited us the next day to the police headquarters in Belfast. So we went up there and he then took us out to meet more people in more bars. Our story seemed to get everyone's imagination working.

There was one person everyone said we had to meet: a police informer and drugs dealer Pat nicknamed Jimmy McKiller, who said he was on the death list of both the Loyalists and the IRA, which apparently gave him the right to carry a gun. But alcoholism made his behaviour erratic and he had recently had his firearms licence revoked after brandishing his gun in a pub and thrusting it down the throat of some Republican thug who had annoyed him. The IRA had declared a ceasefire at the time and most of the Republican guns were out of circulation. 'You're not so clever now, are you?' Jimmy had shrieked down the thug's ear.

Jimmy McKiller was someone else who had lost his leg in a bombing, which really pissed him off because he'd just bought a new pair of boots. He was a real dead man walking, though he had also had some lucky escapes. He owned a bar where, after hours, he would usually carry on drinking with friends and family upstairs. One night, after he'd closed the bar, he couldn't be bothered to go upstairs, so they carried on drinking where they were. He must have left the lights on up there because that same night somebody fired a Russian shoulder-held RPG7 rocket launcher at the upstairs room, which brought the roof down. It's a weapon that is very popular with terrorists, effective and easy to get hold of, used primarily against light-skinned vehicles like armoured personnel carriers. There's no doubt that if Jimmy and his friends had been upstairs when the rocket-propelled grenade exploded, they would all have been killed.

Kevin, the policeman, made a call to Jimmy McKiller's wife, a beautiful blonde who had never met us before, but she must have trusted Kevin implicitly as she came to pick us up from the bar. On the way over to their house, she collected her husband from a meeting of Alcoholics Anonymous. We're sitting in the back of the car, expecting to see this big rough-tough guy emerge from the meeting, yet he couldn't have weighed more than ten or 11 stone, and a good part of that was taken up by his false leg. We drove on to their home, which was only about two or three miles away, but McKiller's wife took a complicated route to make sure we weren't being followed. Eventually we arrived in front of their electrified gates. The gates slowly opened and all the lights flicked on. It was like entering Fort Knox, all the windows and doors protected by iron bars. There was even a floodlight at the bottom of the pond that projected goldfish silhouettes up into the sky.

This guy had known the hunger striker Bobby Sands and run with both sides. He gave us a lot of background, especially about how drugs worked in the Province. Pat tried to tape the conversation but when he played it back the next day, the guy was talking so fast we couldn't understand a word. I couldn't remember any of it either as I was passing out from tiredness, my eyes quite burnt out. Yet despite his history, McKiller and his wife were fantastic hosts, so generous with their time to complete strangers.

Our conversations with Kevin, Noel and the others gave us a sense of Belfast's weird tribal geography, aided by Noel's police maps, which coloured in the different Loyalist and Catholic areas. They also helped us to define our chief villain, someone with a vested interest in derailing the peace process. In the end, it all came down to power, as it usually does.

But we still needed to get a feel for different parts of the city, so we moved from Noel's to the Europa Hotel, which then enjoyed the reputation of being the most terrorist-bombed hotel in Europe. We drove along the Catholic Falls Road, past the Victorian terraces and streets named after battles like Alma and Sebastopol. A hundred yards away you had the wall dividing the two communities, and a hundred yards the other side, the Protestant Shankill Road. You could taste the hatred that kept them apart.

One day we ventured out to the bars of the Shankill Road. There are three quite close together, the Royal and the Rex on opposite corners, and the Berlin Arms. We tried the Royal first, which was protected by wire caging around the windows and door. When you pressed the bell, you'd be scanned by the cameras and if you looked okay, they would release the door catch and let you in. Inside I got chatting to a guy who had just been released from an 18-year jail sentence for a sectarian murder. His release had come a couple of weeks early because his wife had fallen down the stairs and broken her neck. He'd only been out for about two weeks and had visited his wife in hospital just four times, or so he said.

'I'm supposed to be off to see her now,' he said, 'but fuck it, I'm having a pint with you now. I'll see her tomorrow, she's not going anywhere.'

The place could have done with a good lick of paint, and that's being polite. It had wall-to-wall peeling ceilings, sticky floors, nicotine-stained walls and that early-morning smell of beery hops laced with disinfectant.

Pat was round the corner, sitting in a booth, and because he's a journalist, he can't just sit quietly. So he's firing off his questions when suddenly a woman jumps up and shouts, 'He's a policeman, he's a policeman.' These gorillas appear from nowhere wearing leather jackets with braided collars and cuffs. Their arms are so long they are dragging their knuckles in the dirt. They should have been bleeding.

I watched the colour drain from Pat's face and I'm starting to chuckle because I've never seen that happen so quickly, to anyone.

Pat said, 'Would I be a policeman from Britain with a name like Patrick Kevin Hill?'

We were drinking in a Loyalist pub. Pat didn't stop to think that Patrick is the patron saint of Catholics, or that Kevin and Hill are good Catholic names. Pat's a Yorkshireman and about as English as you get. Even as an ex-soldier who had served over there, I hadn't realised that names can say who you are.

They looked about to drag him out the back and beat him up. I was by now laughing out of nerves and terror, and because Pat's face was such a picture of dread that you knew he couldn't be lying.

I said, 'Come on, guys, do you seriously think I would come in here with an undercover policeman? To do what? Pat's a journalist. We're writing a book together and we're just over here to have a walk around, get a flavour of the place. See what it's like living on the Shankill Road and the Falls Road, gauge the character of the people we meet. With the greatest will in the world, I don't have the ability to be deceitful or disguise myself. What would we gain?'

'Okay,' they said. It might seem a little too simple but as soon as you put it like that, they realised the sense of it. They're not stupid people. They might be mad or bad, but not stupid.

After a decent interval we went on to the Berlin Arms, where there wasn't much going on, just a sing-song and some karaoke, then on to another place and back down the road to the Rex. This time a group of young men were barring the door, big lads in their late teens and early twenties. As we stood in the doorway, one of them looked towards a little fellow standing at the far end of the bar with two of his henchman. The little fellow nodded – he turned out to be quite senior in one of the Loyalist paramilitary organisations – and we were allowed inside. Pat said it made the hairs on his neck stand on end and I didn't like it much, either. This guy could let us in on a nod and he wasn't even the owner. It made us both edgy.

At the bar we ordered beers. 'How much?' I said.

'No charge.'

Though we really wanted to get out of there, they had lined up five or six beers for us on the bar, so we had to drink those first. I was taken to have a brief audience with the little chap at the end of the bar, who wanted to know what we were doing there. I explained we were researching a fantasy book based on the troubles. That didn't seem to worry him. People had written truth and fiction about them; he would be worried only by a serious exposé.

We didn't get anything there – it wasn't the sort of place where you could start asking questions, not even Pat, and certainly not after our experience at the Royal. When we told Kevin about it the next day, he said, 'We wouldn't go in there. It's another no-go area.' He also said Pat had been lucky in the Royal. They could quite easily have taken him out the back, stripped him and beaten him to death. Pat looked sicker still at the thought. We hadn't realised how dangerous the situation was.

As we left the Rex, they said, 'Shall we get you a taxi?'

'No thanks,' I said. 'That's very kind of you but we'd rather walk.' It wasn't just a question of clearing our heads. We knew that taxis in Belfast are controlled by the paramilitaries and we weren't taking any chances.

The following night we were in the Europa Hotel getting ready to go out when a taxi driver stopped at a junction just two or three turnings up the road. A fellow walked out, put a gun to the driver's head and pulled the trigger. The gun had jammed, so he cocked it again, fired and it jammed again. The gunman ran away, but the guy in the cab was an absolute wreck, which was totally understandable. It was like playing Russian roulette with an automatic weapon: you don't get empty chambers like you do with a revolver. An automatic cocks and reloads itself, so unless the piston jams, you're a dead man. When we came out of the hotel, police and military were swarming everywhere and the area had been sealed off, even though they had no realistic hope of finding the gunman.

All the time we were in Northern Ireland I was never any good at telling Protestant from Catholic, though the few Catholics I knowingly met I found absolutely charming, just like everybody else.

I have always envied people religion, when it's looked after correctly. Even if I can't quite get it for myself, I see the warmth and the love in it. But when it's abused and misused as it is by both sides in Northern Ireland, by the militant Loyalists and by the IRA, then that's nothing I envy anybody. To turn something that on the face of it is quite beautiful and use it to factionalise people, turning neighbour against neighbour, friend against friend, that to me is bigotry at its most evil and in its most violent form.

One thing we didn't do while we were in Belfast was have any contact with the British military. This was quite deliberate. Even though I'm known to be very pro the British forces, I'm out of the loop and therefore no longer a legitimate target to the IRA or anyone else. Having any involvement at all with the British security forces over there would have changed all that, so it wasn't worth the risk, and I certainly didn't want to endanger Pat. Contact with the police was a different matter altogether. We went out drinking with them and sat around with detectives in bars. One night they smuggled us into a police station where a policeman friend of mine was sitting in his slippers. We had a couple of beers and a chat, but that was all. It's a weird situation and I can't say I fully understood it. The police can drink in certain places and not in others, do certain things and not others. Then, all of a sudden, you'll get a wild man who shoots up a bar out of town where the police are meeting for a birthday party – thankfully we were not around that time.

But it was a great experience. The police were fantastic to us, and so were most other people, to be honest. The only person who tried to have an argument with us was some pro-Republican guy who claimed involvement with the Peace Movement. He found us in a neutral bar close to the Europa Hotel and started making inflammatory statements about how the British government had, in his words, come crawling to the IRA, doing backroom deals that amounted to complete capitulation. I can't see the problem in giving in to certain things, if it brings about peace and doesn't sell out the Protestants, which would be immoral. The guy was desperate to buy us drinks to continue the debate, but Pat and I were getting quite narked by now because he was really irritating, so we told him to bugger off, or worse. That's the only time I came across any friction while I was there – everyone else was helpful, pleasant and absolutely charming. If you have nothing to do with the Troubles, the country is well worth a visit and you'll have nothing to fear. It's like the Republic but with a different accent.

While we were over in Belfast, I found time to take Pat along to the Fleming Fulton School for children with physical disabilities. Located on the outskirts of the city, it takes children from all sections of the community and I'd been delighted previously when the children had voted me president of their Poultry Club, even though I didn't know a goose from a turkey. They'd been winning competitions until some rotten swine had broken in and stolen all their prize birds, so I was glad to help. Brendagh Hamilton was the dedicated worker who had got me involved. I have visited the school three or four times but distance, family and other commitments haven't allowed me to maintain the contact. I just thought it was delightful to be asked: from soldier and rugby player to broadcaster, author, speaker, charity worker and president of a kids' poultry club.

*　*　*

Once we had finished all the planning and research, settled the characters and the smells and the plot details, Pat would then take a month or so to turn it into book form, working flat out every day. I used to go and stay with him for a few days at a time. We would sit up in his attic where he wrote. I would read over what he'd written and we'd talk about it, making changes as we went along. It was so warm up there that we sometimes fell asleep.

I wasn't actually there when the book was finished. Pat called late one night and said, 'It's done.' So we then had to read it all over again before we sent it away. It was a good feeling. We had achieved something, written a thriller that could quite easily have been turned into a film because the plot was so simple yet it had nice little strands moving off at just the right time, to hook you in. Pat's a good writer and the book thankfully needed few revisions.

Even before we had finished writing *Cause of Death*, we got the idea for our next thriller, *Phoenix*. It took the same ex-SAS character, Jim Scala, into a plot that revolved around bigotry in the British Army, much of it linked to the neo-Nazis in Germany. You get all sorts in the British military – it's a microcosm of British society and the British way of life, all under one banner. You get racists and bigots and sexists and gays and artists and musicians and singers and joke-tellers in society, just as you do in uniform. You're going to experience them in the military the same as anywhere else. And we thought, what if they meet and band together, becoming a bigoted group of maybe five, ten, 15, 20 people – what then? That's how it happens in real life – it's just sheer coincidence that all these people come together at the same time.

With both books, we based characters and incidents on things we encountered in life and let our imaginations run riot. The weird thing was that all the way along, our fiction pre-empted things that actually happened later. For instance, the first story starts with a helicopter crash that wipes out the heads of anti-terrorist operations in Northern Ireland. We wrote this before the Chinook helicopter crash of June 1994 over the Mull of Kintyre that killed 25 senior police and intelligence officers based in Northern Ireland, plus two aircrew. The same sort of coincidence happened with the next book, *Phoenix*. In its opening pages a German hostel for asylum seekers and guest workers in the old city of Lübeck is firebombed, as would later happen there for real in January 1996. Some British soldiers on leave were picked up on the streets as they watched the hostel burn.

The starting point for our research on *Phoenix* was a contact of Pat's, Clive Entwhistle, who was then working as a producer on Central Television's *The Cook Report*. At that stage the plot revolved around a briefcase dirty bomb that had featured in one of the programme's earlier investigations. Although these things are now much in the news, this was back in the mid-1990s, remember. Clive introduced us to an expert, a UN nuclear weapons inspector, who told us how you would set up a bomb.

Clive also put us in touch with a journalist in Finland, Reju Rookerman, a big lad of six foot four and one hell of a nice fellow. He'd been living and working in Berlin until his investigations into neo-Nazis there had put him on their death list. I wasn't especially frightened by any of that – most neo-Nazis are too cowardly to carry out their threats – but Pat's family started to receive dead phone calls at night. The police and BT engineers finally traced them to an insurance company with a faulty call centre.

We took a plane to Finland, where we stayed in a fabulous sailors' hostel overlooking the port. The first morning we woke up to see a great rusting Russian submarine outside the window, the hammer and sickle painted on its sides. Jesus, we thought, what's going on now? It was so cold outside, I remember opening the window to the sound of loud cracking as ice formed instantly on the warm pane. (The submarine, we later learnt, had been bought by a Finnish businessman who wanted to turn it into a restaurant.)

Reju gave us the names of a whole lot of people we should talk to in Berlin. Our story was changing all the time, and the briefcase bomb went out of the window as we got more and more caught up in military connections to neo-Nazis.

To get a flavour of military life in Germany, we stayed with the Welsh cavalry, the Queen's Dragoon Guards, known as the QDGs, in their barracks at Sennelager in central Germany. They looked after us royally and gave us a fantastic reception. Their regimental crest is a two-headed eagle known affectionately as 'the Chernobyl Chicken'. It felt good to be back in a military environment. The main difference from the life I had known with the Welsh Guards is that the QDGs have tanks, so they spend a lot of their time in the transport sheds. But there were anyway several ex-Welsh Guards cross-badging with them, who helped me feel at home.

It was wintertime when we drove over to Sennelager and I was the coldest I've ever been in my life. In temperatures that reached −20°C, everything watery in the car froze, and we had to keep wiping the outsides of the window just to see where we were going. I remember the pain of going to look inside a tank and standing hatless for a few minutes on the top. The back of my head was frozen solid. There's no hair there and not a lot of tissue under the skin.

While we were with the QDGs another strand to the story evolved – the mounting resentment within the military at threatened cutbacks to the armed services. A few years earlier the government had published its white paper *Options for Change*, setting out plans to slash military numbers and expenditure. Although everyone wanted change to be voluntary, the plans would clearly involve a lot of compulsory redundancies among the troops. We thought, what will happen to all those lads who are to be thrown on the scrapheap? You train them to kill and then what do you do with them – toss them aside like an old shirt?

During my time around people in the armed forces, I have spoken to lots of NCOs who were not best pleased with what was happening. As they saw it, whole careers were being wiped out. So we asked ourselves, who would our guys link up with to take out their frustrations? You create hypothetical situations and then you take it from there. Through Reju, we knew of British soldiers who were getting involved in far-right activities, though at no point did we find anyone in the QDGs who showed any interest in that kind of thing.

Everyone in the book exists in one form or another, based on the characters we met during our researches. In Berlin, looking for local colour, we started in the Irish bar inside the Europa shopping centre. From here we were led on to an expats' bar run by a disillusioned Irishman, ex-SAS or so he claimed, always dressed in immaculate three-piece suits. Like a lot of people we met, he felt he was better off in Germany than back home. In the bar I was chatting away to someone really boring while Pat got himself fixed by this guy who gave him a thousand-yard stare.

The man said to Pat, 'Have you killed anyone?'

'No,' replied Pat, 'I might have bored a few people to death, but no.'

'Well, I have,' said the guy, who then started talking about all the things he'd done in Vietnam and elsewhere, though officially the SAS never went to Vietnam.

I said to Pat afterwards, 'How come I always get the boring guys and you get the interesting ones?'

'You could have had him with pleasure,' said Pat. 'He scared the shit out of me.'

But Pat got his own back when we turned him into one of the central bad guys in the story. I hope he never reads it but he's probably too miserable to recognise himself.

We finished our research for *Phoenix* towards the end of February 1995, for delivery in the first week of April. Pat took time off to write it, working late most nights and writing the last line at quarter to one in the morning. As before, I went to stay with him for much of the writing. The publishers never really appreciated the speed at which we put it together, we felt, nor did they get 100 per cent behind promoting the book when it came out. Through Pat's contacts, we arranged a full-page interview in the *Sunday Times*, along the lines of 'Falklands veteran talks about neo-Nazis', and slightly different stories for the *Sunday Mirror* and the *People*.

The only rubbish review we got was from the *Daily Telegraph*, which pretty much said that Simon Weston is a nice enough guy but he's misled us about the problem of neo-Nazis. Well, it was a thriller – a factional book rather than a factual book, though I stand by everything that appears in it and later events have proved us right.

The *Telegraph* claimed that all our information came from a guy in north London called Gerry Gable, who runs a magazine called *Searchlight* which keeps an eye on neo-Nazi activities at home and abroad. Gable would see a Nazi symbol lurking in a kindergarten sandbox, said the *Telegraph*. They were wrong about our sources but when their journalist contacted me, I wasn't going to reveal where our information had come from. At that time Reju was still on the neo-Nazis' hit list, and I certainly wasn't about to give him away, or any of the others.

Unfortunately the events the *Telegraph* claimed could never happen became all too logical. In Germany alone, we're told, there are almost a million registered members of the far right. A couple of 18-year-olds secretly filmed a senior German government figure attending a meeting in the Grünewald Forest, on the edge of Berlin, with hundreds of Hitler Youth in full kit, close by a memorial to the SS. We saw some of the film footage, but I wasn't going to discuss any of that with the *Telegraph*. From my own experience, I've known a handful of guys in the army who were involved in things that were very far right. They used to visit skinhead bars in Berlin and never get beaten up when the rest of us wouldn't have stood a chance.

In the same way that we had written the book together, Pat and I threw ourselves into promoting it around the country through interviews, radio, readings, talk shows, literary events and what have you. We developed a kind of irreverent double act, where we'd explain what the book was about, then invite questions and answers.

Pat would stand up and say, 'For all those who don't know, this is Simon Weston.'

'And for those who don't care,' I added, 'this is Pat.'

Someone would always ask us how we managed to write together. I would hold up my damaged hands. They're like large chipolata sausages held together by grafted tissue from my belly, and one finger is missing. 'I can't really type with these.'

'No,' Pat threw in once, 'but he's very good at shorthand.'

Quite a few of those promotional trips turned out to be journeys from hell. There was one in particular when we were travelling up to Norwich from Windsor, and the driver was doing drug deals on his mobile phone as he drove. After we'd been stuck on the M25 for something like six hours, we finally stopped at a service station on the M11. We were all ravenous by then. The car pulled up outside the shop, where Pat, myself and the lassie who was accompanying us all piled out to go to the loo and get something to eat.

'I'm just going off for a smoke,' said the driver. He was a big lad with clear white eyes, but when he came back his eyes were on organ stops and they had turned a muddy brown colour. He then managed to miss the turning off the motorway and reversed back down the M11. That was before he went the wrong way round a roundabout, right into the path of a huge juggernaut coming straight at us.

The man was knackered and obviously out of his gourd. 'Do you want me to drive?' I asked. 'Because I'm more than willing.'

'No, no,' he said, 'I'm okay.'

He might have been okay but we weren't. There was nothing we could do – we certainly couldn't walk. I have no idea if he made it back from Norwich, but by that time we couldn't give a toss. We got the publishers to call the cab company and say that we were never ever getting in a car with him again.

After Norwich we were scheduled to appear on *Good Morning with Anne and Nick*, produced in Birmingham and hosted by Anne Diamond and Nick Owen. Pat knew them both from his time on the *News of the World*. I was driven on to Birmingham in a beautiful Jaguar limousine by a very good driver who was learning to be a pilot. Pat went home, collected his car (an old Astra estate) and drove on up to our Birmingham hotel. The hotel staff told him to park his car out the front, where they could keep an eye on it.

We'd been out for a bite to eat and a look around and went back to the hotel, where we noticed a couple of policemen hanging around reception. It had to be for Pat, because if anything is going to go wrong, it'll go wrong for him. That's why I love travelling with Pat to anywhere dangerous, because at least you know it's not going to happen to you. Sure enough, when Pat gave his name, the receptionist said, 'Would you mind having a word with these policemen? They're waiting to speak to you.'

'Er, Mr Hill,' said one of the officers, 'I'm afraid your car has been stolen.'

It seems the hotel staff had watched the drama unfold on closed-circuit television. Parked next to Pat's was another estate car stuffed full of computer equipment. The thieves had taken all the stuff out, loaded it into Pat's clapped-out Astra (which had already gone twice around the clock) and driven off. The staff called the police, who came straight away, just as Pat's car was winding its way out of the car park. According to Pat, his car was too quick for them and the thieves got away. In reality I could have caught up with his Astra in a milk float.

Pat never got to appear on the show, either, as the publishers hadn't told Anne and Nick he was coming. As he says, 'I got my car nicked for nothing.' And his hopes of claiming on insurance were dashed when he got a call from the West Midlands Police a few days later, saying they had found his car abandoned at South Mimms service station in Hertfordshire, where it spent several more days before he got it back. The worst thing was that the thieves had left the windows open and it was soaking wet inside.

We had both enjoyed working on the books together, and might have continued had the publishers really put their weight behind us. The feedback from the promotional events was brilliant but they never pushed the book. Though we sold something like 12,000 copies of *Phoenix* in hardback, they never went on to do the paperback. There had been a change of policy, we were told, and I lost heart. I think we both did. Someone else approached us to do a historical novel, a kind of Catherine Cookson meets Wilbur Smith, which we were going to set in Merthyr Tydfil at the time of the riots of 1831. We even got started on the research. In my mind I had a great image of the sky glowing red from the foundry and when it snowed, the snow was black before it even hit the ground. But nothing came of it.

8

In the Public Eye

I'M OFTEN ASKED WHAT I miss most about the Simon Weston before I got injured, and the answer that most commonly comes to mind is anonymity – the ability to pass by without anybody noticing. Fortunately and unfortunately, I'm easily recognisable. In the early days people stared at me because of my injuries and now more often it's because they recognise me from the telly or the newspapers.

Most of the time, I am quite happy with who I am and what I am now. Each time I have a wash or a shave, there it is in the mirror. I see a burnt guy but that's me – it's the burnt me. I've been alive longer burnt than unburnt, and certainly more aware of who I am. You don't fully appreciate what your features are like or who you are until you're about seven or eight. So really, I only ever had about 14 or 15 years of getting to know the person I was – physically – before, and more than 20 years of living with the burnt me.

As other people get more used to my disfigurement, I don't face the same problems as I did in the beginning.

You still meet people who are insensitive or rude, the sort who come up to you and say, 'Oh, they said you were a bloody mess and they were right, weren't they? But nice to meet you all the same.' Stupid remarks like that you can pretty much ignore. And there are other people who have no idea what to say, and get embarrassed. They're the ones I talk to because they are obviously feeling uncomfortable. Once they get used to you, they don't notice. I believe it's up to people like me to help them overcome their embarrassment, because I have the experience and they don't. It's not their fault.

The BBC documentaries that Malcolm Brinkworth made about me certainly helped me become more comfortable with myself and confident with the person I'd become. Along with all the press coverage, they helped me immeasurably and probably unfairly in the eyes of some of the other guys who got injured, but I can't do anything about that. I had to make the best out of what had happened to me, and that's what I've tried to do.

A lot of opportunities that have come my way are not ones I have consciously gone out and sought. The same goes for a lot of the publicity and celebrity. People think I have but I haven't. A lot of it has come searching for me because of the way I have conducted myself, and that's why I'm still where I am, because people have seen something positive and worthwhile in the way I've conducted my affairs, something they can use in their own lives. I think that's the only reason why I'm still in the public eye. I'm not someone who makes up fairy tales or says things for effect. What I say comes from the heart, and from knowledge. I wouldn't berate anybody or rubbish anything if I didn't know it to be the right thing to do. Sometimes I get a bit passionate about things and go over the top on occasion, but on the whole I say things as I see them and I think people have recognised that and warm to it. I don't make statements and criticise or argue about things for no good reason, because basically I'm not an argumentative person. I have absolutely no desire whatsoever to get into an argument but if someone else wants one, then I'm your man.

You do sometimes encounter people who have decided not to like you, no matter what you do. There was a girl I met on my first return to the Falklands who accused me of cashing in on my face. She was drunk and determined to pick a fight. 'You're rich, you are,' she shouted at me. 'You drive a BMW and a Mercedes.' I remember talking to Michael Parkinson about it. He was as baffled as I was. 'What difference does it make what car you drive around in?' he asked.

The strangest thing for me is that it's mostly women who've had a pop at me. I don't know if it's resentment or jealousy, or what. 'Why are you the focus of attention?' is what they're saying.

Well, I didn't set out to create the attention, it just happened. Do they think I wanted to get burnt? Do they think that as I was flying home injured, I wrote to all the film companies asking them to make a film about my life? None of that was a conscious choice on my part. Each time Malcolm had to convince me it was the right thing to do. And because he's such a nice, gentle man, he became one of my best friends. He talks a lot of good common sense and there's a certain amount of steel about him. He tells me things straight and that's what I love about him. But it was Malcolm who persuaded me to make the films – I didn't set out to make them.

I never watch them, either, as I feel uncomfortable seeing myself on television. Lucy might watch, and the children, but if I'm home I'll go off and do something else.

* * *

After Pat and I had finished writing the thrillers, I found I was getting more and more invitations to appear on the media as a kind of D-list celebrity. To be honest, I'm not sure where I fit in. On Geoff's advice, I have made a point of never appearing on celebrity quiz shows or things like that, though in the end I did let the BBC film my house (in fact my last two houses) for *Through the Keyhole*, that television programme where the camera tracks through an empty house and a panel of studio-based guests has to guess who lives there. The programme makers had first approached me back in the 1980s when I still lived in Liverpool and I said no, assuming that would be the end of it. I lived in a tiny little house, very clean and presentable, with lovely neighbours, but it just didn't seem right.

After I had moved with Lucy to Quaker's Yard they asked us again and this time I said yes. One good thing about having our house filmed was that it forced us to do some decorating. Like everybody else, we always have things that need doing and those jobs you get around to doing only when your granny or your picky great-aunt is coming to stay.

It's quite a kitsch show and great fun to do – for me, the novelty was whether the panel would guess, which they did both times. If they ever filmed me again, I would confuse them by removing every scrap of militaria, like my collection of metal soldiers, though there really isn't very much here anyway.

Loyd Grossman was still doing the show then. I liked him from the moment I met him. There's a tremendous politeness about him, and I never saw him treat anybody with anything less than great respect. I like that in a person.

I still didn't watch any of the programmes when they were broadcast. We each live our own lives 24/7 and as a distraction I like to get engrossed in somebody else's world rather than my own, which is all too familiar. I was intrigued to see Ken Hom's home in Portugal, for instance, where he has a fantastic wine cellar and a beautiful kitchen he uses to cook classic Western food as well as Chinese.

Soon after the programme was screened, I was delighted to record my choice of records for *Desert Island Discs* with Sue Lawley. The show has such respect, it's one of those markers for people who'd like to think they're getting somewhere. They invite you months in advance, but you only have to hand over your list a couple of weeks before the show is recorded, so that they can get the music. Then they'll record several shows in one day.

She's a very good-looking lady, Sue Lawley, very pleasant. You don't really chat much before they start recording, in case your stories lose their freshness, but you've already talked to one of their researchers some weeks before, to help Sue with her questions.

My gran had told me to choose something from opera as that would make me sound intelligent. I ignored her advice, as usual, and chose instead records that brought back different bits of my past – 'Down Under' by Men at Work, which makes a nonsense of everything; the Beatles' 'She Loves You', which was the first song I can ever remember (I had chickenpox at the time and was cutting up jelly on a dustbin lid as a service brat of three or four); and 'Bat out of Hell' by Meatloaf, the first record I remember in training when I joined the Guards. To honour my regiment, I chose the band of the Welsh Guards playing 'The Rising of the Lark' – in all honesty, I would probably have preferred the more evocative pipes of the Scots Guards, but you must stay loyal to your regiment. There were two more songs to remind me of magical squaddie days in Berlin and Kenya: Billy Joel's 'You May Be Right' and Gerry Rafferty's 'Stuck in the Middle with You'. Then, for Lofty, I chose the theme tune to *Match of the Day*; and because I'm a genuinely happy guy, I ended with the one I would take above all the others: Louis Armstrong's 'What a Wonderful World'. Every time I hear that song it makes me feel so good. I don't know anyone who could make the world sound a better place.

My gran would doubtless have been happier with the choice I made a few months later for Classic FM. I went through a whole load of classical music trying to find the music that was applicable to my life. I knew the music but I don't always know the names, so it took me quite a time. The trouble is that now I have great difficulty remembering exactly what I chose. I'm pretty sure it included Samuel Barber's *Adagio for Strings* from the soundtrack of Oliver Stone's war film *Platoon*. Then there was a piece of music they played at the time of the first moon landing in 1969. I was seven at the time and it was the first television of any real importance I was allowed to stay up and watch. We ate scrambled egg, I remember – it's the stupid things that come back to you. Now I marvel that we ever got the astronauts back – those guys were going on blind faith that they could re-enter the earth's atmosphere. At the time, though, I doubt if I realised the leap it represented for the human race.

I chose music from another war film, *Apocalypse Now*, when the helicopters come flying in to Wagner's *Ride of the Valkyries* played at top volume on a chopper loudspeaker. I found that a brilliant film about the insecurity of war and its terrible consequences. You never normally see war films that pursue the theme of accountability.

* * *

The year 1996 was, for me, a time of settling into a new skin as a person on the media, it was also the year of a devastating role reversal within my family, when my mother discovered she had breast cancer. They caught it very early, thank God. She'd already had one mammogram and a colleague at the hospital where she worked persuaded her to have another. 'Come on, Pauline,' she said, 'push to the front of the queue. You're a nurse, you're allowed to.'

If there's any story worth telling, it's my mother's. She survived a broken back in a car crash many years ago, when my grandmother had pretty much forced her to pick up one of my aunts from the hospital where she worked. My aunt had had a row with a fellow and phoned my gran, who phoned my mother, telling her to go and pick her up. Mam hit some black ice on the way home. No one else was hurt but Mam broke her back and she was bedridden in hospital for months. I was only a kid at the time and wasn't allowed to visit her. But she survived, as she did all the other trials in her life. I give my mother one thing: her stayability and stickability to her family is unbelievable.

Of course, being a nurse, she also knew all the complications that might arise from the cancer, so now I was the one who had to try to stop her worrying about herself and taking life far too seriously – all the things she'd done for me when I was injured.

She was on treatment for a while, taking the drug tamoxifen, which was developed with help from the Tenovus cancer charity, started by ten businessmen from South Wales (the 'ten of us' of the charity's name). As I understand it, the drug locks on to the cancer cells and stops them dividing. But it can also play havoc with your system. It would be freezing cold outside and Mam would be gushing with sweat, or it could be absolutely boiling and she would be freezing, but those are minor side effects. She's here and I'm very thankful.

She also had surgery and radiotherapy, yet throughout all this she took only three weeks off from her job as a district nurse. When she was having the radiotherapy, Lucy would drop her off on her way into Cardiff as she was taking the kids to school and Mam would be at work soon after 9.30. She never told them at work about the cancer, either. They thought the three weeks she took off was a holiday, and gave her stick for leaving her colleague to do everything. Now 63, Mam is still working full-time.

Lynda Lee-Potter wrote about my mother's recovery in the *Daily Mail*. 'My old Mam comes across as very strong,' she quotes me as saying, 'but she's not as strong as she makes out. She's a lovely person deep down, though sometimes she puts on this hard exterior.'

It's just as well that pretty soon after she read that, I was 8,000 miles away in the Falklands, where I went to record a Christmas show for ITV, *Christmas with the Royal Navy*. It was my first stab at TV presenting and live snippets were broadcast throughout Christmas Day. Anthea Turner was the lead presenter, on HMS *Belfast* in London, and there were other links to Royal Navy personnel in Bosnia and Puerto Rico.

I missed my family terribly but it was also unbelievable fun, I suppose because I had no responsibilities and very little to do beyond wishing everybody a happy Christmas. It was all shot at Government House in Port Stanley, where there was a party going on in the background that included a display of line dancing, and I had to introduce the service people who were linking up with their families. I've never been a fan of line dancing at the best of times. I always thought dancing was about free spirits and expressing yourself but clearly not in this case.

I flew over with the young director who had stepped in at the last minute when the guy who should have directed the show got an emergency call from home as he was driving the others to the airport. He dropped everyone off and then had to turn back. The chap who came was absolutely brilliant. We got him totally bladdered. He was like Bambi on ice, his legs shooting out in all directions.

Christmas day in the Falklands was glorious: crystal-clear skies, a temperature of 21°C and not a breath of wind. We stayed at Emma's Guest House, run by a lovely woman who has sadly since died. In the 150 yards from her house to the Uplands Goose Hotel, you could experience every kind of weather – rain, hail, sun, 70mph winds. It really is an unbelievable place and the people are uniquely Falkland Islanders, as anyone who has been there will tell you.

Perhaps because this time I was going back to the Falklands for career reasons, there was very little emotion involved in it for me, though there were moments when it all came back. As the weather was good, the Tornado squadron was able to get out on low-flying exercises. Whenever I saw them fly over, that sent a few hairs on my neck standing on end because of the horrific memories it brought back. But most of the time I felt I had already dealt with all that. I was just so pleased to have been given the chance to go back and realise I had nothing left of the horrors inside me. Or so I thought and would continue to think until I went back to the Falklands one last time in early 2002.

But I'm getting ahead of myself. Nineteen ninety-seven passed pretty much as the previous year had done. I was busy with Weston Spirit and the Royal Star & Garter Home, and doing more motivational speaking. Lucy became pregnant again and we started looking for a new home for my mother. Where she was living in Nelson was getting too rough. A shotgun had been fired in the street; drugs were becoming a problem, and there was talk of porn movies being made with young girls in one particular house. When I was growing up there, it was a very loving community but all that was changing. Society shifted gear when drugs became more available and people realised they could make millions from them.

In the summer of 1997 I flew out to Hong Kong to make a programme for BBC Radio Wales (later networked to Radio 4) about the last British regiment to be stationed there before the handover to the Chinese. A couple of years previously I had mentioned to the BBC producer Tim Green that I had always wanted to visit Hong Kong to make a programme about a Welsh regiment serving there. I'd forgotten all about it until he called me up one day and said, 'Do you remember we talked about Hong Kong – do you still fancy going over there to do a radio show?' Instead of doing a programme about a Welsh regiment, Tim suggested we do a programme about the last regiment there, which happened to be the Black Watch, and I was keen.

We arrived a couple of weeks or so before the ceremony. The Chinese were still building the parade ground, and the huge building that was supposed to symbolise a seagull was nowhere near completion. People were living on ships or hot-bedding it in the building itself as they built it around themselves. I said, 'They'll never finish that on time,' but when I got back to Britain and watched the ceremony on television, it looked immaculate.

We had a great time while we were there, going on the Star Ferry and up the Peak. The RAF flew us over the border and we went out with the navy on anti-smuggling patrols. There was a lot of smuggling going on, and the

British had to keep up their patrols until the day of the handover. With my hands, I wasn't much use roping in the boats, but Tim went splashing around on the junks we came alongside, fish guts spilling out everywhere. We had dinner on board with the Royal Navy and I think they gave me a plaque. It will be somewhere in my attic, there's loads of stuff up there. God knows what the Queen gets given: she must receive a skipful every day. I can never bring myself to throw any of it away, because it is given with a certain amount of affection.

* * *

Our daughter Caitlin was born on the morning of 6 September 1997, the day they buried Princess Diana. We called her Caitlin Felicity after Dame Felicity Peake. In contrast to James's birth, Caitlin was born in minutes and we only just got Lucy to the hospital in time. There's obviously a knack to giving birth and you don't always get it first time round.

For me it was a bittersweet day. We had this bundle of joy, and we drove her home late that morning along roads that were completely empty, dead. You could have gone anywhere in Britain that day at lickety split. There was nobody around, absolutely nobody anywhere, and it felt so strange.

This woman who had the potential to do so much good with her life was no longer with us. Despite all that she had done already, the media's hunger for disaster was greater than their love for her as a person. The press totally thrived on her downfall, they were like sharks in a feeding frenzy. To them she was just someone who could meet their compulsion to sell more papers. The TV media were no different: they were just the same flies hovering around the dung heap. The moment she died they had a field day because they could write what they liked. I just felt for the family. I felt for the boys. I felt for Diana's family. I felt for all concerned. A lot of people were saying things about what the Queen did or didn't say. Who cares? The girl was dead and that was the saddest thing of all.

I liked Diana. I thought she was a nice person. She wrote to me years ago when I got injured and she saw one of the documentaries. I met her many times after that, at Welsh Guards events and a cycle factory in the north-east. I had met her before I got injured, in fact, but she wouldn't remember that because I didn't stand out from the crowd.

I met her again at a garden party at Buckingham Palace and Charles said, 'Oh, Diana will be really pleased to see you again.' He went and got her, and she came over. 'Oh, hello,' she said, 'how are you? What are you up to now?' She was chuffed to see me, she was just that type of person. I think meeting people of my station helped keep her feet on the ground. They're detached from everything, the royals, living a life that is top-heavy with work in a very cosseted environment. I think she probably enjoyed meeting people who are grounded. It helped to keep her real as well.

The terrible sadness was that the two of them fell apart. I actually like Charles, I think he's a very decent man. Whoever falls out of love first, does it matter? People have been too quick to judge in all this. He stopped loving her. Some people say he never did, but I don't believe that for a minute. 'She's just a heifer to have the calves' – what a terrible thing to say. I hate these royal correspondents who write this stuff and are just so rude about people. 'Ah well,' they say, 'my inside source tells me—' What inside source gets to know that much? None. I just think that what went on there is an absolute tragedy, and people should mind their own bloody business. Two people falling apart like that so publicly, and their sons who have turned out to be two fantastic young men – they've had a lot to deal with, and their dad has tried his very best to help them deal with it as best they could, and their grandmother. Let's forget about her being Queen right now, she's their granny. And in the middle you have Camilla, who is getting called all sorts of cruel names. What has she done to anybody? She didn't break up Charles and Diana. If it hadn't been her, it could just as easily have been somebody else.

I think relationships come and go. They break up or they stand the test of time. Whatever the royals do, they're no different. They're human beings and sometimes that happens. You realise you've met your life's mate or sometimes you realise you've made a mistake. Who are we to judge?

I still have the Christmas cards Diana sent me. I probably shouldn't say this but you can trace the break-up over the years, as the cards stop coming from Charles, Diana and the boys, and come instead from just Diana and the boys.

None of this affects how I feel about the Royal Family. I have no problem with them. I'm a royalist. Not a huge royalist – I don't collect royal memorabilia or anything like that. But even if we wanted to get rid of them, what would we replace them with? Another President Bush? Please God, no. An out-and-out ruler? At least now we have devolved power from our sovereign. She's the head of our state, not a god as the Emperor of Japan once was. We don't believe her to be of divine anything. And she works bloody hard, as the rest of the family do.

People complain that the royals travel the world first class, but trust me, the little travelling I do is damned exhausting. It's absolutely shattering. To meet and greet and make idle chit-chat with all these people: if you think that's dead easy, try doing it for four weeks and tell me at the end if your brain isn't fried. I think they do a great job and whenever I've met them, they've always had something intelligent to say, something witty or worth listening to. And at least the Queen has started paying taxes like the rest of us. She didn't have to but she volunteered and that's great, a clear sign that the Royal Family has moved on in this respect and become as normal as everybody else.

9
A Big Year for Weston Spirit

NINETEEN NINETY-EIGHT WAS Weston Spirit's tenth anniversary. When we started out, we had no idea how long we might last and here we were, with centres in Liverpool, Newcastle, Cardiff, Sunderland, Merthyr Tydfil and London and a reputation that saw us growing into a big player in the youth-work field.

We might have had a centre in my home town of Nelson if things had worked out differently. Paul and the others were out scouting for a new place to open in Wales and on their way to me they got hopelessly lost. They saw a guy by the roadside and Paul said to the driver, 'Pull over and ask him the way to Nelson.'

'Excuse me,' said the driver in a broad Scouse accent.

The guy turned round. He was wearing a big black patch over one eye, just like the admiral. 'Oh, er, sorry,' mumbled the embarrassed driver, 'can you tell me where . . . Cardiff is?'

That's how we ended up in Merthyr Tydfil. We never did open shop in Nelson.

But 1998 was a great year for the charity, and we were all pleased to celebrate how far we had travelled since the Liverpool beer mat that had got us all on this road. As with any organisation that starts from nothing, there had been lows along the way. For Paul and Ben, one of the biggest lows was in 1992, after the euphoria of the very early years and before the charity had become properly established. I was a little out of the picture at the time, getting involved in other things, but Paul and Ben were there all the time, working with another guy who had been brought in over their heads to make up for their supposed lack of business experience.

The money was running out and with only £50 to stave off insolvency, the board called an emergency meeting to set about winding up the charity. There was talk of giving whatever money could be salvaged to another charity with a longer-term future. At this meeting Paul made an impassioned speech about why they couldn't shut the place down. Paul and Ben were asked to leave the meeting and when they came back, the board members had had a whip-round and £500 lay on the table. We were being given one last chance. Within a few days a further £30,000 was raised (from Barclays Bank and the Prince's Trust) and the organisation began to turn around. It was passion and spirit that did it, we're all convinced of that. Soon after, Ben took over as chief executive and we never looked back.

The Duke of York, our patron, gave us his support from the earliest days, when we were still very small, and has been hugely supportive ever since. There was a tricky period when we had to challenge the board we had at the time. Most public figures would have ducked away but Andrew took a leap of faith and let us know he would help in whatever way he could. He has remained a very hands-on patron, turning out for us several times a year. I hope we've repaid him over the years by the number of young people we've helped and by the way we've gone about it. I would hate to let him down. In those early days he had an awful lot more to lose than we did if we screwed up big time.

Once he found himself fog-bound in Cornwall where he had planned to jump in a helicopter to join us at a big reception we were holding up in Liverpool, hosted by Vernons Pools. He called and said, 'Don't let anyone leave. I may be an hour or two late, but I'll make it.'

He arrived in a great big motor cavalcade, horns blaring, and kept every single appointment that day, ending up in Manchester for supper with his Falklands aircrew. That sets the mark of the man, to me, as he could so easily have blamed the weather and cried off. But he had given us his word and he stuck by it. And in the end, your word is all you've got.

With people like Prince Andrew and Dame Felicity Peake involved, we were able to attract some of the very best corporate sponsors – companies like Barclays Bank, Kellogg's, the Royal Mail, Marks & Spencer, United Biscuits and Vernons Pools. Opening new centres in the regions has brought in new sponsors, such as Accenture in the north-east. Individuals have helped too. When we announced over the internet that we welcomed electronic donations, the very first payment – for £500 – came from a young lad who had joined one of our courses. Painfully shy, he used to spend hours alone in his room on his computer. After Weston Spirit he went on to get a job creating computer games and the donation was his way of saying 'thank you'. We also got £500 out of Jeffrey Archer when he gave away his libel winnings to charity. Unlike Jeffrey, we were never asked to pay it back.

But the real measure of success lies in the life stories of the young people themselves. Round about the mid-1990s, one of our real high points was when a handful of youngsters who had come through the programmes joined as fully trained youth workers; that's always good to see. Others came to work for us, then decided to go and get trained as youth workers. There's Marie Mumby up in the north-east, for instance, very bright and industrious, who comes from one of the most disadvantaged estates up there. The first person in her whole family to go to university, she went through the programmes and now runs one of our offices in the north-east. We're very proud of her, as we are of all our young people. No one can say she doesn't know how it is for young people today. Weston Spirit's power as an organisation lies precisely here, in the way our workers really connect with the young people who find their way to us.

Our programmes also aim to give young people continuing support after they move on. Keeping everybody together helps, and many of the youngsters on our programmes have stayed in touch as friends ever since. The worst thing we could do would be to get everyone fired up simply to face subsequent disappointment and disillusionment. It's like the astronauts going to the moon. When they came back to earth they got into alcohol and heaven knows what else, because what do you do once you've been to the moon? All the same, whenever I talk to young people I hope to inspire them to aim that high. People without dreams are without futures. Shoot for the stars and you can be anything.

Around the time of Weston Spirit's tenth anniversary, Malcolm came back on the scene with an idea to make a fifth TV documentary, *Simon's Journey*, which was eventually screened in April the following year. After the previous one, about going back to the Falklands and meeting the Argentine pilot Carlos Cachón in Argentina, we had been out of contact for a year or so but now the friendship was back on track, and Malcolm wanted to film the shift he had observed in my life. He was also keen to help me get back in touch with Carlos, whose courage in meeting me had helped in my own recovery. Maybe Carlos needed help in return.

Meeting up with Carlos again wouldn't happen until the end of the year. Before that, we had the whole jamboree over the tenth-birthday celebrations, jumping out of aeroplanes and a lot of other stunts to help finance our operations.

I was also able to take part in the Royal Star & Garter Home's Cadet Challenge over in Finland, a sponsored trek dreamed up by their fund-raiser, Patsy Willis, who has become a very good friend, along with her husband, Bernie. The aim of the challenge is to get young people interested in our work – military cadets, school children involved in cadet training at school, in fact anyone over 16 who fancies a challenge. Some of the young people we take along are doing their Duke of Edinburgh Gold Awards. They do much the same as everyone else but carry more kit. We also take participants from the Army Cadet Force's outreach programme, which helps youngsters in trouble to get back on track.

Over the past few years we've run treks in three different areas of Finland. The first two treks were in Lapland, starting off from Kittilä, close to the border with Norway. After that we did several treks along the Russian Bear Trail through eastern Finland, right on the border with Russia. We've also run one trip that goes right over the top, walking across Sweden, Finland and Norway through the total wilderness of the Arctic tundra, right above the treeline. All you see are reindeer wandering about.

I went on the second trial run of the Lapland trip in the September of 1998. Finland has at least 180,000 lakes and the largest woodland in Europe. If you can get out of the forest to look around, you'll find it's an incredibly beautiful place, though infested with mosquitoes that ate me alive. The Finns call them the Finnish air force and boy, they must be the most ruthless air force in the world. They take absolutely no prisoners.

We were doing the trek as a trial, before the youngsters got involved, and the people with me came from all walks of life. There was a policeman, a journalist, a millionaire father and his son re-engaging with each other, all sorts. We became good friends and we all had a great time. Some of us were walking and others were cycling, which we don't do any more. Part of the walking was a doddle but a lot of it was incredibly tough.

I like the Finns and find the Scandinavians pleasant people in many ways. It's in their nature to be a bit abrupt and they like a booze-up, which suits me fine. In their endless harsh winters they must find it very hard to get around and consequently they lead isolated lives. Britain seems like a consumer paradise in comparison.

It was really good up there. We stayed in a place with a nightclub that we nicknamed 'the Swamp Stomp'. People used to drive there from miles around. I remember seeing four people, two boys and two girls, fast asleep with their heads locked together, absolutely stocious. And never in my life have I seen so many different shell suits, not even in Liverpool in their heyday. Pink and blue were the favourite colours. There was one fellow who came dressed in bright yellow with matching shoes. He even had yellow sunglasses and a yellow telephone, which struck me as pretty brave.

We were having a quiet drink in there when a Finn came over. 'I am arm-wrestling champion,' he said, and insisted on going round the table, wrestling with everybody. He lost every time because he was completely crap. After that he decided to do his party piece for us, so he took off his baseball cap, got one leg and put it over his shoulder, then he did the same with the other leg. He's got these two legs coming over his shoulders, puts his baseball cap back on and continues to drink his beer. By this time I am laughing fit to bust, honest to goodness, I am actually crying.

Thinking back, it was such a funny trip altogether. In the place where we were staying there was a young helper called Bekker. He was only 28 but he looked 93. All he did was smoke and drink. He used to wake up in the middle of the night to have a cigarette, and then go back to sleep. I don't know how he managed to work and drink like he did, and he had a lovely pretty girlfriend. He'd come down to breakfast and the first thing he'd do was drink a bottle of cider. When we left we gave him a bottle of whisky as a thank-you present, a good Glenfiddich, which is really expensive over there. He drank the whole lot there and then. We could have given him the scrapings off the bottom of the barrel and it wouldn't have mattered. He was a really nice guy, just always drunk.

After that we went right up to the border with Norway, staying in a place that also ran a café providing food, drink and a sing-song. I had reindeer stew smothered in Tabasco and lots of beer. It played havoc with my innards. The next day we were driving on to Norway by bus and everybody was hanging out of the windows whenever I broke wind, it was that rank. Outside it was −5 or −6°C, and feeling even colder because of the wind chill, but they still left the windows open.

That first time was really quite cold and the snows came early. About four or five inches of snow came down – it was glorious in the middle of the woods and the wilderness, walking through snow flurries and everywhere totally white. After a day or so it thawed and disappeared. The real snows came about two weeks after we left, when you might get four or five feet of snow. But it was magical, all the same. And because most of the population lives down in the south, you could be 20 to 30 miles from your nearest neighbour.

The flight back to Helsinki was very turbulent and we were bouncing up and down when the door to the cockpit opened and the pilot came out. 'Jesus,' said a mate sitting next to me, 'I was half-expecting to discover it was Bekker flying this bloody plane.'

* * *

It would be another year before I did the Russian Bear Trail. You set out from a large industrial town in southeast Finland called Joensuu. It's a great trek. At one point you come to a river where you can look across into Russia. There were still lots of watchtowers and border guards with Kalashnikovs. On the trail itself you don't get to see any bears because they hear and smell you long before you get within sight. Instead, you are encouraged to stay overnight in a place like a large bottle bank with lookout slits around the sides. Outside the shelter they throw down carcasses and the bears come out to feed. You could be trapped inside this thing with four or five other people for 12 hours or more, and you're not even allowed out for a pee. All you've got is a bucket. It doesn't matter if you're there with friends or total strangers, you've got to use it at some point. Modesty doesn't count, sorry. It stinks when you go in, but by the time you come out it absolutely reeks. You can't sleep, either, because the bears might stay only for five minutes or so. But they do come and if you go outside they'll attack you. Compared with the

American grizzly they are not very big bears, but they're big enough. I wouldn't do it, I'm afraid, as I wasn't prepared to spend 12 hours in a bottle bank, even with bears as a reward.

After Lapland I had a few weeks at home before flying out to New York to meet one of Weston Spirit's backers, the actor Paul Newman. This guy is a big, big movie star, one of the few genuine Hollywood legends we have left. Meeting him was very nice because he's such a pleasant guy – very strong-willed and determined. He has those ice-cold blue eyes that all women seem to love and still go on about, and a little impish grin, even at his age. He was also incredibly fit, working out in a gym every single day.

He came to back Weston Spirit through his company, Newman's Own, which makes cooking sauces and salad dressings, donating all of its profits to charity. The story is that he used to make his own sauces using only natural products, not enhanced by chemicals or additives. He was having a dinner party and one of his friends said, 'Wow, this salad dressing is fantastic, why don't you market it?' 'That's a good idea,' said Paul. 'Let's do it all for charity.'

His company had approached the food distributors in Britain to name suitable charities and that's how Weston Spirit came to be chosen. Having experienced tragedy in his own family, he's concerned to see that all young people on this planet get the best out of their lives, no matter how long they've got.

When we arrived at the New York hotel where we were to meet Newman, we were taken up to the penthouse. I was there with Ben Harrison from Weston Spirit, plus Malcolm and his camera crew, who were filming the meeting for the new documentary. Newman had donated several thousand pounds to Weston Spirit and as a mark of respect for him, I was wearing a suit and tie.

His representative came into the room and said, 'Oh, my God, you should have dressed down. Paul doesn't like suits.'

Paul followed him into the room. You would never have noticed him in the street. He was wearing corduroy trousers that had bits of cord missing, a pair of slightly scuffed white deck shoes and a little rain mac over a jumper and shirt. He looked just like an ordinary guy on a day off from work who was dressing down to relax like everyone else. And that's the way he was – he impressed the hell out of me. I felt horribly overdressed, but when that happens you've just got to live with it. There's no point getting fussed.

I found Paul a very witty guy. To explain the cut to his forehead, he said, 'I was reaching for the last piece of carrot cake and Joanne my wife hit me with a tyre iron.'

I started asking him questions about what he was up to and he asked me about Weston Spirit. All the time the cameras were recording our conversation, which was just as well, or I wouldn't have remembered one word of it, I felt so in awe of him. And, of course, that's the one reaction he doesn't want.

He was curious about how I had got involved in community service. 'It's a strange trajectory, after the turmoil in your life of the last 17 years. No, not strange,' he added, 'I shouldn't say strange, but it's a unique trajectory.'

I explained it was because I didn't want to be pigeonholed as someone who's disabled, although that's clearly how I appear to the government and to the military. 'I'm disfigured quite obviously, but I didn't want to be labelled as that.'

I told him about meeting Paul Oginsky in New Zealand, and the ideas that were running through our heads. 'We knew we wanted to do something for inner-city youngsters, because there were a lot of problems in Britain at the time that were highlighted by the riots. An awful lot of youngsters were involved and we just thought we could do something – we weren't terribly sure what we could do, but we knew we could do something. And I just decided that's where I wanted to go – helping young people.' I told him about my background, and how the army had been my way out.

'You know,' said Newman, 'one of the things we've discovered is that small personal units like yours actually serve the inner-city kids a lot better than these huge organisations. It's the smaller organisations that are seen to be getting the job done.'

We talked about Weston Spirit's expansion plans, how we already had centres in Liverpool, Cardiff, Newcastle and London and had plans for another centre in Merthyr Tydfil, close to where I grew up. 'It's had its problems over the years since the coal mines closed down and the iron industry disappeared. When the foundries went, they took the heart out of the town. It's got a lot of problems with drugs and a huge housing estate reported to have one of the worst vandalism rates in Europe.'

Paul told me about a project in New Haven, in the States, that sends college kids into the housing developments during the summer to live with the young kids and tutor them in things like computers and baseball. They meet the kids hanging around the street corners and find out what they want to do. 'But I've got to tell you,' said Paul, 'we walked through this place and the young kids that were just standing around – it was like the opening of the Red Sea. I mean they were very deferential, because the kids thought, well, maybe I ain't gonna make it but my kid brother is 'cos this guy is helping him. So it was very rewarding.'

Paul asked me about the New York marathon, which I was scheduled to run the following week.

'How long are you going to last?' he asked me with a laugh. 'And have you ever actually run 26 miles?'

'The most I've ever run is about 17 miles, and that was when I was in the army.'

'It's the last seven that are the kickers,' he said.

'Yeah, so they say. I know that I'm going to be breathing through my ears and every other bit of me that can suck in wind. It's going to be very difficult, primarily because I've had an Achilles problem since I did the Great North Run a few weeks back. That's a half-marathon run in Britain. And I trod on a water bottle someone had thrown back into the road with the top screwed back on. It was like hitting a stone. My foot just rolled over and I tore the ligaments in my ankles.'

'Wow,' said Paul. 'You'd be better off breaking your ankle than pulling a ligament.'

'I think I'm going to have a lot of problems with it but I'll just keep going and get around the best I can. I'll run as far as I can, then I'll walk a bit until I rest it, then I'll run again. I've made the commitment, so I've got to do it now. It'll be strapped up and it's only a forward motion. It's not like playing sport.'

'Are you going to attach a wheel to your shoe? You know, they have these skis with wheels so you just kind of work your arms.'

We got talking about racing cars, because I still loved the sport and Paul co-sponsored a championship car team, Newman-Haas, that won the Indy Car World Series in 1993 with Nigel Mansell driving as a rookie, though he'd won the Formula One championship the previous year. Paul himself was just off to Daytona, where he was taking part in an antique-car race. The main criterion for entry seemed to be that the cars cost $1 million or more.

These cars would be hurtling round the track at 150mph or whatever, and any second they could be written off. I thought that was brilliant, taking risks with a million-dollar car that wasn't even his own. It was a lifestyle that reminded me of the late King Hussein of Jordan, who had paid for my flying scholarship at Kidlington. A group of us trainee pilots were sitting around talking of buying a second-hand plane for maybe £20,000, throwing in £5,000 apiece and wondering where the money would come from. King Hussein said he had the same problem when he was buying the Jordanian air force, but he was talking £500 million to our five grand. Newman was just the same, yet there was no 'I'm a huge film star and everybody has got to respect me for that'. He commanded respect just by being the man he is, that's all.

He was also a guy with very little time, yet he spent an hour and a half chatting with us, and then took us out on to the roof to have some photographs taken. I felt privileged to spend so much time with him. As a guy from the valleys, I don't stand in awe of many people, but with someone like Newman you can't help but feel a bit humble.

'I tell you what,' he said, 'you come down and taste some Newman's Own food produce I have lined up. I've got to do an interview for the *New York Times*, so we'll go down and do this food tasting. I've got all these barbecue sauces for chicken. You're British. You know the British taste. You tell me which ones we should bring out, because we've got to choose five out of seven.'

I went down with him to the hotel restaurant and chose the five I liked best. I have no idea whether I'm a good sampler of British taste – bland and boring, I'd say.

We'll eat anybody's food except our own. But I certainly knew which ones I liked. Paul said, 'Yeah, those are the ones I liked too.'

While we were down there, a photographer from the *New York Times* asked a couple of women in the restaurant to move their pushchairs so that she could photograph Paul in a better light. When he realised what had happened, he got quite upset. 'I'm here to do an interview about my foods,' he said to the photographer. 'Don't you dare inconvenience people on my behalf.' He went over to the women and apologised for what had happened. 'Please, it's all on me,' he said. They tried to refuse. He said, 'It's the least I can do.'

This guy was growing every second in my estimation, which was already very high because of his charitable attitude. He looks upon himself as just somebody who acts, and that's his job. As far as he was concerned, it didn't give him the right to interrupt anybody else's day. He paid for the women's lunch and everything.

Four or five days later I was on a plane back to New York to run in the New York marathon. My ankle still hadn't healed since tearing the ligaments in the Great North Run and it was very painful. If it hadn't been for Weston Spirit, I would have pulled out, but Paul and Ben and a number of others from Weston Spirit were running it with me, including some of our young people, and I couldn't let them down.

Paul and Ben are hugely fitter than I am and would have been hours quicker on their own, but we all three stayed together and had a laugh. They took it in turns to video me for Malcolm, which involved jogging backwards a lot of the time and lots of jokes about minding your back. Actually, I think we were running on stupidity rather than spirit. Paul kept asking me to smile for the camera. I was more in the mood to smack him in the eye, to be honest.

There were about ten of us on the team, all good people, and we raised something like £80,000. I'd gone on stage a few months before the race to encourage volunteers. 'I'm built for comfort not speed,' I said, hoping to reach out to others daft enough to accept the challenge. One who came forward was Howard Griffiths, a great stalwart who lends us audiovisual equipment for our fund-raising events. Then there was little mad Frankie as usual, a Scouser and veteran of many a marathon, who runs in an Everton shirt and cap, which makes him a potty blue. Frankie works for Guinness, who have been hugely supportive of his fund-raising runs over the years.

My aim was to finish running before the mop-up bus goes round to pick up all the stragglers. I don't remember how long it took us but at least we finished before they turned the lights out. There are so many false ends to that marathon. You think it's going to end round the next corner, and it never does. It goes on for bloody miles. You touch the edge of the Bronx and I remember some huge black lad who was muscles all over, stripped to the waist and holding a big sign above his head, 'Run faster, you are now entering the Bronx.' Run faster? I would have if I could, but when I saw a fellow in a rhino suit overtaking me I knew I was in trouble.

The last six miles or so take you through Central Park. It's only when you try running round it that you realise how colossal it is. By the end I was in absolute pieces. Even before the Great North Run, I'd been having injury problems and had to wear inserts in my shoes that cut into my feet. So I was getting blisters from those, and the problems with my ankle and my Achilles tendons were making my knees collapse. It was not an enjoyable experience. All the same, I ran for nine or ten miles before I had to start walking in between the running. The one part that was hugely enjoyable was finishing. That was really, really good – picking up my bag and putting on something warm, because after a while you stop sweating and just get cold and tired and all your energy levels drop away. When you finish, though, you start fantasising about doing another one, if only to repeat the euphoria of coming to a halt.

The Americans are completely crazy. They were out on the streets cheering us on for hours. Six or seven hours after the winner had crossed the line they were still out there. New Yorkers are bonkers, everybody knows that. They can be so aggressive and they're absolutely barking, yet that day they were very good to us.

When we finished, I didn't want to go down any steps into the subway. Anyone who has done any running will know how hard that is. We tried to get a cab, which was daft as the New York traffic was bumper to bumper, so we went to the nearest burger bar and filled our faces with the biggest, most stupid things we could eat and then we braved the subway – thank God there was an escalator. On the train I was scared to sit down in case I never got up again. Just negotiating kerbs was impossible, my thighs were so stiff.

That night I went out with the others and threw a few beers down the back of my throat. I'm a hardy party animal when I start, even knackered after a marathon. And the following day we went sightseeing. I could barely walk but you never know when you might make it back again.

10
Meeting Carlos Again

As MALCOLM SAW IT, there would be two strands to *Simon's Journey*, the film we were working on throughout 1998. The first was about a purely personal journey, from Falklands War victim to somebody who would run the New York marathon and fall out of aeroplanes, if not for joy then at least for charity. But there was something much deeper he wanted to unlock around the theme of reconciliation, which he saw operating at all levels: personal, political and symbolic. The key to this, he felt, lay in bringing Carlos Cachón over to Britain to renew the contact we had made in Argentina in 1991 for the earlier documentary, *Simon's Return*. Carlos had written to me in the intervening years, but I'm no letter-writer myself and I hadn't found anyone to translate his letters and emails for me.

In fact on a personal level, I didn't have anything I needed to reconcile with Carlos. The conflict between us was professional, not personal. He was a pilot and I was a soldier and we were both doing our jobs. I might have wished he had done his job a little less well on the day, but it wasn't something I held against him personally.

Carlos and I get on exceptionally well and he's somebody that I really like. I know it doesn't suit a lot of people for me to say that I like the guy who blew me up, but I do. I can't help it. He's a lovely man with an enigmatic smile – a genuinely nice guy who did his job as best he could. And he bested me on the day. He wasn't the first and he won't be the last.

Before I met him that first time, I had wanted to see if he had life in his eyes. I remember waiting in that Buenos Aires apartment, feeling very nervous, though in reality I don't know why. There was nothing Carlos could do that was going to hurt me again unless he carried a gun or a knife with evil intent and I doubted that very much indeed. But I suppose this was such a big moment and one that could have a huge impact televisually, to witness the reconciliation between us, even if I thought there was little to reconcile.

The door opened and this little guy came in with a great big moustache. I only wish I had a moustache half as good as his – mine is more like a busted couch, but there you are, I'm not going to get rid of it. He had a very gentle way about him, almost apologetic, though quite rightly he wasn't about to apologise for his part in the war. You should never feel ashamed of serving your country, no matter if your country is right or wrong.

'I'm sorry—' Carlos started to say.

'You don't need to—'

'—for your family,' Carlos continued.

'That's okay then, because you didn't do it to me personally. It's not like you did it to Simon Weston.'

The body language of that first meeting says it all. We sit down on the sofa. Carlos puts his hand on my knee and I'm very defensive, leaning away from him, really quite cold. I'm not sure that everyone connected with me back then realised quite how many things were going on in my mind, but that's fine. We all had our jobs to do and our reasons for being there. At the time, I also had no idea there was so much anger in me – clear, identifiable anger and hostility. It's only now, over the last couple of years, that I've been able to reflect on it properly.

We had two more meetings in Argentina before we flew on to Chile and the Falklands: once in the van, when Carlos came out to find me; and later at the war memorial to the Argentine dead, where Carlos hugged me in a clinch snapped by Pat Hill and splashed across the *News of the World*.

Those first meetings with Carlos released me from something very dark and oppressive that had been hanging over me for ten years. I had tied myself with crazy mental bonds and until I met Carlos I couldn't break free. Meeting Carlos did that for me. Other things might have worked, but without seeing a psychiatrist or a psychologist, it's hard to see what.

Carlos too had carried his own problems and baggage to our meetings. He had his own worries and fears and nightmares about the terrible thing he had done. He didn't know at the time just how terrible it was, because he had no idea how many men were actually on board the *Sir Galahad*. In any case that shouldn't have swayed his judgement when he did his job – which, unfortunately for us, he did incredibly well, probably because he was trained by us anyway. But, you know, we have guys who went into the first Gulf War as pilots and navigators who targeted buildings and what have you. Only later, when they saw the television footage, did they realise how much devastation they had caused. They've had nightmares since and some couldn't go on. There will doubtless be more from the 2003 war just past. Although the damage you inflict as a pilot is remote and therefore impersonal, the people flying planes are still human. They still have feelings. They still have dreams and nightmares and aims and aspirations. They still have families, and that leaves them open to nightmares. And because Carlos felt like this too, it made everything a whole lot easier for me to live with.

Yes, the idea of meeting Carlos again was a delight. As I said to Malcolm at the time, 'I'll be meeting him with no baggage whatsoever. I carry no baggage from the conflict, apart from a few bits and pieces that come from things that have been said about the Welsh Guards – ill-informed insults really.

'You take the lessons of history forward, but you can't keep on dragging the baggage. Far too many conflicts have reigned for far too many years because of people's inability to discard the baggage and learn from the lessons of history.' And maybe, I thought, I could help Carlos in my turn.

Malcolm arranged for Carlos and his wife, Graciela, to fly to London in December 1998. Reconciliation was clearly in the air because a couple of months previously the then President of Argentina, Carlos Menem, had come over to Britain on an official visit, the first since the conflict more than 16 years before. He laid a wreath in the crypt of St Paul's Cathedral to honour the 237 British service personnel killed in the South Atlantic. Margaret Thatcher did not attend the ceremony.

I wasn't on the original guest list, either, which wasn't a problem for me, but then the press kicked up a fuss that brought me a late invitation and it would have been churlish not to attend. So I went along and stood in the crypt among the crush of Foreign Office people, press, military and everyone else. I would have seen more on TV because Menem was surrounded by some of the tallest Argentinians I have ever seen. I don't know where they rustled them up from. Every ten minutes or so somebody asked us to move somewhere else; at times it felt like we were doing the hokey-cokey. Sir John Nott, the former Secretary of State for Defence, introduced himself, and I was constantly being asked what I thought about Menem's visit. Did they think I was going to lamp him, for Christ's sake? He was just a guy to me, not a god or a villain, just an Argentinian with bad skin, a guy with a job to do, like Tony Blair.

Malcolm had asked me the same question in the taxi on the way over. I was genuinely pleased that relations with Argentina were getting back to a state of normality. 'The past has been done and gone,' I said many times over; 'this is all about the future. The Falklands is very important to Falkland Islanders, obviously, but at the end of the day, I have to get on with my life. I can't live in the Falklands. Some people do. I don't. The Falklands War was the start of the rest of my life.'

* * *

Meeting Carlos and Graciela again was every bit as good as I had hoped. We really were meeting again as friends, re-establishing a friendship that had begun in Buenos Aires seven years before. Malcolm had arranged for them to stay in a hotel in Richmond, close to the Royal Star & Garter Home, and caught much of that first reunion on camera. I tried to ignore Malcolm and the others, wanting our meeting to be as natural as possible. We must have succeeded because I barely remember the cameras at all.

'Simon!' exclaimed Carlos as I entered the room, a warm grin on his face.

'Carlos, how are you?'

'Fine, and you?'

'Yeah, very good. Nice to see you again.'

'Well, okay. Please, do you remember my wife?'

'I do, yeah. Graciela – nice to meet you again. How are you?'

'*Ola*,' she said, in a very Latin way.

'How about Lucy?' asked Carlos.

'She's okay. She's taken the children to school, so she can't be here. But we'll meet her tomorrow.'

'Okay,' said Carlos, 'and your children is good?'

'Good, very good.'

'James, how's James?'

'Oh, James is good.'

'My James too,' said Carlos.

'Yeah, your James is , er—'

'Twenty-two years.'

'Twenty-two years, yeah.'

It's weird – I called my eldest son James Andrew, and Carlos called his boy Santiago (the Spanish St James) and his daughter Andrea.

We started talking straight away about things that were maybe trite and irrelevant to a lot of other people but very relevant to us – about families, opinions, rugby, sport, jobs, the places where we lived, the weather in Argentina and Wales. They were very interested in baby Caitlin.

'Does she walk or talk?' asked Carlos.

'She's walking and just starting to talk, one or two words. Not many people can understand what she says. But she is definitely the boss. She's a typical woman, bossing the boys about, bossing the family. She controls every-thing.'

'I'm not the boss,' said Graciela. 'I obey.'

I didn't believe that for a minute.

'Last year,' said Carlos, 'I wrote a letter for the arrival of your daughter. I don't know whether you received it?'

'I received a letter but I couldn't find anybody to translate it at the time. I still have the letter at home, with the photograph of the four of you. I'm afraid I haven't been able to translate it.'

'It doesn't matter,' said Graciela, 'through that letter you must have received our love.'

'I did feel there was a lot of warmth in the letter, yeah.'

'Tell me a little of what you are doing now,' said Carlos. 'You look very well. You have very much recovered from the last time I remember. You know, perhaps I noticed you were a little cold, a little distant if you like, at the first meeting, but now I see you very well and I am very happy that it seems to be like that.'

'Well, the first meeting we had . . . I had lots of things to sort out in my own mind. And when we met, that did so much for me . . . You were incredibly brave to meet me, because the situation was . . . I don't know, it was very difficult. I can't thank you enough for that meeting. From that point on, I have really been able to start to live a different life, as much as I was happy before. I still had ghosts I had to put to rest.'

'What can I tell you?' said Carlos. 'To see that you have a family, to see that you are very much loved in the family, that is perhaps far more important than the contribution of my person in your recovery. Which is why I am so intensely happy that you have such a wonderful family now, and we pray that it shall always be so. And, of course, that you consider us your friends.'

'Yeah, no problem at all, I am delighted to call you a friend. I mean, this is the strangest friendship you could possibly have, when we were once soldiers and at war, but that's just sort of assigned to the past, where it should stay. The future is what's all-important.'

'I never dropped my bombs on Simon Weston,' said Carlos. 'I saw a big block of iron. That was it. I never knew what was inside. That's true, very true. That I feel very much, but it's a part of history and there's a lot of things to do in the future, for our families and for ourselves. I see that Lucy looks after you very well because you lost some weight.'

That was the closest we came to looking back. We laughed and I told them about running the marathon, and recent games of rugby between Wales and Argentina. They gave me a lovely book of verse (in English) about the hard life of the gauchos, the Argentine cowboys descended from the Spanish, which I promised to read.

'Of course,' said Carlos, 'you'll probably have to work less to find the time.'

'Work less? I wish.'

Carlos told me an old Argentine saying: If you want to earn money, don't work so much, unless you want to be the richest man in the cemetery.

He talked a little about what he was doing, travelling as a sales rep for some packaging companies and organising a centre for ex-service people, and he told me about an uncle's place in the country where he and Graciela would escape for a bit of peace.

'He makes us barbecues and rides horses,' said Graciela.

'So you ride?' I said. 'I sat on a horse once and decided it was better for other people to do that.'

We talked about happiness too.

'I am very glad to see that at least you managed to transform your life,' said Carlos, 'from what was hell to what seems to be a paradise. That's very important. To feel internal peace, inner peace, you have to enjoy the smaller things in life.'

Before we left London for Wales, I took Carlos and Graciela to the Royal Star & Garter Home as I wanted them to see the splendour of the place. We went into the machine shop where one of the residents was making an old Spitfire. In the occupational therapy room, a lad who'd been injured in Northern Ireland was working on Remembrance Day poppies. 'It's not just about British service people,' I explained to Carlos, 'it's to remember all the people who have died and suffered in all wars.'

Malcolm had already driven to Wales with the crew, ready to film Carlos and Graciela's arrival at our home. Lucy and I were still living in Quaker's Yard, though getting ready to move into a new house in Cardiff early in the New Year.

The plan was that Carlos and Graciela would stay with Malcolm and the others in a hotel in the Brecon Beacons, close enough to us but far enough away to give them space and time to themselves. It wasn't going to be all filming. I wanted to show them a bit of Wales, take them around the Brecon Beacons and introduce them to the places that meant a lot to me.

Lucy had been quite apprehensive about meeting Carlos and Graciela, more for my sake than her own. She always likes to make up her own mind and certainly had no wish to appear stand-offish. As I expected, though, she liked them from the start. Like she says, Carlos has such a smiley face and they both wanted to fit in, despite the language barrier between us all. And Lucy knew as well as I did that without Carlos we wouldn't have met and there would be no young Westons, either.

It felt right welcoming Carlos and Graciela into the house, just like any other friends in fact, apart from the cameras and an interpreter. It made me think that a stranger is often just a friend you haven't yet met.

Caitlin woke up from her nap and there was a lovely moment when Graciela took the baby in her arms and

Caitlin snuggled in, a secret little satisfied smile on her face.

'You can come and see me any time you like,' said Graciela to Caitlin through the interpreter.

'Oh, well,' said Lucy, 'she'll fit into a suitcase nice and easy.'

We showed them the house, then Carlos and I looked at some maps of the Falklands and we quickly got into a discussion of what had happened that day – where we were in San Carlos Water and the point at which Carlos had actually seen us. In fact it was one of the other pilots who spotted us. Carlos himself had already turned his plane towards Port Stanley, because that's where he thought the ships were supposed to be. Carlos changed direction.

'I saw the ships,' he said, 'but only the aerials and then we put our engines on full power. We were protected by this small peninsula you see there. We went past it and saw the two ships, *Sir Tristram* and *Sir Galahad*, in their positions. The attack lasted about four seconds and very quickly we made our escape back to our base on the mainland. The impact of my bombs was seen by the planes behind me. The rest I just saw later on television.'

We talked a bit about my injuries as well. Carlos had heard that I had problems over sweating. I told him what it was like, with memories of the New York marathon strong in my mind. 'When I go running, for instance, my face goes bright red like a big tomato, and I'm sure people think I'm having a heart attack. But it's just the fact that the scars don't sweat, so the heat comes out in my face. Apart from that, it's not too much of a problem. But my hands are the worst.' I showed him how they looked now, and what they had done. 'They sewed my hand into my belly. Because my hand was all closed and they couldn't open it, they cut it all and put it in there, and grew my belly into my hand, so I've got a fat hand now as well.'

All this I explained through the interpreter, who stayed with us most of the time. One subject we avoided was any political discussion about the Falklands. Along with many other Argentinians, I suspect Carlos still believes that the islands are rightfully theirs. Geographically and logistically they may well be right, but historically they are wrong. First the Spanish and the French occupied the Falklands, then the Brits kicked everybody else off and occupied the place, but the Argentinians never did. Just because you are right geographically, it doesn't make you historically or morally correct. Geography isn't everything. But it was something we chose not to talk about, even through our interpreter, who spoke Chilean Spanish rather than Argentine Spanish. Carlos himself didn't speak enough English and I'm a multilinguist only when it comes to ordering beer.

The next day, when Malcolm and the crew were filming Carlos and Graciela back at our house, we had a visit that took us all by surprise. My Mam came bouncing round in her nurse's uniform to show me the *South Wales Echo*, which carried a full-page picture of me. Even though we lived quite close, she would only call round maybe two or three times a month, so it was very unexpected. There we all were, just sitting down to tea in the kitchen with the man who had injured her son and left a lot of other families grieving for lost husbands and sons. As soon as I heard her voice, I went into the hall.

'What are you doing there?' I asked. She looked genuinely shocked. Malcolm must then have asked if he could film her meeting Carlos, and checked with Carlos and Graciela that it was okay. It wasn't set up in any way and Mam knew she was quite free to say no.

'We've been doing this for 16 years now,' said Malcolm. 'You know the rules. If you don't want to, I won't film it.'

'Oh, all right,' said Mam. Deep breath time. 'Just give me a couple of minutes to compose myself.'

Jesus, I thought, let it run. If it turns sour, it turns sour. When she was ready I took Mam into the kitchen to join the others. 'Mam, this is Carlos,' I said, then watched from the hallway. There were too many people in the kitchen and maybe I wanted to stay out of harm's way.

You don't know my mother. She can be quite volcanic at times, and this wasn't a meeting I had bargained for. The first time I went back to the Falklands, she hadn't been at all keen that I should meet Carlos. She felt for all the Welsh Guards who had been killed, and their families. She didn't want anyone in Wales to think that I had let them down. After she had seen the film and read what I had to say about meeting Carlos that first time, she felt a bit happier. Time helped too. I think she was curious about what he might have to say. 'I'd just like to have a look at him, you know,' she had said to Malcolm some time before the meeting. 'I just want to see what makes him tick really.' Maybe subconsciously she had called round hoping she might see him, though on the surface that was the last thing she expected.

When I went back into the kitchen, everybody was still quite calm. Mam hadn't kapowed Carlos in the chops or anything dramatic like that.

Afterwards she said she'd been quite happy to meet Carlos, purely and simply because I had told her already he was such a nice man. I don't think she could warm to him especially, because of what he'd done and because of everything he had put our family through, and the other families that had lost loved ones. The meeting didn't lay any ghosts for her, because she hadn't held on to any bitterness at what had happened.

'I didn't feel anything,' Mam said to me. 'I didn't feel a weight was lifted off me from meeting him. I just feared for the loved ones that had gone, and the families – that was my big problem, I didn't want you to get a bad press. But a lot of time had elapsed since all that. If you had ended up in the gutter, it might have been a different story but no, if I felt anything at all it was, "Gosh, this poor man is in a strange country and we could all attack him." He looked quite bewildered. But really it didn't mean anything to me. It was just like meeting the postman.'

Whatever Mam says, I know Carlos and Graciela were pleased to have met her. Graciela, whose son was then 22, had actually put herself in my mother's shoes and at one point had left the kitchen in floods of tears. It had been a very difficult moment for her too, she said, but they overcame their difficulties. Having my mother there, serving tea, doing the dishes – 'Those are the same customs we have,' she said, 'and it was very beautiful.'

The rest of their visit passed all too quickly. In a mirror image of a visit I had made in Buenos Aires, I took Carlos to the memorial for Cardiff men killed in the Falklands. We went walking in the Brecon Beacons, which was lovely, and I showed them the range where I had trained for the Falklands. There was an exercise going on at the time, so we wandered around to explosive bangs in the background. The terrain is much the same as in the Falklands, with similar valleys and hills, although the ground there is much stonier and empty of trees. Sheep wandered all across the range in spite of the signs telling them to keep out, but these were Welsh sheep and the signs were in English.

We had lots of time away from the cameras, eating together and just talking. Malcolm tried to film as little as possible, honestly wanting us to be able to explore common ground in our own way and our own time. Carlos and Graciela were such fun to be around. It was nice to get to know them and also to learn something about the Argentine people. They are very philosophical, which came as a surprise. A lot of what they say is based on old teachings and philosophies. So there was a lot to learn but also a lot of fun to be had. Carlos has a wicked sense of humour. They were both delightful and I enjoyed my time with them very much. It was just a bit sad that the weather didn't hold, so they didn't see the Brecon Beacons in their full splendour; it's such a beautiful place. But apart from that, I think they enjoyed themselves immensely.

I would love one day to take up their invitation to meet again in Argentina. At the moment Lucy and I find it difficult to get time together, and the Argentine economy is none too stable. I wouldn't want to expose Lucy and the kids to that situation. We'll go there when the time is right, I'm sure.

11
Private Dad

I OFTEN FIND MYSELF feeling flat and blue around Christmas time. Lucy does most of the preparation and though I enjoy parts of it, I have to admit to feeling glad when the holiday is over. It seems to go on for ever – two or three weeks if you have kids. I much prefer the American idea. They just have Christmas Day and Boxing Day off, and then they're back to work.

But Christmas 1998 was especially horrible. Gill, who had acted more or less as my PA at Weston Spirit, lost her son to cancer of the heart. He died on Christmas Day in her arms, five days after his 22nd birthday. It was hugely sad. Gill has always been a good friend to Lucy and me, and we drove up to Merseyside for the funeral early in January. I find going to the funerals of young people perverse and can't reconcile myself to the fact that they die so needlessly. Some time after, Gill moved on to work for another charity. There had been some personality clashes at Weston Spirit, and I suspect the memories were too strong. That was one of my saddest moments – a personal low, rather than a professional one. It was amazing to get on so well with a colleague and we remain the very best of friends.

Pretty soon after, Lucy and I moved with the kids to our new home in Cardiff. The main reason was to be closer to the children's school. We're just the same as any other family. Life revolves around the kids, and one or other of us (usually Lucy) was driving 60-odd miles every school day on the two school runs, from Quaker's Yard to Cardiff, and that's before parties and after-school activities.

We also had to contend with new neighbours moving in next door. Though they were generous-spirited and exceptionally friendly to us, they marched to the beat of a different drum. They turned the downstairs loo into an aviary for an owl and the house soon filled up with people, kids, grandparents, snakes, lizards, birds. Our first sighting of them was when we came back to the shared driveway and the dad was up a ladder putting a flashing Santa and reindeer on the front of the house for Christmas. Inside there wasn't a stick of furniture. Later we saw the baby of 18 months running out to the snow in bare feet and nappies. One of the oddest episodes was when they threw out a hibernating lizard because they thought it was dead, wrapping it in newspaper before chucking it in the bin. When they next opened the bin, the shocked lizard was trying to climb back out. It was all just too bizarre.

By the time we moved, Caitlin was not quite a year and a half and already she was getting away with murder compared with the boys. She's a little minx – witty, cute, pretty, quick with one-liners, the real little sister, spoilt rotten but not in a tantrumy, spoilt-brat way. We don't let her have her own way all the time. If she throws her toys in the dirt or sits sulking on the stairs, that's it. 'Come back when you've changed your attitude,' I'll say. But we do ruin her because she's the baby, I suppose, and because she's my little girl. I just can't help it with her.

At heart I'm a family guy really, not someone who enjoys the lifestyle of a public person. I love meeting people and talking to them, but I also love my own space and my own company. Best of all, I love being at home with Lucy and the kids. Although I work very hard, I'm fortunate that I also have time, and I try to give them as much as I can.

I very rarely go out drinking when I'm home. I may go out once a month or so with my mates from the old days in the army, Cappa and Rodney 'Wrong Charge' and the others. Rodney was my number one in the mortars. He got his nickname from a live firing exercise when he messed up the orders for the direction and elevation of his mortar tube and got the settings all wrong. Everyone else's mortar bomb had been fired in a straight line but Rodney's went sailing off in the wrong direction, straight into the artillery's *parc fermé*, where you park all your vehicles and equipment and regroup for the night. There was a huge shout of '*Incoming!*' and everyone jumped down. You put one hand on your head and one down below and just hope that none of it gets blown away. Hot shards of metal scattered across 360 metres but thankfully nobody was hurt. All the time he was in the army Rodney was the only man I knew with Velcro on his stripes – they were on and off his arm so many times it was unbelievable.

Cappa, another ex-Guardsman, was in 2 Company. In fact I didn't really know him that well in the military, but I got to know him afterwards as he and Rodney are great friends. Cappa is a big gentle giant who is now a social worker. He's a good drinking buddy of mine and has a super wife, Elaine, whose two young daughters he took on as his own.

I will also occasionally nip out for a pint with John, my neighbour from across the road. He's a grip in the film industry and great company. His wit is very dry and I enjoy the company of people who make me laugh. Lucy gets on well with his wife, another Elaine, who is such a pleasant person, the sort who could make friends with aliens. She's also a great host. My problem is that I'm always one of the last to leave, but then I live the shortest distance away and it's all downhill, so I just have to let my legs roll. But really, I'm happiest at home with my family.

One thing we've had to get used to as a family is the attention I get when we go out together. I took the boys to Tesco in Cardiff and one of them said, 'How come you know everybody, Dad?' 'I don't, son,' I explained. 'They know me.'

When people recognise you, they'll sometimes want to seize their opportunity and stop and speak to you there and then. Because of the way I was brought up, I feel I have to stop and talk to them too, but sometimes you really don't have the time. I'm always surprised when people do this, because I forget about the public side of my life. You're ferreting through the sales looking for a pair of slippers or whatever and someone catches your eye. It can be a bit disconcerting for other people with me, as it really is bizarre to be stopped in such a pleasant way by complete strangers.

I took my mother and Lucy out for the day recently, to an outlet centre in Swindon. We'd just sat down for a sandwich and a cup of coffee and this woman came out of the shop. She came straight over to us and said, 'Somebody told me you'd walked past. I rushed out and was ever so disappointed when I found you weren't there. I've always wanted to meet you, you're one of my heroes.'

'Thanks very much,' I mumbled. Still, after all these years, I feel slightly embarrassed and totally humbled that anyone should think like that. It's lovely too, don't get me wrong, but I'm lost for words. I wish I was quicker with the wit. I'm always left treading water with my tongue.

Another time I was at a Simply Red concert when the brother of an ex-wife of somebody I grew up with came up to me and said, 'Would you mind coming over to meet my friend? He's terribly shy.' To say they were both six foot six is probably selling them short.

It can be a bit hard on the family at times. My sister got attacked in a restaurant once. She was out with the girls around Christmas time and somebody told this chap that Helen was my sister. 'He's the most selfish guy,' he started screaming, or words to that effect, effing and blinding for absolutely no reason. 'He doesn't do anything for anybody else. Everything he does is for himself and his own gratification. He's horrible.' He grabbed hold of her and was threatening to punch her in the face. They had to drag him off her and all because she was my sister. I can only assume he was jealous, but jealous of what?

Lucy has never mentioned a problem with things like that, but she's not someone who goes out pubbing and clubbing. She's her own independent person. I know my mother gets hacked off being known as Simon Weston's mother instead of me being known as Pauline Hatfield's son. She comes back from the hairdresser's after listening to someone else claiming they were at school with me. 'You must have been in the biggest class in the world,' she says. It's a bit remarkable, considering I hardly ever went.

Even if I wanted to go out drinking more, it isn't always that easy. One night I was out with Cappa and Rodney when this guy came over. He was drunk and fawning all over me. It was very embarrassing. After about three or four minutes Cappa turned round and said, 'I don't know about him, but I think you've said enough. If you're not boring him you're effing boring me, so if you don't eff off, I'm going to rip your head off.' Cappa's big enough to do it too. To be honest, it's a bit difficult for the people I'm with. Some people when they're sober wouldn't dream of approaching you, but a drink or two gives them a bit more Dutch courage. I don't get offended by it but I do understand why a lot of people don't particularly enjoy the experience. At least we've found one little pub in Cardiff where people just seem to ignore you, out of friendliness rather than rudeness.

But to the children, I'm simply their dad, which is how it should be. They see me on the telly sometimes, and that's still a novelty to them. 'I love it when you're in the papers or on telly,' Stuart said the other day, but they don't see me as a public figure. I heard the actress Ruth Madoc say the same thing when she celebrated 40 years in show business: her children only ever see her as their Mam.

My kids enjoy school and as far as I know, have never been bullied because of me or who I am. I remember my sister's youngest boy, Jonathan, telling me something derogatory one of the other boys had said to him about me. I said, 'Don't worry about it, kid. When you go back, ask him what his dad has done. Does he race motor cars? Does he fly aeroplanes? Has he cycled across America? If his dad really has achieved something with his life, then he can say whatever he likes about me.' The lad never did come back at him after that.

I always find it very refreshing being around children because they'll ask questions if they want to know things. Sometimes they stare, sometimes they don't. Sometimes they see things, sometimes they don't. When we were up at my parents'-in-law recently, one of my nieces and her girl cousin asked me loads of questions about my missing little finger and the baldness down the back of my head but they didn't seem to notice my face. How children react will usually depend on how you behave; if you feel terribly self-conscious, they will too. I'll explain things if they ask, but I don't volunteer it and I don't shy away from them, either.

With the kids, I'll take the mickey or say something funny. If you're nice to children, they tend to forget what you look like. They don't recognise colour or size or weight or wheelchairs. They only recognise people and qualities like kindness or aggression. Well, they may also be intimidated by very big people, but there isn't a human being I know who isn't wary at first when they go near someone else's child and that's how I'll behave.

My kids' friends don't seem to have a problem with me – like all kids, they respond to how you are. Of course, if they respond negatively then you have to back off because you can't expect an eight- or nine-year-old to get over any initial problems or feelings of intimidation straight away. But they'll talk to my kids or to their own families and then they realise the way I look is just because of something that has happened to me.

My own father left home when I was ten. Unlike my stepfather later, he had played very little part in my life anyway. The only time I can remember doing anything with him was just before he left, when he took me and my friend Carl camping for a week in the Brecon Beacons. I really enjoyed that, but otherwise we never did any of the things dads do with their kids – he never took me to rugby or football matches or taught me how to play cricket. He did buy me a fishing rod for my birthday once, but it was my next-door neighbour who took me fishing. My boys will never be able to say that about me. I've taken them to international rugby, club rugby, local village rugby, the same with football, and there are lots of military things we've done together. At the invitation of Captain Paul Mason, for instance, I took them to see the Army Air Corp's Apache Longbow helicopter and they had a great time crawling all over that.

There are some things I can't do with them, though. I can't play ball games any more because the skin on my hands won't let me. Stuart has loved basketball ever since he was little, and now he's into American football. He wants me to throw a football or toss a rugby ball but I can't catch small balls and rugby balls make my hands sore. He wants me to kick an ordinary football but I'm no footballer, either. I feel as if I'm letting him down terribly but there's nothing I can do about it.

At least the things that have happened to me are there in my books, so there's a lot I don't have to explain. James is reading the first one at the moment, and enjoying it, I think. He laughs at some of the daft things I've done. I expect some of it he finds a bit emotional but he hasn't really talked to me about that. I'll tell him when he's ready to ask. 'Did you really do that?' he'll say. 'Did you really say that?' Other people know more about my first book than I do, especially James, because he's still in the very retentive phase of his life. I'm over 40 and I've forgotten almost everything in it.

Lucy and I have a very even partnership, or it wouldn't work. I go out and earn the money, making sure she doesn't want for anything, and she looks after the house. It's a fair distribution of work, because I work hard and I know how hard she works. She hates me doing any sort of housework because I get in the way. She reckons that I start in one room, move into the next and start something there, which really irritates her. I'll help her with the dishes most of the time, providing my hands aren't falling apart, but Lucy does most of it.

The kids tidy up with a hand grenade. You walk through the door and everything explodes, but that's just the way they are. They're a joy to be around. You can take them anywhere, even if they're always misbehaving back home with us. But if they can't swing from the lights in their own home, where can they? You'd go ballistic if they did it in somebody else's house, or in a shop. They've got to have somewhere to release all their energies.

The one thing Lucy doesn't do is clean the shoes; that's my job. I just believe people should have clean shoes. I was travelling on the London underground recently and there were all these nice shiny shoes. That's not a bad start to the day, I thought. I got talking to the guy standing next to me, who just happened to be a military guy, and he was absolutely pristine. I looked down at his shoes and they were like mirrors. From top to toe he looked the part. Isn't that what it's about? If you look the part, it's half the battle in most cases.

I enjoy work immensely but find I have to kick-start myself back into it after I've had time off. One of the things I don't like having to do is put on a suit and tie again – I would be much happier leading a beachcomber existence. I've got something like 20 suits, partly because my weight keeps fluctuating and partly because after the initial investment, wearing different ones stops them looking tired. When you stay away from home for a couple of functions, it also means you don't have to get up at six in the morning to iron your suit for the next event. I don't enjoy a trailer lifestyle, though. You'll sometimes see me in a back lane or in service-station toilets, getting out of my tracksuit trousers and into my suit.

There are times when you dress completely wrong. I remember turning up on behalf of Weston Spirit to receive a cheque from a Rotary Club in Usk. I was wearing an open-necked shirt while everybody else wore suits. The man who introduced me made a joke about something he remembered his mother saying, how it's not the suit on the man you come to see but the man in the suit. I got up and said, 'That's valley talk for "you're a right scruffy git".'

As the years go by I find I get busier than ever. I try very hard to keep the weekends free for my family, but when you work for two charities, promoting what they do, it comes as no surprise that much of your work takes place around the weekend. I sometimes wish I had a typical week, so I would know what to expect, but I like the fact that there is so much variety in my life and I am always bouncing from one place to another. When I think about how busy I get, I realise there are times in the year when I don't know whether to wind my arse or scratch my watch.

As well as promoting the charities, I still do a lot of media work. I get asked because people like the common sense I talk and because I try to give an honest answer to the question, unlike politicians, who say what they wanted to say all along and try somehow to attach it to the question. I've been on Richard and Judy's shows a number of times, ever since they were up in Liverpool, and on ITV's *This Morning* with Fern Britton and Phillip Schofield. I've got to be honest, I like all four of them. I find Richard and Judy lovely people to work with and Fern Britton is just a delight. She and Phillip laugh and giggle constantly on and off camera like a couple of school kids. They are two very professional people who have obviously hit it off with that magic that happens when you suddenly click with people. Whenever I've sat with them, you'll be running through your stuff and the next thing you know they start breaking into howls of laughter.

It's sad that Lucy can rarely get away with me now, unless she can get help with picking up and taking the children to school, so she'll only come to the higher-profile events. I love it when she does come away with me because it's great to have company and I'm in love with her still. Eating out at night in a hotel restaurant on your own is dead miserable, you might as well have a book, so I'll usually eat in my room. If Lucy's with me it's lovely to go down into the restaurant to enjoy the atmosphere.

My family are great at helping out. Mam will babysit when she can, though she prefers to have the children up at her house as she says my 11 p.m. is more like her 3 a.m. and she doesn't like having to drive home afterwards if she's working in the morning. I also get a lot of help from my sister Helen, who has been coming over once a week for years to sort out all my paperwork and deal with things like email. In our house the computer is the last thing that gets switched on by me, after the telly, the radio, the kettle and all that stuff. It's going to have to come to a stop soon because Helen's about to qualify as a teacher and always takes on far too much. I'm not going to let her off that lightly, trust me. There'll still be things she will do for me in the future.

I love my sister and I'm proud of her too. I only wish she'd realise how much she has achieved. She has brought up three children, much of the time on her own. My nephew Richard has become a policeman and has never brought a moment's trouble to the door. My niece Becky is working and taking A levels in her early twenties, having decided to go back into education when she realised she had wasted the first part of her life. Strangely enough, I felt the same. Only last year Helen got her degree; a good degree too. Now she's doing her teacher training in some pretty tough schools. Sometimes I think she feels she's living in my shadow but she really doesn't need to. There's nothing glamorous in driving away from home in the mid-afternoon and not getting back till well after midnight, having shaken hands and grinned at God knows how many people. But there's no point in griping, you just get on with it. It's not a bad way to earn a living, after all, providing you throw your heart into it. As long as you believe in what you are doing, you can enjoy anything.

12
Learning to Say No

ONE OF THE CONSEQUENCES of being in the public eye and doing a lot for charity is that you get more requests for help than you can possibly manage on your own. It comes with the territory and one of the lessons I have had to learn is to be hard-nosed about what I can and cannot do. The rules I worked out with Geoff have helped enormously. He's been like a mentor to me, though I make my own decisions and take counsel from other people, turning to Geoff for advice only when situations threaten to explode in my face.

Weston Spirit and the Royal Star & Garter Home are the charities that have the biggest claim on my time. By focusing on just those two, I can achieve my goal of helping to raise their profile and as much money for them as I possibly can. Geoff and I worked out that I can usually take on one other big appeal a year, providing it doesn't clash with either of those two. I want to give quality not quantity, and you can't spread yourself too thinly.

But however clear you are in your own mind, the requests for help still keep flooding in, from organisations and individuals. Last summer, for instance, a national newspaper sent on to me a letter that had come to them from the husband of a woman who was approaching her 60th birthday. He had promised her anything she wanted for her birthday, jewellery, a watch, anything he could possibly afford, and what she wanted most was to meet me. She's from Wales and clearly off her head if meeting me was so important to her, but according to her husband, that was her fondest wish.

Helen, my sister, got in touch with him on my behalf. 'Well,' said Helen over the phone, 'Simon's at home on Saturday and he could slip into Cardiff and meet you there for a cup of coffee.'

So that's what I did, spending a delightful hour or two chatting with them over coffee in a Cardiff hotel. As people get older, the chances of meeting at some public function are getting slimmer, and as long as it's not too far, I'll do what I can.

Afterwards the woman phoned up Helen to thank her for her help in arranging the meeting; she was practically in tears. You can't do it for everybody but occasionally you can and you do – not for yourself but because you want to see people go away with a spring in their step. After all the kindnesses and effort people have put in for me, it helps keep my feet on the ground if I can do something for somebody else in return.

Schools are another area where I get lots of requests each year. There was a time when I was trucking round the country speaking to loads of schools, but then I realised that unless you set yourself a quota, it can all too easily turn into a treadmill you can't get off. So now I set myself a limit of ten or 12 schools a year and make sure that each one gets the best of me.

Oddly enough, the requests that are easiest to turn down are the ones offering you money to do something, because then you don't have any guilt. Whether you do it or not becomes a commercial decision, which is very different from facing a heart-rending situation and no money. Those are the requests you try your absolute hardest to fulfil.

A year or two back I visited a school in Swansea where a young pupil had been very badly burnt in a fire. The school had got in touch with me to see if I would speak to the lad and his friends and family, and then to the whole school. He was only 11 years old, the same age as my son James, and the school was concerned about how he would be able to integrate into school life.

So I went along, met the boy and his family, then talked to the youngsters in the main hall. I was pretty blunt with them. 'If you think it's big and clever to poke fun at people who have been disfigured or burnt or just look different from everyone else, it's not,' I said. 'You can call me anything you like – I'm big enough and tough enough to take it. But it's just not funny to poke fun at your fellows.' I also told them they should listen to their teachers, who wanted them to stay safe. If they were warned to stay away from fires or railway lines or whatever, they should do what they were told or they might end up looking like me. 'When I was younger,' I said, 'I thought it was clever to miss school. I regret it now, and even though things have luckily worked out for me, it's a hell of a way to become successful.'

The school was fantastic, really supportive of the boy and all the other kids there. The fact that they had asked me to help meant a lot to me, as I felt I could share so much of my own experience with the boy at a time when he was embarking on a new venture in life. His mum was there, a lovely lady, and the boy himself seemed a lively enough lad, surrounded by loads of friends who gave him massive support. Afterwards I had a private chat with the lad and his mum. She told me that a pizza shop across from the school had ordered him away from the window, worried that he was frightening off potential customers. It's hard to believe they could be so unthinking and not give a damn about the kid's feelings. I didn't go over to sort them out as I felt I might have punched somebody in the face. And it wasn't my business anyway. The boy would probably stay at that school for a number of years and I reckoned it was up to the school, his parents and, most importantly, the boy and his friends to deal with that one.

The lad still had a long way to go, and he'll have to face up to a lot of pain as well. I hope that my involvement will help him see that being aggressive and resentful towards other people over what has happened to him will get him nowhere. Sticking up for what you want for yourself is different. But there is absolutely no point in being angry or aggressive because you feel yourself to be a victim. That will just waste time and land you in a whole lot of bother. But in this case the lad seemed to be going about things the right way.

The boy's experience in the pizza shop reminded me of a holiday I had taken with Lucy in Switzerland, in the very early days of our courtship. I had planned it as a romantic week away over Christmas. We were staying at a hotel on one of the Swiss lakes but there was trouble right from the start. At the train station, nobody would tell me which platform would get us on the right train – everybody was totally aggressive and unhelpful. Then, at the hotel, people would literally stop when they saw me and run back to take another look. I had people laugh in my face until eventually the hotel asked us to leave as they said I was putting off the other guests. As you can imagine, I'm not keen to go back there, ever.

It was a five-star hotel in a beautiful setting yet I was treated like a 14th-century leper. The insensitivity was quite unbelievable. They made me feel like the Elephant Man – you know, 'Roll up and see the circus freak.' It was even worse for Lucy because there was nothing she could do about it. We didn't see any disabled people while we were over there, nor did there appear to be any wheelchair ramps or provision for anyone less than perfect. I don't know what they did with people who have any sort of disability.

After about three days I took up the hotel's suggestion and said, 'Right, we're off. We're going home.' As our flights were booked for a specific day, it cost us double to fly back early. We were back at our Liverpool home on Christmas Day, eating egg and chips for Christmas lunch because the shops were shut and we hadn't been able to get in any proper food. To cap it all, at the Swiss airport I had pushed my trolley right over Lucy's foot and broken her toe. 'Stop making a fuss,' was my sympathetic response.

It's something I have noticed, that people from continental Europe are often awkward with me, and don't really know how to cope. I met one of Chirac's deputy ministers, the little terrier who was espousing Chirac's anti-war stance, and he looked distinctly uncomfortable in my presence. It's as if they only see beauty as far as skin-deep, though I've no idea if that really is the case. But they don't seem to know how to deal sensitively with my appearance. Once when I was visiting the Welsh Guards in Germany, an old woman came up to me in a bar and asked what had happened to me. One of the lads with us spoke some German, so I told her through him that I was a British *Soldat* injured in the Falklands.

'Are you being looked after well?' she asked.

'Not particularly.'

'Ah,' she said, 'Adolf, he would have looked after you. You'd have got a good war pension from him.'

There we are then, lovely girl, I thought, that's all I need. A nice fat pension from Adolf Hitler.

My experience of Australia was different altogether and I loved being over there. Although Aussies are renowned for being really hard, rough-tough folk, outspoken and brusque in their speech, I found myself giving a talk to a group of nurses who were all in absolute floods of tears. Their attitude can be really abrupt, which I like because you know exactly where you are with them, but underneath they can be amazingly gentle.

Despite the need to ration the claims made on me, I find that I often get approached to help in the case of children who have been burnt or injured. I'll do what I can, though it takes its toll and I have to filter quite a lot because there's only me. I can't take on board everybody's woes and pains and it's very, very difficult if I'm always being asked to help in the case of burns and disfigurement.

One kid I remember really well is a little girl from Ipswich, who had been trapped in a cot fire when she was only two. I went up there a year or two after to lend some support and draw public attention to her case. Even I was deeply shocked when I saw her, though I am well used to being around burns. She had no hair, no features, and the only fingers she had came from her feet.

I remember another little girl from Northern Ireland called Melanie. As a baby, she had been badly burnt when the parked car she was in exploded into flames because of a wiring fault in the roof. Her little sister died, and Melanie was pulled out with her hair and clothes on fire. Their mother had left them in the car for a couple of minutes while she popped into the supermarket at Enniskillen. Melanie's face, she said, had just melted away.

As I was going over to Northern Ireland anyway, I was happy to visit the little girl and her family. Melanie featured in a BBC documentary, *Face Values*, in which she was shown getting on happily at school, swimming, riding, playing the piano. 'All Things Bright and Beautiful' was the piece she chose.

Melanie's mother had my Mam's strength and determination, and a similar insight into what the future might hold. Trying always to be positive, she wanted to counteract problems before they became serious. Her greatest fear was that Melanie might reach her mid-teens and simply shut herself away in her room and not try any more. Yet all those who knew the little girl were convinced she would succeed, and that being on TV might help in the process.

'It'll do Melanie an immense amount of good,' I said in the BBC film, 'because she doesn't have to explain herself. She doesn't have to give an excuse as to why she's there or why she's injured. She just is. Just accept her for what she is. Let her love you and love her, she's a lovely girl, and she just cares and she deserves to be cared for, not just by her family but by friends and everybody else.'

Also appearing in the same documentary was James Partridge of the charity Changing Faces, which tries to help people come to terms with their injuries. It's a charity I help when I can, along with another very new charity, the Healing Foundation, set up to help fund research into all aspects of transplantation – organs, limbs, faces, skin and all the psychological effects of transplant surgery. I'm hoping the two will work together on various projects in the future.

While I believe strongly in the aims of both these charities, I don't consider myself to be fighting a personal crusade to make disfigurement more acceptable in society, not consciously anyway. I do hope to make a difference in my own way, by appearing on television and in newspapers. If an ordinary guy like me can live happily with the physical and psychological consequences of my injuries, then so can anyone else. Whenever I meet people who seem embarrassed by my appearance, I try my very best to make them feel more at ease because if I'm happy with who I am, I don't see why anybody else should worry. And if certain people are repelled by my appearance, that's their problem, not mine. But overall, my life is about much more than disfigurement and that's why I don't claim to be fighting any particular crusade.

Recently, though, I found myself getting involved in the whole issue of facial transplants. While you might think I'd be a prime candidate to get a new face, I wouldn't want it done at any price. I wrote about it at length for the *Daily Mail*.

For me, the idea of wearing another man's face is just a non-starter. Not only would I have to suffer all the physical problems in having somebody else's skin but I have grown to like who I am. And anyway, how would my family react to me in a new mask? How would Lucy feel kissing a dead man's lips? How would the children react to seeing me in a stranger's face? However brilliant the surgeon, there's no way a transplanted face can ever match its host. Besides, we are all different and a face is like a physical autobiography; it tells the story of our lives. In my case, the story is all too obvious. I see the Falklands each time I look in the mirror, but every face reveals the truth about its owner, whether you're looking at the smoker's sallow complexion or the laugh-lines of a kindly grandparent.

I don't see any ethical problems in facial transplants, however. If somebody else wants one, fine, though I would definitely draw the line at people clamouring for new faces purely for cosmetic reasons. The first person to get a new face will attract enormous public attention – the chances are they will become either a pariah or a millionaire. So I was quite happy when the surgeon Peter Butler asked me to join a consultative panel involved in developing a psychological profile of good candidates. It's a terrific challenge, when you think of it, selecting the sort of person who would be able to handle the psychological effects of a new face under the harsh spotlight of public-ity, and we're still trying to sort it all out.

The whole idea of facial transplants set me thinking about other sorts of transplants. One part of me I would not want transplanted into anyone else are my eyes, which I look on as the gateway to the soul. I don't want anyone else to look at the world through my eyes; through my thoughts, maybe, through my hopes and my desires, but not through my eyes.

A common thread running through many of the chari-ties I help is about giving people a future, whether it's the disenfranchised young people at Weston Spirit, the vet-eran residents of the Royal Star & Garter Home or burnt and injured youngsters. Public service is another theme, and I was happy to take part in a campaign to encourage more recruitment to the police, alongside people like sportsmen Lennox Lewis and John Barnes.

'Real-life heroes' we were called. I don't know about that, but even before I got injured, one of my own real-life heroes was Douglas Bader, who not only learnt to fly again without his legs but got himself banged up in Colditz as a prisoner of war because he was a constant escapee. He showed that no matter what life throws at you, you can always rise to meet your challenges. 'Never let the bastards grind you down,' as Ronnie Barker said in an episode of *Porridge*. Bader was also a fine rugby player and – as I learnt when I visited RAF Cranwell – a bit of a prat in some people's eyes, but that didn't stop him being a great man and it's said he lost a lot of his arrogance after he lost he legs. I liked him because he had that special something – he was destroyed and yet he found the strength to rebuild himself. How many people does that happen to? Having Kenneth More play him in the film made about his life, *Reach for the Sky*, can only have helped, too.

I really enjoyed making the TV advert for the police. For me it was a new departure, like being an actor. Although the adverts were scripted, you were able to ad-lib. Again I felt my mouth flapping when John Barnes came up and introduced himself some time afterwards. 'We both did the same adverts,' he said, 'but I thought yours was much better than mine.' My advert was about how hard it must be to go to somebody's house to tell them that their loved one has been killed by a drunk driver. I just remembered how hard it had been to identify the body of my stepfather, Lofty, and then the pain of going to my mother to tell her I'd done it. Imagine how much worse it must be telling a total stranger that their loved one is dead – that surely takes a special kind of courage?

I like to think the advert brought in at least two new recruits – my nephew Richard and a young officer I met at a Star & Garter event for army cadets at Winchester. He came up to me afterwards and said he was changing careers to join the police force because of my advert.

It's just as well that Geoff helped me early on to prioritise the requests for help that come in, or I might have sunk under their weight – I would definitely have sunk under my own. He probably turned down loads of stuff at the beginning I never really knew about. The media will use you for their own purposes, which can do you a lot of good but you can also fall off the tree because you've been over-exposed, so you have to be very careful how you respond.

Geoff and I are also very careful about the charitable commitments I take on. You have to stay in control of what you do and make sure that any appeals or campaigns are properly run. People work in charities for all sorts of reasons and you can't afford to get mixed up in their agendas. My reason is simple: to raise as much money as I possibly can for the causes I support. Sometimes you have to learn to say no to something because you can do more good – and raise more money – in other ways.

You also have to be absolutely straight in what you do. I remember a woman in Scotland who got in touch with me after I had done a mailing for the Star & Garter. Instead of giving money to the appeal, she wanted to give some money directly to me. It was quite a lot of money, several thousand pounds in fact, and she wanted to buy me a holiday. I called Geoff to see what I should do.

Geoff said, 'There are two ways we can play this. We can either play it properly, or you just turn her down.'

We talked it over some more and agreed that what I should do was to ask her to give the money to charity. I then spoke to her on the phone and said, 'Look, if you really want to make me happy, give whatever you can to the Royal Star & Garter Home.'

And that's what she did. I couldn't take the holiday, either. You have to play by the rules or life becomes terribly messy and it was far better that the money went where it was genuinely needed. But I don't want to sound in any way saintly, or strangle myself with my own halo. 'Neither a saint nor a sinner' – that's what I'd like as my epitaph.

13
A Fistful of Honours

GETTING HONOURS AND AWARDS is another side to the public coin. It can be hugely exciting but they don't occupy a large part in your life. They happen. You go up to receive them. But you don't go around thinking about them much of the time – you just get on with other things.

Of course, for anybody to recognise your efforts and endeavours is immensely rewarding, though part of me feels embarrassed at the same time. I accept awards not because I think I have the right to receive them, but because of the spirit in which they're offered and the fact that they're honouring everybody involved in my life – Mam, Lofty, Lucy, my family, Weston Spirit, the Royal Star & Garter Home, everybody who works their socks off in the charity world.

The first award I ever got was Pebble Mill Man of the Year. I couldn't go to the ceremony as I was lying flat on my back after two major surgical operations, so my mother went on television to accept it on my behalf. I watched her from my hospital bed, and told her afterwards that she was wearing so much make-up she looked like a tart. After that there was Man of the Year (they made my Mam Woman of the Year too), Man of the Decade (that was for the 1980s), Motivator of the Year, the Snowdon Award Scheme's Special Award and (for 2002) Speaker of the Year from the Association of Speakers Clubs. Once I even got named Tie Wearer of the Year by the Guild of British Tie Makers, and have a specially woven tie to prove it. I also have a handful of honorary degrees from various universities: from Glamorgan, UWIC (the University of Wales Institute, Cardiff), Liverpool John Moores University and most recently, the Open University. This might seem a touch ironic, given my school history, but it's good to get them from places where you have some connection.

I don't remember ever turning an award down, though I was a bit doubtful when I was first offered the OBE. They ring you up before it's announced, to see if you will accept.

'What's it for?' I asked suspiciously. 'If it's for being injured, I can't take it. There were more than 750 other guys injured, besides me.'

'No,' she said, 'it's because of your commitment to charity.'

'That's okay, then,' I said, happy to accept it on behalf of everybody involved and all those like Geoff who have helped me steer my course.

Once they've announced your award, you've then got to go along for the investiture ceremony when you receive it from the Queen, which happens three or four months later. I turned up at the Palace with Lucy, my Mam and Lofty (this was 1992, two years before he died). We were all looking so smart – Mam in black, which she says isn't her colour, Lucy in crimson, Loft and me in morning suits, the whole works.

You're all milling about together in the same room for a short time, then your guests get taken off to the ballroom, where there are hundreds of chairs laid out and tiered seats rising up on three sides. The place is absolutely magnificent: chandeliers and red carpets and an orchestra playing away in the gallery. In all the hundreds of faces, I remember catching sight of Patricia Routledge from TV's *Keeping Up Appearances*, who was then at the peak of her fame. She was just another face in the crowd, there to watch somebody getting an award.

One of the officials shows you what to do and tries to keep everybody calm. When it's your turn, you move forwards to the usher, stop, wait to hear your name read out by the Lord Chamberlain, advance several paces, stop, left turn, bow, advance three or four paces to the dais – it's like being in the military all over again. You've already been fitted with a hook in your jacket, so that the Queen can snap the medal on quickly. She's had plenty of practice by now. There are more than a hundred people lined up in the queue, so it's a bit like a conveyor belt.

The Queen says a few words to you as she pins on the award – congratulations or something like that. Unless you're someone like Sir Steve Redgrave or one of her favourite actors, there's not much she can say. She shakes your hand, then you take three steps back, bow, right turn and walk off into a small room where they whip your medal away and hand you a different one back in a box. It's all over pretty quickly, but it was a great day for all of us, apart from the fact that Lofty had been taken ill with chest pains the night before. Mam didn't tell me at the time, though we've talked about it since and she now thinks that Lofty's illness dated from then. Loft himself gave no hint about how he was feeling, as he didn't want to spoil anybody's day – that's the kind of man he was.

Afterwards there was quite a fuss in the press when Vivienne Westwood, the designer – who was getting an award at the same time – came out into the courtyard and lifted up her dress. She had nothing on underneath. I thought, what a way to cheapen yourself in one easy movement. It's amazing how some people in the arty world think they've got to act strangely. Don't get me wrong – I'm not knocking her, I've never met the woman. I just think what a strange thing to do, but such is life. It wouldn't work if we were all made the same.

* * *

Sometimes, being honoured can give you a terrible fright. I remember when I was set up for *This Is Your Life*. Malcolm had asked me to take a bunch of young people from Weston Spirit down to the Welsh Guards' assault course at Pirbright, supposedly to film a TV charity programme. Geoff, unusually, had arranged to be there too and had taken me out for lunch on the way down, saying he wanted to come and see me at work so that he could talk to others about what I do. I still didn't suspect anything until Michael Aspel appeared from behind a wall clutching his red book and I went into shock. 'This is a joke,' I kept repeating to the camera, flapping my lips like a fish unable to breathe. They had to take me for a walk along the Thames so I could calm down, and then we all went on to the television studios to record the show because it gets done in the same day. Michael Aspel said to me afterwards, 'You had that look on your face, I thought you were going to thump me.'

But at other times, you really do have fun. One of my proudest days was attending a luncheon with the Queen in November 1999 to celebrate men and women of achievement. Five hundred or so had been asked, though not everyone could attend. I remember seeing lots of sports people there, like Sir Bobby Charlton, Dickie Bird, Bill Beaumont, Sharron Davies, Tanni Grey-Thompson, the rugby player Martin Offiah (commonly known as Chariots); entertainers like Ronnie Barker, Andrew Lloyd Webber, John Cleese and Shirley Bassey; plus all the other famous faces. In fact before we went in I was one of the few people hanging around I didn't recognise. At lunch I sat opposite the guy who discovered DNA fingerprinting and there were all these other people who are unknown to most of us but who have created much of what goes on in the world of science, engineering and technology. It was a whopping big stroke to the ego, and the wine was lovely. If you had to go for just one cracking meal, that was it.

After the meal Shirley Bassey sent an aide across to see if I would mind if she came over to meet me. *She* asked if she could come and meet *me* – Shirley Bassey. And she planted a big smackeroony on my lips. 'I think you're great,' she said, uttered a couple of pleasantries and slipped away before I could say anything back. I just thought, she knows who I am and she gives a damn. Then it dawned on me that Shirley Bassey had just kissed me, what a claim to fame, and she had instigated it. *Wow*, I thought.

My other abiding memory is of Ronnie Barker, who was being photographed with somebody else as we were going into the building. 'Go on, be quick,' he said to me, 'we'll all get in here.' So the three of us had our photograph taken, and there I was standing next to this British legend, a man I've laughed at and enjoyed for years. I still love *Porridge* and *The Two Ronnies* and *Open All Hours*. I'd love to have a copy of that photograph, which I'd hang in my downstairs loo in a rogues' gallery.

I didn't meet the Queen that day – it would have been too much to expect her to talk to everyone – but I came away happy.

One honour I was very proud to receive was the Freedom of the City of Liverpool, which I accepted as a tribute to everyone who has worked so hard to make Weston Spirit a success. Merseyside has a very special place in my heart: it's where Weston Spirit started out and I'm very grateful for all that it has given me, freedom of the city, an honorary degree, a wife. Others who received their freedom before me include the Beatles, Nelson Mandela and football manager Bob Paisley, so it was quite a company I was joining.

It didn't happen first time round, though, as the original ceremony was scheduled for 11 September 2001, the day Osama bin Laden's al-Qaida network hijacked four planes in the US and flew them into the Twin Towers of the World Trade Center and the Pentagon in Washington, causing thousands of deaths. We were with Lucy's parents, at their home in the Wirral: me, Lucy, my mother and the children. As I had to go on ahead, I was just getting dressed and putting on my tie when I switched on the television. It was about 2.45 p.m., 8.45 a.m. New York time. The others were all busy downstairs.

I went to the top of the stairs and shouted, 'Turn the telly on, quick.'

'What is it now?' called my Mam.

'Just put the telly on.'

Like me, they saw the second plane being impaled on the tower and the next thing we knew, the towers just sank to the ground.

We were all sitting there completely horrified when the chauffeur-driven car arrived to take me to the ceremony. The others were to follow on afterwards as the guests were not expected until 5 p.m. I went along to the Town Hall, where all sorts of people had already gathered, TV crews, Weston Spirit supporters, marathon runners and all the other people from Merseyside.

Of course the ceremony was cancelled after a short consultation with the Mayor and the leader of Liverpool City Council – it had to be – so we just ate some of the food that had been laid out and drank what was there. I mixed and mingled, then the car took me back to Lucy's mum and dad's and we went on home to Wales. As we were driving home I remembered my excitement and anticipation of the night before. I felt the incident had robbed me of a magic moment, but far worse was the huge weight of sadness at what it had taken away from the world, which would never be the same again. If there is a devil, he certainly showed his colours that day under the banner of religion, though I don't believe Osama bin Laden and al-Qaida speak for Muslims generally.

The ceremony proper was held the following January and I enjoyed it immensely. Family and friends turned out in force, along with the mace carriers, the sword carriers and the Lord Lieutenant of Merseyside. Lucy's mum had by this time broken her leg coming downstairs and had to sit with her leg up in a plaster cast while people brought her food and drink. It was the first time she had been pampered in years and she tried to maintain a level of decorum, though actually she got quite squiffy and enjoyed herself very much. There were speeches and I was especially proud of the tributes that came from people connected to Weston Spirit – Ben Harrison, the chief; Leon Lopez, *Brookside* actor and former member; and one of our recent members, Sarah Povall.

They gave me a beautiful casket with a very fine illuminated scroll in it. I think there are certain privileges attached, though I've yet to discover exactly what they are. I believe I can park my sheep in the streets of Liverpool and hang out my washing in Dale Street. I can't park my car but sheep are allowed anywhere. All I have to do now is go out and buy some sheep and an apartment in Dale Street – that's Liverpool's main street – so that I can hang my washing out of the windows.

Like I said, you don't let honours go to your head. I don't walk around the streets of Liverpool thinking, I'm a free man, get out of my way. In fact I bet I'm one of the few free men to walk down Matthews Street with a drink in my hand. But it really did mean a lot to me, especially as it was voted for by Liverpool's councillors on behalf of the people of Liverpool. For them to acknowledge or recognise anything that I have done is a massive honour. I love Liverpool and miss being there. Whenever I go, I never fail to have a bloody good time. Every Scouser has an anecdote to tell, and they're sincere as well as witty.

It was at Liverpool John Moores University I best remember the farce of dressing up for the ceremony when you get awarded an honorary degree. The robe isn't a problem, but they put a great cloth cap on your head like a big pillow. You could stuff it quite comfortably and sit on it to watch telly. I think they look awful. At Liverpool, football manager Gérard Houllier put his on and looked quite stylish while mine looked more like Bagpuss. That sums up style for me – continentals can get away with murder. The gown incorporated colours of my own choosing. I had asked for the Guards' colours, blue and burgundy, then on the day itself Mam ticked me off for forgetting to wear the Guards' tie.

Another time the occasion was let down by the outfit was when I picked up the Queen's Jubilee torch from Newport on the final leg of its journey from Wales to England. There were more than 5,000 of us taking part, so-called community heroes, athletes and sporting stars. The kit looked like an explosion in a paint factory: on my chest it had purple and yellow splodges across a white background, as if somebody had been drinking cider and blackcurrant with a good dollop of custard, then woken up in the morning for a Technicolor yawn.

It was nice to be on the bus with a whole lot of people who had all represented their communities in different ways, though breakfast could have been a little more substantial: just a couple of Celebrations chocolates. When it was your turn to run, you got off the bus and waited by the roadside for the previous runner to hand you the baton. The flame flickered to your pulse and you know what they say about strobe lighting: mine was pulsing so fast that drivers must have been passing out all around me from epileptic fits. After about 500 metres the bus picks you up again, not before time. There was no way I was going to be seen dead in that outfit any longer. The next time anyone asks me to give something away for charity, they can have it.

Some honours are really special, though, because of what they mean to you. In 1999 I was asked to speak at the Festival of Remembrance at the Royal Albert Hall, alongside Sara Jones, widow of Lieutenant Colonel 'H' Jones. The Right Reverend Michael Mann KCVO introduced us. He had soldiered in World War II, and lost a son in Korea, killed in action at the age of 24. For me, a private soldier, it was a huge honour to stand in front of a worldwide audience with an officer and the widow of a colonel who had won the Victoria Cross.

My sister had helped me with the words. I talked about comradeship and my grandfather's stories of the war, which had made me think that veterans were old men, like my grandfather. But the friends who served with me in the Welsh Guards and died so tragically were not like the veterans I used to imagine. These were young, vibrant, energetic young men just out of boyhood, who sacrificed their futures for what they believed was right.

* * *

Getting awards is one thing. It can be just as big an honour when you are asked to judge awards being given to other people. In 2001, I was one of the judges on the *Daily Mirror*'s Pride of Britain Awards, along with Richard and Judy, Sir Richard Branson, Denise Lewis, Lord Robert Winston and the paper's editor, Piers Morgan. These awards pay tribute to the men, women and children – for the most part ordinary folk – whose stories inspire us all. Choosing the winners for all the different categories is hugely difficult and humbling at the same time. Their stories just go to show that no matter what goes on in life, there are people willing to sacrifice themselves for others, and willing to work and strive to make other people's lives better.

Last year and this year the *Daily Express* asked me to help judge their awards as well, and I remember many years ago, when I was doing a poppy appeal, being asked to nominate children of courage, which was a very great honour. To help anybody recognise somebody else is very humbling, because you see what they've done. A small bit of me is also envious: these people have done something so heroic and you want to know if you have the same spirit within you. You won't ever get to find out until you go through something similar.

I really do get impressed by firefighters and policemen, by nurses and ambulance workers, by these school kids and scouts who have saved people's lives, by pilots who manage to bring down planes in trouble, by people who do dangerous things on aircraft to save other people's lives, by flight attendants who have to deal with dangers every day. Only very special people actually do these things, as opposed to all the others who only talk about them, like those great movie scriptwriters who have never done anything more dangerous than get in a New York taxi.

Another award I was asked to help judge was the Edexcel Student of the Year. I remember one young girl who was playing volleyball, basketball, tennis, learning things, doing art, doing theatrics, doing charity work and doing well at school. She was packing so much in, you couldn't help but ask, 'When do you have time to be you?' Part of the reason she could do so much was that she had a great home life, in contrast to another lassie who had many more difficulties to overcome, including dyslexia. When younger, she had been written off by so many people, much as I had been after I'd got injured. To write young people off in this way, shattering their dreams before they've even started to achieve anything, is utterly wrong and I'll do whatever I can to help turn things around.

14

A Final Return
to the Falklands

EARLY IN 2002 I went back to the Falklands with Malcolm to film *Simon's Heroes,* the sixth in the series of documentaries we have made in the 20 years since the Falklands War, and most probably the last. We might work together again, but there's not a lot left of the Simon Weston story to tell, unless something really extraordinary happens.

We always intended *Simon's Heroes* to be very different from the other films in the series. Although it would complete the gaps in my own story, its real purpose was to gather together the stories of other people involved in the conflict. Because of what happened on the *Sir Galahad,* the Welsh Guards never really saw action yet there are plenty of people from other regiments whose courage and bravery remain largely unsung. The plan was to take a half a dozen service people back to the islands, where they would walk us through their experiences. Out of their stories would come a wider picture of the Falklands War and

what it meant to those who fought in it. The bombing
and evacuation of the *Sir Galahad* we would cover by more
interviews in Britain and a visit to the replacement ship,
then docked at Southampton for minor repairs.

This gave me a very different role in the making of the
documentary, and one that I very much enjoyed. I would
conduct some of the interviews out in the Falklands and
later record a commentary (sitting with Malcolm in his
front room) that would help pull it all together.

Malcolm interviewed a number of possible subjects
before making his final choice. It included two Royal
Marines, two Paratroopers, a helicopter pilot and an army
field surgeon. All these guys were heroes in the most genuine sense of the word. Risking your life for others – that's
what a real hero is, somebody who puts his or her life on
the line for other people. There were thousands of heroes
down there and it's a real shame that many of their stories
will never be told.

In January I flew out to the Falklands with Malcolm
and the small crew, cameraman Nigel Meakin and sound
man John Pritchard, both great guys who had filmed
around the world with Michael Palin. With us came the
first group of veterans: army field surgeon Charles Batty
and the two Marines. Now a colonel, Peter Babbington
had been a company commander in 42 Commando at
the time of the conflict, winning the Military Cross,
while Chris Ward – known as Sharkie – had been a 26-
year-old corporal who won the Military Medal for his
part in the assault on Mount Harriet. The others would
join us a week later: helicopter pilot John Greenhalgh,
who had flown missions and evacuated casualties in
appalling conditions, and the two Paras. Phil Neame
(now out of the military) had been one of the company
commanders of 2 Para, under Lieutenant Colonel 'H'

Jones, while Chip Chapman had commanded a platoon in B Company. The arrival of this second group was timed to give us all a night out together in Port Stanley before the first group flew back.

For me, the trip back to the Falklands really did represent the final chapter of that part of my life. I don't think I shall ever go back again, unless somebody gives me a very good reason or I take Lucy and the family (Mam says she would never go). It's not that I dislike the islands or the people – I don't. I have grown to like the islands more each time I visit and find them unbelievably attractive. The place can be very cold and inhospitable when it wants to be, but it is also very beautiful and has weird little pockets where you feel as if you are entering a different country. When you leave Port Stanley for camp, as they call the countryside, in the summer, you actually enter a different time zone where farmers have the option of gaining an extra hour's daylight. As many of the roads are still bad, where they even exist, distances don't really matter – it's the time it takes you to get to places that counts.

I like the people as well. They are very warm and friendly and life moves quite slowly, which is hardly surprising when you think that Stanley is just the size of a small village with maybe one or two thousand people living around there. I've heard it said that 75 per cent of the population are historically related in one way or another.

But it is certainly a very different place now from when I first went there, much more modern, as if the war has brought it up to speed. There's a coach park now and a coach depot catering for the tour groups that arrive for the wildlife and the battlefield tours. When we first returned, in 1991, the war memorials stood in virgin ground, reached by a simple track. Ten years on they were building roads and pathways in anticipation of the

20th-anniversary celebrations and it all looked very tacky, but that was probably because the work was still unfinished.

The memorials themselves are very moving, as I found on my first return, beautifully tended by a guy who lives close by. The Argentine cemetery by contrast struck me as very sad because it was such a long time before the families of the dead were allowed on to the islands to see it. And when they finally came, the islanders behaved badly and spat at the bus taking the families to see the graves of their loved ones. I understand the islanders' fears, but with the size of the British garrison there, nobody would be foolish enough to attack the islands again. Why belittle themselves when they could have welcomed the families with dignity?

One thing that really did disappoint me this time was the amount of litter and debris everywhere – dead penguins, oil drums discarded on the shoreline and seabirds killed by toxins that had leaked into the sea. Throwing rubbish out to sea was fine when it was mostly perishable, but now people are discarding car batteries full of acid by the water's edge, or dumping vehicles by the roadside out in camp. I said on local radio how disappointed I was with the way people were treating this beautiful wilderness. It's a very fragile environment and people shouldn't spoil it. If it was worth defending 20 years ago, it is worth defending now.

But for those of us involved in the filming, the trip was lots of fun and everyone got on famously. They were all exceptionally decent blokes, hugely professional yet good company and very funny. Most service guys are like that. They all have a great sense of humour, I suspect because adversity stares them in the face so often and adversity brings out the best in people.

Phil Neame would sit arms crossed at his bar stool, lord of all he surveyed, and then he'd come out with something disastrously funny that had happened to him while he was mountain-climbing. He's twice had a stab at Everest, though each time something got between him and the summit. The night the two groups met for a meal in Stanley, at the Malvina House Hotel, Chip Chapman (from the Paras) and Pete Babbington (a Para who had cross-badged to the Marines) exchanged banter about which was the better regiment. They're both colonels now, and their banter turned into definite point-scoring that revealed their strong, friendly rivalry and made the rest of us laugh. Nothing changes, even when you reach the senior ranks. Charles Batty had a wonderful Scottish sense of humour, very dry and entertaining, whereas John Greenhalgh's humour was completely different, manic and utterly hilarious. Sharkie and I got on extremely well because we are basically pretty much the same guy, and had I survived in the army, I could quite possibly have made it to his rank of WO1, Warrant Officer first class.

Throughout our time on the islands we stayed at the military barracks out at Mount Pleasant, where I was lucky enough to be given one of the two VIP suites, the only ones with a private bathroom. I had a lounge and two beds all to myself, so if one became scruffy I could use the other, and someone came in each day to make my bed and tidy up my room. I thought it was great, and while I would happily have swapped rooms with one of the officers if anyone had asked, I wasn't going to volunteer, believe me. But those guys are used to roughing it and sleeping in ditches. As long as they had somewhere clean and dry and a place for their kit, everyone was happy.

Our days quickly fell into a rhythm. We would set off filming at around eight each morning, returning by 7 p.m. in time for dinner in the officers' mess. As a serving non-commissioned officer, Sharkie would eat in the sergeants' mess, joining us later for drinks at the bar. The army is without doubt the last bastion of the class system, but you don't think twice about it. I still call my old commanding officer 'sir' as a mark of respect, and will do till the day I die. But as I had never served alongside the officers who came with us on the shoot, we used first names to each other, which was how they introduced themselves.

Later, in the bar, we would talk about mundane things like the weather – which really is something else in the Falklands – or start chatting about the Falklands conflict. Over the years I have learned a huge amount about what really happened from guys like these who have read all that is going on the war and are always worth listening to.

It was altogether a very different shoot from my first return to the Falklands, when I was ten years younger and my stress levels were bubbling away close to the surface. This time the days we spent filming were exceptionally long and by 11 p.m. we were all whacked. Malcolm never stopped working the whole time we were away. He might have a glass of wine or a beer after dinner before getting back to work on the next day's schedule. The only time he was less than fastidious was when he had the trots and was caught short out in camp, desperate for a large rock or a bush but there was absolutely nowhere to hide. He did manage to find a ditch, which was little more than a hollow, and the sight of him scrabbling around for non-existent paper made us howl with laughter, I'm afraid.

Malcolm's favourite expression throughout was 'That was great, but—' He was always exclaiming over the landscape, 'Oooh, look at that skyline, look at that field, oooh, look at that light,' and he'd stop to shoot loads and loads of film to add atmosphere and blend in with the soldiers' stories. I'm sure they could use it to promote the islands if they wanted to bring in any more tourists.

The way Malcolm had planned the filming was to walk every inch of the battles these men had fought. They stand among the real heroes of the Falklands, and their stories tell you a little of what that war was really like. Unlike the long-range bombing seen recently in the Gulf, much of the Falklands conflict was fought in hand-to-hand combat. You can't bomb mountains or send in the cruise missiles – well, you can, but there's not much point. You can tell the difference from the casualty figures: over 1,000 casualties in the Falklands (dead and injured) compared with just 34 dead in the second Gulf War and only six or seven of these actually killed in action. That tells you just how dangerous the Falklands were.

Each one of the men who came down with us had an extraordinary story to tell. Phil Neame fought on the flank of the battle for Darwin Hill and Goose Green, advancing down the beach in the face of enemy fire in a way that undoubtedly helped to secure one of the decisive victories in the war. Having read a little about what he did that day, I think his actions clearly merited far greater recognition than he actually got, and it's equally clear that the awarding of medals is hugely political. While 'H' Jones and A Company were bogged down at Darwin Hill, Phil had noticed Argentine soldiers retreating down the beach and believed he could follow their route. But Jones turned him down twice in no uncertain terms. Shortly after, Jones was killed in a solo assault on an Argentine position. With a new officer in command, Phil Neame was given the go-ahead to move along the beach line, but they soon ran into enemy fire from Argentine positions on the hill above them. As Phil says on film, it was a 'heart-churning moment'. But with the arrival of B Company they set up a double act and very soon every enemy position was flying the white flag. 'I don't know whether it was flags or underwear,' said Phil, 'but it was white and that was good enough for me.' To my mind, he is a quiet, very impressive man.

I liked the energy of paratrooper Chip Chapman as well. At the time of the Falklands he was a young leader of men in his early twenties. He described the first night's battle at Goose Green as the most exciting night of his life – almost better than any sex he'd ever had, though he didn't want his wife to hear that.

From Pete Babbington and Chris Ward, you got a sense of what the battle for Mount Harriet was like. It was mostly fought at night. Pete was sat on a big rock controlling operations through his radio handset. Rounds of enemy ammunition were coming down all around him, and he was calling to his signaller, 'Give me more slack in the cable,' because he had trouble stretching it to his ear. 'Eff off,' said his signaller. 'You can have some more, but not until they stop firing. I'm not coming out from cover.' With all this crap coming down on them, Pete was orchestrating his men from the rock, telling his platoon sections to move round because he could see the enemy. He somehow didn't stop to think that if he could see them, they could bloody see him as well. He wasn't thinking of himself, only of his men.

Chris Ward's story is one of courage and close combat in the battle for Mount Harriet. The hand-to-hand fighting that took place up there typifies one difference in the way the US and the British fight their wars. I remember speaking to an American policeman once who said the British are actually much more violent that the Americans. The Americans will shoot you from across the street, whereas the British – because we don't have guns in our society – will end the argument with a knife, up close and personal. In our psyche we're used to that kind of fighting. In this country you're not so much frightened about being shot in the street or even shot by an intruder, but you are concerned about somebody coming at you with a knife. It takes more out of you to do that, I'm told, because you can smell the person you're killing.

When our guys are in somewhere like Northern Ireland, they can't simply bomb the place, or call in an airstrike. They can't do what the Israelis do, which is to call in a gunship and destroy whole towns, because we care about what happens to the people living around. I'm only drawing comparisons, not making a moral point. We are not a murderous bunch but we are capable of upfront, instinctive combat and Chris Ward did that magnificently. He got the Military Medal for his actions that day and, to my mind, he deserved a lot more. He should have got a gallantry medal like the George Cross or the Victoria Cross, the VC, which his company commander said he merited.

Chris led the charge that secured Mount Harriet for our advance. Chris put the suppressing fire down. He sent in the rockets to the Argentine positions and followed it up with hand-to-hand fighting, shooting, giving it gun, which is hugely courageous. He took it upon himself to do this because his friend had been injured and he thought the only way he could get his friend out without suffering further injury or even death was to take out the whole target. So after he'd sent in the rockets he said, 'I'm going,' and he was off, gone, and all the others could do was follow him some three or four bounds behind.

The simple fact is that Chris was leading the charge, which takes courage above and beyond the call of duty, because he could have taken out that target in other ways. But he knew that to help his friend, he had to do it asap. They couldn't move his friend under enemy fire because they were too close to the situation, and in the name of his friend, he needed to be decisive, which is what you call upon people to be in battle. The Americans have a saying, 'If you snooze you lose', and Chris couldn't afford to snooze. His friend had been shot in the legs and had they nipped the main artery, he could have bled to death before anyone could check whether he was bleeding internally.

If we're going to talk about VCs, they are supposed to be for people who achieve something. Chris Ward's actions saved people's lives and also gained the initiative and the objective. He helped the speedy recovery of his own side's injured so that they could get them to a medical aid station as swiftly as possible. His company fought most of the battle on their own, so Chris led the shout for his battalion all the way down the shooting range.

As courageous as all the other guys were, John Greenhalgh stands out as one of only three living pilots who have been awarded the Distinguished Flying Cross. To my mind he's one of our modern equivalents of a World War II pilot, a true hero tinged with a certain amount of justifiable arrogance about his skills and his ability – altogether a hugely decent man with immense amounts of courage boosted by pounds of lunacy. You would have to be mad to live under the constant fire and pressure that was his life for those five or six weeks of the conflict.

It was John's job to fly into the front line in his zippy Scout helicopter, drop off ammunition and collect the wounded. He also carried out any lightning raids that were needed, like the one to Swan Inlet House when he took in Chip Chapman and the other Paras. Their objective was to make a telephone call to the settlement at Fitzroy to find out if the enemy was still in place, but no one was sure if the Argentine section was still camped in the house. Within 90 minutes of the raid being first proposed, John and the other Scout pilots were airborne, Paras hanging off the aircraft, machine guns at the ready. As soon as they got to within three or four feet of the ground, the Paras hit the ground in a bomb burst, already in fighting order, and immediately assaulted the house. Finding nobody there, they were able to make that vital telephone call to Fitzroy on an antiquated telephone with a crank handle.

'British Army here,' they said, when somebody answered the phone. 'Are the Argentines still with you?'

'No, they left this morning,' came the relieved reply, so we knew the way was clear to advance without delay to Fitzroy and Bluff Cove.

Army field surgeon Charles Batty links my own story to those of the dead and injured from other units. The main field hospital, nicknamed 'the Red and Green Life Machine', was set up in an old meat-refrigeration plant at Ajax Bay, across the water from the D-Day beaches at San Carlos. I was taken there by helicopter to be assessed by doctors, after first being choppered off the *Sir Galahad* to the community hall at Fitzroy settlement. There wasn't any surgery Charles and his team could do for me, so I went on to the hospital ship, the *Uganda*, where they saved my sight by taking split skin grafts off me to cover my eyes. My eyelids had swollen up because of the burns and as the swelling decreased, the skin on my eyelids had begun to shrink and I was in real danger of going blind because I couldn't keep my eyes moist or offer them any protection. Once on board the hospital ship I was completely out of the game, protected by the big red cross painted on the side and not even a legitimate target any more.

Going back with Charles was my second visit to the field hospital. It still wasn't a pleasant place, but at least this time I walked away under my own steam. Here Charles had operated on the wounded in a windowless meat-hanging room right at the centre. As the hospital was situated next door to an ammunition dump, they weren't allowed to paint red crosses anywhere on the building. The building was attacked while Charles was operating on a badly wounded Argentine soldier. With an unexploded bomb quite literally hanging over their heads, he carried on operating as best he could and the patient lived. That tells you everything about the man – a great humanitarian and no doubt a fine soldier as well, who would have picked up a rifle as readily as he picked up a scalpel. It's said he once operated for 17 hours without sitting down; they even fed him standing up.

I remember Charles telling me about a time he had gone to one of the settlements to conduct the triage, when you prioritise the wounded for surgery. You usually take care of the worst injured first except in certain types of combat, when priority is given to those who can be operated on and returned to the battlefield as quickly as possible, on the basis of 'worst injured, last treated'. To be brutally honest, this makes perfect sense because a man who can still fight has to take priority over others when you're running out of reserves and don't have unlimited numbers you can simply throw into the battle.

Charles had just finished the triage when he noticed a young soldier sitting there, looking immensely grey and uncomfortable.

'You all right, lad?' he asked.

The lad said, 'Yes, sir, I'm fine.'

'Why don't you lie down?'

'I can't breathe when I lie down, sir.'

'What do you mean, you can't breathe?'

'Well, if I lie down I can't breathe at all.'

Charles looked at him, found he had a gunshot wound to the chest and as the guy sat there, he stuck a shunt into his lung and drained off about three or four pints of fluid, saving his life instantly because he was bleeding into his lung.

Through Charles's story, Malcolm had come full circle to his original inspiration for the documentary series, which had been to film the work of medical units in the Falklands throughout the conflict. But unluckily for Malcolm, his clearance came through the day after the last plane had left for the war, so he had to make do with filming the casualties as we came home. Had he caught that plane to the Falklands, we might never have met and my own life might have been very different.

To all those guys I went back with, they have my utmost admiration. I would like to thank them for the stories they told, and all those that remain untold. Without them, I would never have come through in the way that I did. Charles in particular really did play a part in my recovery.

After the film was shown I received a number of letters from people asking why they hadn't been included, including one or two from Scots Guards. The Marines and the Paras didn't win the war on their own, they said. Well, I didn't choose who went down with us to the Falklands, and at the tenth anniversary we had gone back with a Scots Guard, Gary Tytler, a very decent guy whom I like and admire immensely. For this film, both our budget and our airtime were limited and to have covered the battles fought by the Scots Guards as well was pretty well impossible. But I wouldn't want anyone to think that I was trivialising the part played by the Scots Guards. They fought the hardest, the fiercest and the most ferocious battle of the Falklands, at Tumbledown, and I would never want to sully their military history or the way they do things. They're a fine, fine regiment. Without everybody doing their job properly, we would never have been so successful. There were lots of other small units who played their part too, and especially the medics, who never get mentioned anywhere near enough.

The more you learn about the Falklands conflict, the more you realise that this was a politician's war that could have been avoided. A lot of people are not going to thank me for saying this, but the war didn't need to happen. I'm not complaining about this. I chose a career, not the conflicts I was going to fight in. It's simply a fact and if people don't like facts they should stop living, because there are good facts and bad facts out there. Mrs Thatcher clearly knew something was going on in the South Atlantic well before the scrap-metal merchants landed on South Georgia. It's common knowledge that we had a spy ship down there equipped with an early-warning system intended to keep the Argentinians at bay. Apparently when the Argentinians found out the ship was being withdrawn, they got in touch with the British consul or whoever and said, 'Does this mean what we think it does?' In effect, the Argentine junta took it as a green light to go ahead and invade the islands.

The Argentine leader, General Galtieri, was a complete nonentity, a serious alcoholic and abuser of human rights in his own country who was never going to leave his mark on history, apart from the minor blip he caused over the Falklands. His recent death left me with nothing except a load of phone calls from the press. Did I mind that he had died? The answer was no, but I couldn't have cared less if he had lived, either. He meant nothing at all to me. Galtieri was just a thug and a bully and a criminal who served three years in jail for military incompetence – but you could lock up many generals for that, including one or two of our own.

Mrs Thatcher, of course, went on to become a major player for a time, winning an election on the back of her Falklands victory, which makes me wonder if that wasn't part of her reason for sending off the troops in the first place.

Over the years I have met Mrs Thatcher on many different occasions and I cannot remember her sharing a single conversation with me; nor has she ever looked me in the face. The first time I met her it seemed to me she couldn't wait to be distracted away to go and talk to somebody else. We were introduced and somebody said, 'This is Simon Weston, he was burnt on the *Sir Galahad*.' She shook my hand, somebody said something to her and she was gone. She didn't come back. She didn't say, 'Excuse me, I am talking to this gentleman,' she just upped and went, which to my mind was rude at best and ignorant to say the least. Every time I have met her since, it has been exactly the same. I remember being at a benefit evening run by Jim Davidson for the British Forces Foundation, a charity he set up to help provide entertainment for the troops. She would quite happily stand and chat to Jim, who has met her on many more occasions than I have, but she wouldn't talk to me.

It was the same old story when we met aboard the *QE2* at a function to celebrate the 20th anniversary of the war. As she wasn't terribly well, Mrs Thatcher wasn't supposed to be getting up to make a speech, so I had been asked to give one in her place. Lucy came with me and though we were there in the captain's room together, again we didn't speak to each other. She made her speech anyway, apparently, after I had left early to go by helicopter, car and plane to another function in Dublin. In my view, if you want a leader who will take you to war, there is no finer than Mrs Thatcher because she's ferocious, a modern Boadicea. But the fact that she has never looked me in the eye speaks a million words.

Her behaviour makes me feel pity rather than anger. She did not make my choices for me. She did not make me sign up for the military. I did that myself and I am not going to blame anyone else for my decisions. Our lives are dictated by the choices we make. She has never spoken to me, so I cannot speak for her, either. I don't feel anything for the woman. She's not somebody I hold in special reverence or think we should cast in bronze (though she has been). A lot of my friends can't stand her. A lot of the people I served with think she's terrible, while others think she's great. If I have any bitterness towards her, it concerns the way she destroyed the political system as her legacy, so that people voted against the Tories rather than for anything in particular. But I certainly don't hate her because she did Simon Weston a bad turn; that would be pretty pathetic. She's a chapter in history and a chapter in my life and that's all there is to say about her.

My conviction that the Falklands war could have been avoided received confirmation from a surprising source. A couple of days after *Simon's Heroes* was screened, I received a letter from Sir John Nott, Defence Secretary at the time of the conflict:

Dear Simon Weston,

I watched your programme on the BBC last night and I thought it was absolutely excellent. I do congratulate you in demonstrating to millions of viewers some of the horrors of war and the terrible traumas which you and so many others suffered as a result of an unnecessary war. It was a great programme and your commentary was brilliant. I'm afraid that we've only met once and that was briefly at the service of conciliation with the then Argentine President at St Paul's. As I'm not a member of the South Atlantic Association I do not get invited to their meetings so I do not know as many of the Falklands veterans as I would like. If you would like to telephone Ian Dale at Politico's in London he'll send you a free copy of my book so that you can read what it was all like in London as you risked your life and future in the South Atlantic.

Yours,

John Nott

I was completely stunned to receive this letter in which he referred to the Falklands as this 'unnecessary war'. But whatever happened has happened. Whatever he says now does not make a blind bit of difference. We can't turn the clock back. We have to look at it and be real about all these things.

And in the end, I believe we were right to go. British people deserve British help. I would say the same today if Spain invaded Gibraltar, even though I like the Spaniards. Once the politicians had failed to resolve the crisis for whatever reason, then it was our job as soldiers, sailors and airmen to do what they couldn't do, which was to bring the conflict to a speedy and successful resolution, hopefully as expeditiously as possible and with as little loss of life as possible. Politicians are our employers, so when you're in the services, whether you agree with their policies or not becomes totally irrelevant.

Before we flew to the islands I went with two former Welsh Guardsmen to visit the replacement *Sir Galahad* at Southampton. The original was sunk as a war grave off the Falklands, too badly damaged to be salvaged, but it's a strong name, a proud name, the name of a knight who was good, honest and kind. The two who came back with me were Mark Pemberton (Pem) and Jimmy Salmon. Pem was my section commander in the mortars, while Jimmy helped save my life on the burning ship. We had also done our army training together in the same platoon, sleeping in opposite bed spaces. After the bomb had exploded on the *Sir Galahad* and I had finally made it to the deck, Jimmy cut off my trousers and threw them overboard, along with my wallet and all my winnings from poker dice. Then he gave me morphine and wrote a large 'M' for 'morphine' on my favourite green T-shirt for good measure. I remember asking him to check if my wedding tackle was still intact as without that I didn't think life would be worth living. He took a look, then said, 'You're fine. Well, that's a point of debate.' My son James is named after him, taking his middle name Andrew from two of my friends, Yorkie (Andrew Walker), who died in the explosion, and Andrew Davies, Jed the Head. Everybody has the right to be ugly but Jed abuses the privilege. That's what we always said to him in the Welsh Guards but hell, look at me now, who am I to talk?

Walking into the ship with Pem and Jimmy brought the memories alive. It looked narrower than any of us remembered, but you could still place exactly where you were when the bomb came through. I found the spot where we were playing cards beside boxes of blood lined up against the wall. My friend Yorkie was sleeping up on top. Lots of stupid things came back, like everyone stripping off their tin helmets and throwing them into a box, saying, 'These aren't worth a carrot,' then somebody shouting, 'Air-raid warning green. Green, green, air-raid warning red, everybody get down' – it wasn't a drill we had practised before, though most of us guessed what it meant – and the bomb coming through just as I was getting down into a crouch.

'It's like being hit,' said Pem as the three of us looked around the empty *Sir Galahad*. 'No noise, no bang, just your ears ringing, like when you have a big smack in the face that makes your eyes water. You know something has gone. Everything is orange. Your eyes are open but everything's orange. No pain or anything, just everything sort of up in the air.'

'Yes,' I said, 'it just knocks your senses all out of you.'

'Your breath goes,' said Pem, 'your wind is gone because of the air being sucked in. You're winded and you know that you're hurt but you don't feel any pain until a lot later. I just think that's the adrenalin, probably.'

I kept coming back to the colours. 'The yellows, and the oranges and the golds, intertwined with black smoke. They just seem to be swirling and swirling, bowling towards you, and there's nothing you can do about it. There is nowhere you can go, nothing you can do.'

'And you can't see anything for a while either, because of that orange.'

'It's a feeling of helplessness, isn't it?' I said.

'You couldn't see anything. It was all hands along the wall and along the boxes and things like that.'

'I just turned and ran out. I mean, once I realised I couldn't help this guy. He was in no state to be helped. He was dead. So I just turned and ran and I came out. There's smoke, thick smoke, black smoke, acrid smoke down there, and I couldn't breathe. I remember seeing one guy who was alive at that point but then he never came home. The story is he came back in here to try and help people.'

'I think the guys who died along here from our platoon,' said Pem, 'if they didn't get out, they died very quickly. Eight of us got away out of the 30 that were in here.'

'I think the ones who didn't get burned were some-where else on the ship at the time.'

'It was pot luck.'

'Just depends where you were sitting, simple as that.'

As we were talking, the three of us, I remembered coming out on deck, where Jimmy was already helping the injured, alongside medics like Pierre Naya, who is still haunted by post-traumatic stress and whose story I tell in the next chapter. I looked at my hands. They were like lumps of sausage meat, swollen beyond recognition, so black and charred you couldn't tell how damaged they were. I remember looking at other people and saying, 'Oh, God, you're in a bit of a mess,' and they're going, 'You're not looking too clever yourself.'

Talking later to Malcolm, Pem described our return to the ship as eerie. 'When we first walked in,' he said, 'it doesn't all flood back straight away. As you spend time down there, different things come back. Some things you've forgotten, perhaps, but you picture the things that were important to you at the time. I didn't see people burning or people in pain, until I got off the ship.'

Pem remembered, too, the guilt we all share. 'We were cocky, fit, self-confident lads. The training makes you self-confident and you honestly believe that nothing is going to happen to you. When it does, your training and your instinct for self-preservation kick in. But afterwards you realise it was just a lottery. When the guy sitting here is dead, and the guy sitting there and the guy opposite . . . You get a guilt trip, I think we've all had it, you know. Why did I get out and they didn't? Everybody is different but you get on with life as best you can after that. When we see people we haven't seen since the Falklands, old comrades, you can get emotional because you are sharing the same guilt. Simon, Jimmy and I, we get emotional having a chat over a pint, about things, about people, because we're sharing the same guilt as everything else. Yes, we're lucky and we're thankful we're off, but you know, you are always thinking, why did I get off and they didn't?'

One more figure from my Falklands past came on to the ship that day, Philip Sheldon, then a pilot with 825 Squadron from RNAS Culdrose in Cornwall. Very motivated, very professional and very brave, he had choppered off many of the wounded from the *Sir Galahad*, fearful that the ship might blow up at any second.

He and I talked about what it meant to return to the places where you experienced these terrible things. 'This is closure for me now,' I told him, 'complete closure. I didn't realise I would be emotional coming back to the ship but I had a little moment earlier on when I felt a real lump in my throat. I think the same may well have happened to the other two who are with us today. It played such a big part in our lives and I suspect will continue to do so, but in a much less offensive way. I didn't realise how much I needed to come back here and see this. I'm glad I came back.'

Philip told me about going back to the Falklands in 1984 on a different mission, and how important that was to him. With a young Marine who had served in the conflict, he went back to the freezer centre where Charles Batty had carried out his operations.

'By then it was completely abandoned,' said Philip. '"The Red and Green Life Machine" was still written above the door. We walked through that door on a sunny afternoon in '84 and it was just . . . an empty void, you know. And there were some demons in there.'

'I'll bet there were.'

'There were some real demons in there. And we wandered around the area where the surgeons had carried out their work. There was a whole area at the back where you guys were in rows on stretchers and you may not know this, but there was quite a lot of graffiti on the walls where guys would just scrawl something. So while they waited to be taken off to the hospital ship or whatever, blokes would put one or two thoughts on the wall.'

'Were they still there when you went back?'

'Yes,' said Philip. 'It was a really eerie afternoon in '84. There was a lovely bit where some poet had written, "Nott and Galtieri: two bald men squabbling over a comb." I thought that was quite a poignant thing to say about the Falklands.'

* * *

Making *Simon's Heroes* and talking to guys like Philip and the others really did allow me to lay my Falklands ghosts finally to rest. It was a good thing to have done, because now I could draw a line under the Falklands for myself, though maybe not for others. Until I went back to the islands this third and final time, I hadn't realised how much was still left inside – sheer sadness at the magnitude of loss we had suffered, not just for me or the Welsh Guards, but sadness for every guy who had died. If I had religion in me, I might have found more of that sense of spiritual contentment and all-encompassing forgiveness on my first return. But it took two more visits to reach the heart of the experience.

I had been through an emotional journey with all those who went down with us. I'm glad I went through the experience and came out the way I have. I owe a huge amount of the journey to Malcolm, to Geoff, to my family and to the people I went down with – they all added to the colour of it, as did the reception from the islanders, who most of the time were very positive; only occasionally were they derogatory or ambivalent. But on the whole the journey was very worthwhile.

Right at the end of filming I cried on camera for the first time. It was a very pleasant day, much like the day I was blown up, and I was sitting up on Wireless Ridge when Malcolm said to me, 'Do you realise this is the last piece we'll do together? This is it, there is no more to say. You've said it all.'

I had been working with this guy for 20 years, over which time we had become good friends. He must like me or he wouldn't go on working with me, and I certainly like him. It was hugely emotional for me – not sad, because it was good to finish on a note like that, and it was so positive and uplifting being there.

Then I cried about the Falklands, which is a bloody stupid thing to do. I cried because I was saying goodbye for the last time. I was saying goodbye to all the ghosts, to the whole mystery of whether there are spirits. I was saying goodbye to the whole thing; and the guy that was me before I got injured, I was leaving him behind down there.

'To those that didn't come home,' I said at the end of the film, a great big lump of emotion stuck in my throat, 'I'll always miss them. I'll always remember them. And with all my heart, I salute them.'

15
Fighting the Demons

To MY MIND, one of the most shocking statistics to emerge from the Falklands War is that more people who served down there in the conflict have since committed suicide than were ever killed in the fighting. Philip Sheldon talked of the demons he encountered in the abandoned field hospital at Ajax Bay. For many of us involved in the war, fighting off the demons has become a daily reality as we struggle to live with the effects of post-traumatic stress disorder, or PTSD as it is usually known.

According to the current state of medical information I've been given, you can cure most cases of PTSD if you catch it early, within three to six months. But if you let it fester for much longer, it becomes too well entrenched. It's like depression, which can revisit any time it wants. It only needs a trigger and you feel yourself spiralling downwards. An ex-Para in Bolton told me he hates seeing me on TV or in a newspaper, for instance, because it sets him off every time. Even though I have learnt to cope as best I can, I still find myself feeling low or depressed for no good reason and I am in no way and by no means a depressive. I am by nature a happy person, moving around life quite pleasantly and enjoying the company of people I meet.

Those of us who served in the Falklands never had any psychological help when we came home. This meant that although the doctors and surgeons worked miracles on the physical damage caused by my injuries, the mental and psychological scars were left untouched. It was as if the powers at the Ministry of Defence simply shut their eyes to the problem. Psychological help had not been offered at the time of the first two world wars, so why should it be necessary after a much shorter conflict? There have been scores of different conflicts since then, yet not until about 1993 did the MoD start to take it seriously, despite all the research done by the Americans since the 1920s and 1930s looking at different aspects of shell shock, and film footage of electric shock treatments. Even now, I am not convinced they do enough to catch the demons before they take hold.

Flashbacks, nightmares, violent mood swings, depression, hyperalertness, inability to sleep, binge-drinking, feelings of worthlessness and self-loathing – these are some of the ways PTSD manifests itself. Some people can take 20 years or even more to show any symptoms and some take 20 minutes. Those who get rid of it in the very first days are the ones who come out strongest. But once it has taken hold, I don't think you ever escape it properly, despite the things you can do to alleviate its worst effects.

Revisiting the scene of the trauma undoubtedly helps, though the experience can be painful as well as cathartic. Before I went back to the Falklands for the final time, the nightmares started all over again. I remember waking up one night in an unbelievable sweat, I could really and truly feel the heat on my body. I called out to Lucy, 'I can feel myself on fire.' That's how bad the nightmares got – I really did feel I was burning.

The lowest point I ever reached happened about three years after I was blown up, when I actually tried to top myself with a crossbow I had bought from a catalogue because I had the money and nothing else to spend it on. I used to take the crossbow out rabbit shooting with my friend Bobby Brain. We would go to the Wern, on the edge of Nelson, a wooded bog full of rats and rabbits near the railway tracks and an old ironworks.

All this happened some time after the screening of *Simon's Peace*. I was living at my mother's, drinking far too much and filled with self-loathing. I felt so guilty at having survived, at not having done enough to help get the boys out, at not having gone into the shooting match with everyone else. I felt guilty too at some of the things that were going on in my life because I thought I was being too lucky.

When the black mist descends over you, you become solidly depressed, waking up at night because you are still on fire, still hearing the screams and the torment of people dying around you. The worst thing about PTSD is that your nightmares also happen in the daytime. You are living with the nightmares all day long, living with horrors and dreams and noises, like voices in your head. Everybody experiences it differently, but to me it meant living a nightmare, and that is a terrible place to be. When you wake up you don't want ever to get out of bed. Life is awful. The world is awful. What have you got to look forward to?

All of us at some point wake up thinking that life has turned against us. You might just go down to the pub, have a couple of pints and think, what the hell is wrong with me? Then sooner or later you're right again. That's normal. But with PTSD you can lose a whole weekend and not remember a single thing about it. With PTSD you become so down that nothing and nobody can bring you up. Winning the pools or the Lottery, nothing makes you feel right. Seeing your team win or your wife bouncing a beautiful healthy baby doesn't pick you up. You can become violent and aggressive. You can go into a drunken binge that might last a fortnight, or a month, or two months. You can go into an area of darkness and nastiness that distorts the way you approach your loved ones. It's not you, but unfortunately there's no way you can deal with it.

I was like that for a hell of a long time and I don't apologise for what I was. I know I upset a lot of people and I apologise for that, I really am sorry, but it wasn't me wanting to behave that way. It wasn't me wanting to be that horrible person. It was just something I became because of the depression. I would look at myself in the mirror and feel I was becoming as bad as I looked. That's how my personality was coming out. What people saw was what they were getting, and I loathed myself. It was like I was living in someone else's body and I couldn't reconcile the two.

When was I ever going to get a girlfriend? Never, if I continued to be as bad as I was. When was I ever going to get a job? In all honesty, who would ever employ me? A major on the resettlement board had just told me I was completely unemployable. What could I possibly do? I was no longer a Welsh Guardsman, which had been my only status in life. Before I went off to the Falklands, I'd had a fiancée and was due to go on a promotion course when I came back. I was playing rugby. I was having a good life and enjoying myself. And all of a sudden it was gone. Nothing. That went on for three or four years.

The day I tried to kill myself, I was on my own in my room. I have no idea if my mother was in the house. I don't know and I didn't care. The music was on and I was just sitting on the floor. With the bolt ready to load, I tried to cock the crossbow with my hands but my damaged fingers weren't strong enough. As I pulled the twine back on the bow, it snapped back and nearly took my fingertips off.

I thought, shit, that hurt.

I put the crossbow down. Jesus, I thought. What pain. If it hurt my fingers like that, what the hell will it feel like if I don't manage to do the job properly?

That was the closest I ever came to suicide. I took it as a wake-up call. Instead of seeing myself as a victim, I began to see myself as somebody who was lucky. Hey, come on Wes, I thought, you're worth more than this. I stopped drinking for nearly a year, Sundays excepted. I went into training, working out at the gym with my friend Keith Cullen, who was one of the people who helped save my sanity. I started to see the light that would help me through the worst effects of PTSD.

After the making of *Simon's Heroes* I honestly believe I can walk away from the Falklands as my life is about more than my injuries or the scars I carry. But some people have not been so lucky and still find themselves trapped inside the horrors they experienced. One of the people who affected me deeply during the filming was Pierre Naya, a medic on board the *Sir Galahad* when the bomb struck and a long-term PTSD sufferer. The beast in his closet, as he calls it.

Another of the film's true heroes, Pierre is one fabulous guy who saved an awful lot of lives. Originally from Malta, he is one of the most incredibly courageous and human people I have ever met. You sense that, like

Charles Batty, he has tremendous love for his fellow men at the same time as a contradictory ability to be a soldier. On fire himself, he tended to the injured, many atrociously mutilated or wounded. He continued to do so in the weeks that followed and later back in England, where our paths crossed again in the military hospital at Woolwich, though I didn't recognise him behind the medic's mask.

Like me, Pierre was down in the tank deck when the bomb exploded. To this day he remembers the screams of the injured and the dying.

'It's a nightmare,' he said, 'like half a football stadium screaming for help all at the same time. The nightmare was that in groping our way out of it, we couldn't see very far between the swirls of smoke and flames. And of course, self-preservation is uppermost in your mind. Live and don't die – I'm sure that's what went through people's minds . . . In the bowels of the ship, everything's burning up. Ammunition exploding, people getting killed, shrapnel everywhere. Get out! But of course, between here and the exit, I was crawling over people that needed help. So basically, I did my thing as a Medical Corps man, helping people as I stumbled across them, people screaming for help. I did the best I could for them, just crawling through, helping people – you know, half-seeing, half-choking, doing my thing all the way through. Bandaging, tourniqueting, ripping whatever, helping people, dragging or lifting them out eventually after God knows how long, up into daylight. You couldn't get away immediately from the smoke and flames because it was billowing all around us. I was burning myself because my uniform was on fire. And all you can do is pat it. Couldn't do anything about the back, apparently my hair was on fire and the back of my neck was getting burnt, arms getting burnt, you see.

'So I tried to make my way to the bow of the ship where I presumed there would be some cleaner air and all along there, carrying and lifting people, dragging them along, administering to their terrible injuries, really horrendous injuries. Because modern weapons are awesome, obviously designed to kill, but when they go bang they also burn, you know, that's the awesome thing about it. Terrible, traumatic amputations and massive injuries one doesn't normally see, you know, in real life, except perhaps in a war situation . . .

'I had so many around me that required urgent, urgent treatment, really serious injuries, life or death-threatening injuries. So I just— As far as I was concerned, as a Medical Corps man, I just got stuck in with whatever I could find, whatever I could use, whatever I acquired from the Guardsmen, some of whom recognised me as a medic. "He's a medic, he's a medic," some shouted, "give him something." They were giving me their drips, their bandages and so forth. I used every bit I could find, and some I had to improvise, tearing bits of clothing off, kicking a wooden pallet to make a splint because some of them had smashed legs and arms. Totally useless if they fell overboard, they would drown. And, of course, all the time in your mind is self-preservation. Live don't die.'

When Pierre was finally helicoptered off the ship, he was so grateful he kissed the pilot. 'Bless his heart,' said Pierre with a laugh. 'I put the sign of the cross on him. If the Lord keeps me alive, at least the Lord would protect him.'

But for Pierre the nightmare hadn't ended yet. He stayed in the Falklands for five or six more weeks, treating the wounded from both sides of the conflict until the new medical team could fly out.

'My concern was the lads,' he said. 'And like I said, I was trying to do my job. That's basically it. I was a medic and I had to do it, wherever that job presented itself. There are no niceties about war. It's a dirty, vulgar business, you know. As far as I'm concerned, it shouldn't have happened, but there you are. And the injuries sustained by these lads were atrocious, seriously atrocious.

'The thing that always stays with me ... I'm a Medical Corps man. I've got a theatre background and I'm used to the smell of dried, dirty blood. Blood smells, you know. And when it's stuck on you and you can't wash it off, you have to live with it day after day after day, because you're wearing the same dirty, tatty, burnt uniform. There was nothing to change into, no nicety about it, everything was getting burnt and scorched. And whoever vomited on you, whoever bled on you, it stayed with you. You couldn't wash it off. And it smells like that ... I call them trigger points, they trigger things off in me, you know. Almost like a panic, it's seriously distressful. A backfire of a car, a loud plane overhead, a sudden noise, a drop of a plate on the floor, a clang of a metal dish – they make me jump out of my skin. The smell of petrol, burning log fires, you know ... burning flesh. It's a most peculiar smell, especially when it's alive. I'm not being flippant but it's horrible. As a medic you get used to it, but that really ingrained itself into my mind.'

Talking to Pierre and his wife, Nina, brought my own experiences back into sharp focus. Like me, Pierre's family didn't recognise him when they went to meet him at the airport after the long flight home. Pierre reckons that his normal weight of 12 stone was down to little more than seven and a half. Only his youngest daughter picked him out, no doubt helped by the distinguishing red crosses on his epaulettes.

Though Pierre's family were all too aware of the change in him, the army made no attempt to find out what was wrong. They gave him ten days off and then he was back at work, treating the casualties week after week, month after month, convinced that if he told anyone about his problems, he risked instant discharge.

'You came back like an animal,' said Pierre, talking of the months that followed his return. 'I was aggressive. I would have stabbed somebody. I was keyed up to the nines. I was very, very aggressive and I was very angry. I was a very angry man. I was seriously depressed. I still am seriously depressed. But I was a very angry fellow and I dare say some people said, "Oh, God, he behaved like an animal."

'My wife said, "Don't behave like an animal. Why are you doing that?"

'It's self-preservation. I mean, at the slightest bang from outside I was diving under the table. I couldn't get out of the habit of staying alive. Don't die now. Keep your head down, don't let the sniper get you, or something. I was doing the most peculiar things. I couldn't sleep. I had horrendous flashbacks. I still get them now, till today. Nothing but bad flashbacks. And it's like it was . . . just five minutes ago. I can smell it. I can hear it and I can smell it. It doesn't go away. I get depressed, yes, I'm seriously depressed. And I'm getting treatment for it, from my own seeking, because I think it's helpful. I think I should get this beast out of the closet and face it, that's what I'm trying to do. Bring it out into the open. I buried it for too long, and people like me were suffering in silence.'

As my own mother knows only too well, you vent your anger on those closest to you. We all did it to our loved ones. In Pierre's case it was his wonderful wife Nina who bore the brunt of the strain.

'I couldn't survive without her, you know, Simon,' he told me. 'I would have topped myself a long time ago.'

'Ah, my Mam was the same,' I said. 'She put up with so much. I was just able to talk a lot sooner and open my box a lot sooner. But the people who suffer probably just as much are the people who have to sit back and watch it all.'

It was several years before Nina Naya finally convinced her husband he should seek help. For a long time Pierre himself had thought his behaviour was perfectly normal.

'I thought perhaps I'm bad-tempered since I came back from there, and who else wasn't, Simon? I could have stabbed somebody walking in the street if they said boo about the Falklands, you know, or anything like that. I would have stabbed them. I came back a very cross, a very angry man, a very depressed person ... But I was really seriously depressed, you know. And my wife pulled me out of this. She pointed it out over many years. I wouldn't believe her and then presumably it got worse and worse and worse and worse and worse and she said, "Look, do something".

'You did it in the end,' said Nina. 'I mean, Pierre just couldn't accept there was a problem at all, you know. In the end, in 1988, I'd had enough and so I rang the army – doctors that we knew when I was nursing as well. I spoke to them and they referred Pierre down to Aldershot. And that was where he was told what I already knew and he couldn't accept: that he had PTSD.'

Right at the start of our meeting, Pierre had told me that he was dreading seeing me again because I personified so many things for him, a bit like that Para in Bolton. Having known me for many months in my treatment programme, Pierre had shared in my pains. But meeting again after all this time was good for both of us. I was able to thank him for all that he had done to save so many lives and to ease the passing of those whose lives were past saving. It was almost impossible for me to reconcile the lovely, gentle man I was meeting with the depressed and angry person he described for me. Pierre is truly one of those people who did far more than me and never got the meritorious recognition he deserved. I am glad that he too got something from bringing into the open some of the memories we shared. We were lifting another veil from what happened.

'I was frightened of the situation,' he said. 'I thought, I've got to open this box up. But I've kept this box closed for years, Simon, since the Falklands. I've locked this box because it was too painful, with all the beasties in it. It's open now. Like I said. You opened it. We've opened the cover, we're turning the pages of the book—'

Pierre's experience is typical of the way the army dealt with the traumas suffered by some of its bravest and best: it didn't want to know. Though Pierre himself is now out of the forces, service people like him continue to serve this country and make us proud, yet when they need help themselves there is virtually nothing for them. I still burn with anger at the way we expect young men and women to do an incredibly hard job yet when they come home we offer them very little in the way of what I would call long-term help and true support. I've always been well cared for by my regiment, but not everybody felt the same and that's unfortunate and very sad. Some guys injured in the Falklands were made to feel awful, as if they were in some way to blame for what happened to them. They weren't.

It was for people like Pierre that I joined my name to the group action of British veterans suing the Ministry of Defence for failing to offer help in preparing for and coping with the horrors of war, and failing to detect signs of trauma in service people returning from the field of war.

In my own case I wasn't interested in any money we might win, though plenty of other claimants lost their livelihoods and were badly in need of decent damages. Rather, I wanted to draw attention to post-traumatic stress as a disorder that you can treat, and one that the MoD and the military should have been treating for years.

More than 2,000 of us added our names to the action, veterans of recent conflicts in Northern Ireland, the Falklands, the Gulf and Bosnia. Co-ordinating the action on our side was the Manchester-based law firm of Linder Myers. Our complaint was not about being injured – that's a risk you take when you agree to take the Queen's shilling – but at the lack of psychiatric care before and afterwards. For the purposes of the case, we were divided into two groups, depending on when the trauma occurred. Those of us, like me, injured before 15 May 1987 had an extra hurdle to leap because up until then the Crown and its offices (like the MoD) enjoyed immunity from prosecution.

The courts took eight months to air the generic issues involved in the action, aided by 15 lead cases. The argument we set out to prove was that PTSD is detectable, preventable and treatable, and that proper systems would have achieved these objectives in the vast majority of cases. Even if the British military didn't use PTSD as a clinical label until 1992 (unlike the US, which adopted it in 1980), the MoD knew full well that war produces all kinds of psychiatric disorders: shell shock, depression, anxiety disorders, PTSD, alcohol and substance misuse, enduring personality change and what have you. However you define them, these symptoms were there for all to see, and they were treatable.

The verdict, when it finally came in May 2003, was devastating. Although the court accepted the reality and severity of the psychological injuries of war, it found hardly any evidence of systematic negligence on the MoD's part. In only four of the 15 test cases did the judge consider the MoD had breached its duty of care, and even these were apparently not enough to indicate systematic failure.

All those in my group failed in our action, full stop, as the judge ruled that crown immunity applied until the law was changed in 1987. So anybody whose trauma occurred five minutes before the cut-off point was ruled out of court, as if that made our suffering any less. This wasn't the only immunity to let the MoD conveniently off the hook. According to the judge, a historical 'combat immunity' still applies for all active operations against an enemy, including things done well away from any live military action, such as planning and preparation and peacekeeping operations.

But it was on the issues of treatment and detection that the court judgment was potentially so lethal. While concluding that post-traumatic stress disorder can be effectively treated – and setting out benchmarks which may well prove valuable in the future – the judge bafflingly decided that the MoD was under no legal obligation to identify sufferers who might benefit. In his view, it was up to sufferers – like Pierre and all the others – to put themselves forward for treatment, when the whole macho culture of the military was screaming at them to keep quiet. In documents presented to the court, one general went so far as to suggest that people suffering from psychiatric illness were a bunch of wets, completely lacking in moral fibre.

Before the verdict was announced the MoD had put a price tag of at least £100 million on meeting the 2,000 or so claims. Now it looks as if far fewer than expected will succeed, and those mainly on old-style clinical-negligence grounds. Linder Myers looked at the ruling and decided they couldn't appeal on the issue of crown immunity but they were hopeful that perhaps some 30–40 per cent of post-1987 claims might succeed.

The verdict left me stunned and, for once, absolutely speechless. I simply couldn't believe it. Did the judge listen to anything that was said by the claimants or the 16 leading world experts on PTSD? He might have heard what was said, but did he really listen? I found the verdict abhorrent and I can no longer put my hand on my heart and say I have faith in the law. Somebody once said to me, 'Don't equate justice with the law,' and by God how right they were. I never gave a sod about my injuries, they're a by-product of the job, but I have always believed that the MoD has a duty of care towards its service people, and that it should set out to look after us physically and psychologically. This verdict has shattered that faith – all I see are people running to cover their backs, and 2,000 of the boys being sold out.

So what exactly happened to produce such a verdict? Did the government apply any subtle pressure on the judiciary to get the result it wanted? Nobody, not even the government or the MoD, could have expected the result they got. There was clearly some arrangement between the British and US governments not to allow American PTSD experts to come here on behalf of claimants. What deal was done I don't know, but I can see no other reason why the US should deny their experts the opportunity to prove their worth in court. With all these shadows looming over the verdict, just how impartial was it? Or is my total disbelief a sign of my own paranoia? – though I really and truly don't think it is.

In effect, the judgment allows the MoD to walk away from its responsibilities. They are ultimately the employer of the armed forces, and this verdict lets them wash their hands of their employees' psychological well-being, now and in the future. How can we leave it to soldiers and other service people to self-heal? We've taught them to fight, we've taught them to act professionally in one specific sphere, but not in psychiatry, so how on earth can the judge conclude that service people must present themselves for treatment? If the MoD isn't responsible, then who is? Just who is?

The loss of any potential damages is not a problem in my case – I had always planned to give half to the veterans' charity Combat Stress and half to my Mam. It seemed only right to divide any financial gains between an organisation that helps other soldiers and my Mam, who had to live with me for five years, putting up with the sadness, the drinking and the misery. Now virtually the only gainer is the British government, and the MoD can wash its hands of responsibility to people like Pierre, who gave of himself like a true hero, and to all those in the future who will continue to suffer in their private hells because the military has been spared the duty of seeking them out. Can you look me in the eye and call that right and just?

This is one battle I don't propose to simply let go. People are still suffering and we must do what we can to alleviate their misery. The ruling did at least give clear responsibilities to the NHS to care for PTSD sufferers, however overburdened and overstretched our general health services might be. But now the government has nowhere to hide: it must make the money available to ensure that all these veterans are properly cared for, as they should have been since the 1970s, when effective treatments for PTSD became available.

From statements made by various military psychiatrists, it seems that things are improving to a degree but they remain far from perfect. Until we can remove the stigma attached to PTSD, and the fear that it might blight a military record or a career, people are still not going to put themselves forward for treatment.

16
Death of My Grandmother

LAST YEAR BROUGHT TO a close another chapter in my life with the death of my grandmother, Nora, in February 2002. We never really reconciled our differences, and that's very sad. There had been such a strong family bond between us all, one that should have produced a better result, but you can't always write the endings for real life.

My grandfather's dying, followed so soon by Loft's death, caused the fracture in our family that saw it all fall apart. Nora became older and lonelier very quickly after Percy died, but she created a lot of her loneliness herself because she would say things that would drive people away. She became really quite bitter towards the end. People would think, I don't have to put up with this, and they would walk out. Each time you went to see her she would chip away at you and say something nasty. So you didn't go to see her one week, or the week after that, and so it would continue. When people don't get on, the best way to remain happy is simply to stay away.

We were barely speaking by the end and whenever we did, it was stilted and uncommunicative. She might telephone my Mam and if I picked up the phone I'd say, 'Hi, Gran, how are you?'

'I'm fine. Can I speak to your mother, please?'

Once my mother had moved house, the family ties were broken and everyone lived in their own little units. My grandmother might speak to us when she needed something, but it was better not to be in each other's company.

When I was growing up, my grandmother had all my respect, but as I got older I felt she had no right to be rude to me. So we used to fall out, even before my grandfather died. One of the first big arguments I remember was over my Auntie Pamela, who used to bring her boyfriends round to my mother's house and expect her to cook for them.

I complained about this to my gran. 'My mother's got enough to do,' I said.

'Who do you think your mother is?' asked my gran. 'The Queen of bloody Sheba?'

I gave her a few choice words.

'Who do you think you're talking to?' she stormed. 'Don't you ever talk to me like that.'

So I didn't, for three or four years.

When we were speaking, she was always expecting us to come running over, though she would never make any attempt to come and see you, or even pick up the phone and ask you to come over. 'Forgotten where I live, have you?' she'd say to Lucy, who exchanged a few straight words with Nora, which was the worst thing you could do with my grandmother.

There was a further upset when we were moving house for my mother. Caitlin was just a baby and to keep her safely out of the way, we had left her with my niece Becky, who was living across the road. Without consulting any of us, my grandmother took the baby, put her in the pram and wheeled her down to my Auntie Judy's. The first thing we knew about it was when Becky phoned us in a pure panic. That put the tin hat on it. Why did Nora have to get involved? Becky is a sensible girl who had babysat for just about everybody in the village. She was simply keeping an eye on the baby. Lucy was on hand if Caitlin needed anything.

All of a sudden it was like a war of words from Nora and then from my Auntie Penny, who blackguarded Lucy over the phone, calling her all sorts of names. My grandmother thought she was being helpful but really she was just meddling. Nobody had asked her to take the baby, and she put a 17-year-old girl in a very unenviable position. Towards the end it was just her nature to be divisive.

As I had broken free of the chains that bound so many others in the family, I suppose the estrangement between us was inevitable. My Auntie Judy is a similar spirit and she used to fall out with Nora every week. I'd be round at Judy's laughing like a drain over something she said because she really is so funny. If my grandmother walked in she would see me and walk straight out again, that's how she felt about me.

The person who remained in my grandmother's house the longest was my Uncle Jeremy, who was brought up like my brother. There were only ten weeks between us and we often used to have a wonderful time when we were growing up together because I lived at my grandmother's a heck of a lot of the time. Jeremy never really set out on his own until he reached his mid- to late thirties. The only time he really did break away was when he met his current girlfriend. Over the last ten years Jeremy and I have only really seen each other at weddings and funerals. He's a good man in his heart, somebody I have hugely fond memories of, but we're just not close any longer. I wish we were closer but we went our different ways in our twenties and when I got injured, that pretty much separated a lot of things.

I never stopped loving my granny, even at the end. I can't help loving the person she was when she was younger, and the memory of her. She could be the most fun in the world – the funniest, happiest, most carefree person you ever came across. If you needed somebody, she was the strongest person in the world. If you needed love, she was there. But she became such a vastly different person as she grew older, especially after my grandfather and Lofty died. Out of love for her and respect for her memory, I felt it was better and more peaceful if we stayed apart.

When Mam got the call to say that her mother had been taken ill, she went straight round to the house and followed the ambulance to the hospital. They were all there, my aunts and Jeremy. Nora was still conscious, and kept telling everyone, 'This is my daughter Pauline, she's a nurse.' I like to think she felt that with my mother there, she'd get better. But Nora's condition worsened in the night and they took the decision to transfer her to University Hospital in Cardiff (the Heath), where she died just as they reached the entrance.

The funeral service was held in St John's Church in Nelson. There was a further falling out the night before between my mother and my Auntie Penny, who said something like she wished it was my Mam who had dropped dead, which more or less set the tone for the day. I went to the funeral with Lucy, and afterwards we all went round to Judy's, then dropped my mother off and came on home.

It was just one of those days. We wouldn't not have gone, in spite of the distance that had grown up between us. Nora made life hard for people to want to be around her, or to like her. I continued to love her but I didn't like her very much towards the end. And if you don't like somebody, go away, don't interfere in their lives. I had tried to please my gran but you only get hurt in the end, so it was easier to say, 'No, this is my life now. Gran knows where I live. If she wants to come and see me, she can.'

17
A Fair Deal for the Services

I DON'T OFTEN GET ANGRY with newspapers, but the way the *Daily Mail* reported a speech I made to the Tory Party conference in October 2002 caused a fallout that went far beyond the immediate issue and took the shine off the message I was trying to deliver. In the end, the story had a good ending and confirmed my belief that you mustn't be scared of controversy. You can't be a patsy all your life. Sooner or later you have to take part, even if that means rocking a few boats. You might disturb a few people who might not like hearing the truth, but ultimately if you're honest and truthful about what you're saying, it can only stand you in good stead.

The invitation to speak at a fringe meeting (as a veteran, not a party member) had come from my solicitor friend Jonathan Evans, leader of the European Tories. When Tory leader Iain Duncan Smith heard I'd be coming along he asked me – as a fellow Guardsman – to address the main conference. I jumped at the chance to speak out for those whose voices are very seldom heard, British veterans of today and tomorrow, our current service community.

My unscripted speech was one I had been working towards for 20 years or more. In it I linked two themes that are very close to my heart: procurement policies for the military; and my disgust at the shoddy treatment meted out to returning service men and women, especially those who come back injured and needing care. To my mind, the two are closely linked. Give people the right equipment and they'll have less need of support later on, because our boys and girls will be better able to look after themselves and we'll see fewer injuries.

Why is it that we have the very best of our young British men and women in the services, yet we rarely give them the best tools for the job? Our current service community is under-strength and underrated, denied the credit it deserves. This is a country we're proud of, but if we don't give the military the proper equipment, how can they do the job properly and make us all proud again?

The story of the SA80 rifle, to my mind, illustrates all that is wrong with British procurement policies. It has caused so much controversy over the past 15 years, ever since it became the British weapon of choice. On the whole, the weapon works fine in the northern hemisphere, in the European theatre of conflict, but it has consistently failed in dust and desert conditions. Bullets were jamming all the time when it was first trialled in 1986, long after it had first appeared on the drawing board. It failed in the first Gulf War, yet despite all the problems that became clear there, only some five to ten modifications were made. It failed again in Sierra Leone, when our Pathfinder troops were under fire from rebel forces, and it proved inadequate in Afghanistan.

Weapons experts blamed the failures on firing the weapon dry instead of oiling it. To most soldiers, suggesting that a professional army doesn't clean its kit properly is one of the most awful things you can say about it. When I joined the army I was taught to strip a weapon down and put it back together again. Then I was taught to clean it. That's bog-standard basic training. We were also taught that when firing a weapon in hot, dry, dusty conditions you use no oil because oil attracts dust. The training instructions for cleaning weapons come from the Ministry of Defence, so presumably even the MoD didn't understand how the rifle should be cleaned in certain conditions. Certainly the problems should never have been blamed on the men.

It was an armourer who said, 'Have you tried oiling the weapon and changing the cleaning method?' They tried it and it worked, so what they're saying now is that the more oil you use, the better – completely opposite to how the boys were taught. It wasn't their fault the rifles were jamming in the desert.

They say that the modified SA80 A2 is now the best rifle out of all the standard-issue weapons used by NATO forces, more accurate over a longer distance, more reliable and with a better cyclical rate of fire. Okay, but why did it take 15 years to get to this point? And why, when I made my speech to the Tory Party conference, were the SAS and the SBS still not using the SA80 A2 as their weapon of choice, preferring the Canadian DiMarco and the US ArmaLite instead? I could only assume they had still not given the SA80 A2 the thumbs up.

I made my speech to the conference at a time when a second war in the Gulf was looming ever closer. 'If we want to bring people back looking like me or, even worse, in body bags,' I said, 'then we only have to continue giving them the worst.'

When I went to the Falklands, the British Army had to go and buy civilian rucksacks – bergens as they're known to the boys – from the warehouse of a local high-street camping store. Feet were shot to pieces because our boots were substandard – they let in water and fell apart. Twenty years on, nothing much seemed to have changed. Our service people in Afghanistan were still living in tented encampments and as they told me afterwards, they were being kept awake at night by the noise of the air-conditioning units used by the Americans, the Scandinavians and everybody else. They also told me they were going up to use the lavvies of other units because ours were not up to standard. The results were plain to see in the very public outbreaks of dysentery and other health problems.

Equipment shortfalls continued in the Gulf, as we saw reported in the press. The American forces nicknamed our troops 'the Borrowers' because we had to beg, steal and borrow loo rolls and all sorts of other stuff. The newspapers didn't simply report it – they ran campaigns to buy loo rolls to send down to our boys and girls in the field, which is hugely embarrassing. Then all of a sudden that sort of reporting stopped. The government had obviously spoken to the press and said, 'Stop doing this, because it is damaging morale.' The damage to morale was caused by the lack of supply and proper procurement, but I suspect the government feared that this kind of reporting was drumming up more anti-war feeling here, because people felt we were sending out the troops without giving them the proper equipment. Most of our guys down there would have laughed it off, because they get used to being sold short by politicians.

For the most part, the kit given out to elite regiments like the Marines and the Paras is far superior to that enjoyed by the rest. In the Falklands, for instance, the

Marines and the Paras got special Arctic-warfare boots. When the Welsh Guards first landed near Blue Beach and took over positions that had been occupied by the Paras, we found stuff they had thrown away that was tons better than our kit. Pierre Naya remembers the rubbish British helmets that lifted like a pancake, letting the flames go underneath. They were great for plant pots and hanging baskets and that's about it. We had none of the flash gear that might have helped us survive without injury.

Just as shocking is the lack of support we give to men and women returning from the services, especially those who come back injured and needing care. I was lucky enough to get the very best medical care to help me over my physical injuries, but now injured service people must rely on overworked, overburdened and underfunded NHS hospitals.

After I came back injured, I spent long months in the Queen Elizabeth Military Hospital in Woolwich, followed by countless repeat visits. The care I had was excellent – medically and physically, I couldn't have wished for any better. Woolwich was quite a distance from Wales, but my Mam and Loft could at least drive there and back in a day, especially the way Mam drove then. The QEMH has since closed as a military hospital and reopened as a civilian one, allowing the old civilian hospital to be sold off for luxury apartments.

I was on a train recently and got in conversation with a chap who worked for the MoD in Germany. He said they were talking to three or four German hospitals to see if they could treat our injured service people in the event of mass casualties, because we don't have enough beds in this country any more. That, to my mind, is wrong. I needed my family and friends around me to help me recover, to help me move on, to help me live a productive life. We were having quite a rant about this and when I got up to leave I discovered that sitting nearby, well within earshot, was Princess Anne. The security man with her looked at me and winked. At least she would know we were talking from the heart and not making it all up.

Of course, we still have some fine establishments in this country, places like the Royal Star & Garter Home, which has never let down one single person who has ever entered its doors. But as I said at the time of the conference, the home is seriously underfunded – 'not by the British public, but it gets no government funding whatsoever. It doesn't even get any Lottery funding. There's not a British military charity that I know of that gets Lottery funding. We can give them to groups that could be even anti-British, we can give them to anybody else, why aren't we giving them to our ex-service community?'

That throw-away phrase 'anti-British' was the one that caused all the trouble but I didn't know it at the time. I was just getting into my stride.

'These are our people,' I went on. 'They have done it for us and lots of others. They have given of their youth, of their lives. We as service people are very willing to put our blood – to shed our blood – on the line. We don't need anybody else to offer it up for us, we're more than willing to do it. But if we're willing to do it, then give us the best we deserve. We're not looking for special privileges, we just want what is right and fair, that's all. That's all service people demand, that they get given a fair treatment. They give of their best, they never let anybody down. They don't go on strike for more pay. These people can't strike, yet they are ready to go and fill in for firemen. They will do their best, but they can't do it well enough.'

I was getting close to the end of my speech. The threat of war with Iraq was uppermost in my mind. 'When we've finished our fighting in conflict, in the name of this country, in the name of the finest people we have, please don't make them fight for what is rightfully theirs when they come home, to endure the peace in pain and in suffering.'

My speech received a standing ovation. I had been working towards it since the Falklands and now it was delivered, I felt drained yet also hugely sad that I had needed to say those things. I have raised these issues in quieter ways – in television documentaries and sat astride a tank at the Woolwich arsenal – but nothing can match the passion of live delivery to an influential audience in a packed conference hall. I would have been sadder still if I'd known how true those words were to prove in the months that followed. We get plenty of rhetoric from politicians but we still don't get any action.

Immediately after the speech I had to go straight on to an exhibition-opening in Richmond, where I was representing the Royal Star & Garter Home. It was late afternoon and I was just driving out of Bournemouth when I got a call from the *Daily Mail*, asking me about asylum seekers. I hadn't read the papers for a few days and therefore had no idea the *Mail* was running a campaign against Lottery funding for groups it didn't like, especially those supporting asylum seekers and refugees. The paper had picked up on my phrase 'anti-British' and had maybe thought in all naivety that I supported what they were saying. I don't know, but I certainly didn't know what their agenda was either. By 'anti-British' I had simply meant any organisation that doesn't have the best interests of the British people at heart – I didn't have any specific group in mind.

I said, 'I'm not involved in asylum seekers as an issue, my speech was all about the military. But if it's true that asylum seekers have been given more Lottery money than

organisations representing veterans, I think that's wrong.
I'm not saying they shouldn't have it, but what I am saying is, "Give us a fair share of the money as well."' That's
what I was trying to get across to people, and that's what
I tried to explain to the *Mail*. My comments in the speech
had nothing to do with anything I had read in the papers
or anybody else's agenda.

I drove on to the reception and didn't think any more
about it until I picked up the *Mail* the next day. 'WAR
HERO WESTON BLASTS LOTTERY' ran the front-page
story. 'They give to anti-British groups. Why can't they
give to our own veterans?' Though my views on the SA80
rifle and the closing of military hospitals appeared later in
the piece, you could be forgiven for thinking that the
main point of my speech was to have a go at the Lottery.

Oh dear God, no, was my first thought when I saw that
headline. What's the fallout from this going to be? Once
you've been in the public eye, you know that this kind of
thing can only bring trouble. I should say that I don't
hold a grievance against the *Mail* as such. I think it's a fine
newspaper and does a good job, but it hurts when you see
that kind of reporting, because it would be absolutely stupid for me to blast the Lottery, which is, in effect, the
hand that's been feeding Weston Spirit for so many years,
and so many of the other charities I support.

There was more of the same the following day, when
the *Mail* ran a two-page spread on its inside pages casti-
gating the Community Fund's £68-million support 'lav-
ished on groups supporting or working on behalf of asylum seekers and refugees', compared to just £1 million
given to veterans' organisations over seven years. In a
hard-hitting editorial, the *Mail* invited readers to vent
their 'justifiable anger' by writing to the Fund's chair-
woman, Lady Brittan.

Other newspapers gave coverage to my speech and most reported its main thrust. *The Times*, for instance, picked up many of the points I had made about poor pay, neglect and substandard equipment. The *Sun* singled out what it called 'a blistering attack on the Army's controversial assault rifle'. Certainly everyone I spoke to in the military knew exactly what I was saying. They knew I was talking about procurement policies and support for present and past members of the services, rather than having a bash at asylum seekers. Even the officers in my own regiment said, 'Well done.'

But inevitably the controversy stirred up by the *Daily Mail* about the Community Fund's support for refugees and asylum seekers pushed my wider message off the screen. Lady Brittan got bagfuls of hate mail and even death threats. Sales of Lottery tickets took a dive and people who had not heard one word of what I actually said assumed I was the one who was stirring the pot.

If the fallout was bad enough on a personal level, the shock waves quickly reached Weston Spirit and I couldn't allow that to continue. Potential backers started to shy away, confusing the *Mail*'s views with my own. I may not have said what people thought I had said, but in the charity world, perceptions count as much as reality. In the immediate uproar Ben at Weston Spirit replied to a letter from Lady Brittan I hadn't even seen, distancing the charity from words I had never uttered in the first place. 'Simon does not speak for Weston Spirit' was the underlying message. That infuriated me, and I found I was defending myself over things I hadn't said. Even Lucy was feeling the pressure.

I did the only thing I could in the circumstances: I offered to resign from Weston Spirit, and I made public my support for Lady Brittan. I was particularly upset by the hate campaign waged against her personally. If people don't like the organisations that are getting money from the Lottery, they should write a sensible letter of complaint, instead of turning it into a rant. I often think we don't complain enough about the things that really matter to us.

After some fairly plain speaking I was happy to withdraw my resignation from Weston Spirit. 'Let's not go down that route,' said Ben and I was glad to get our wires uncrossed for the good of the organisation and everyone involved. I believe passionately in the work the charity does with young people, and I am just as passionate about maintaining my own freedom to speak out about things that concern me.

For three or four weeks after the speech I continued to deal with the flak until eventually I just shut up, judging that I had done all I possibly could to defend myself over views that weren't mine anyway. The furore gradually died away, though not before I had received a letter from an old soldier incensed by what he saw as my cowardice in backtracking from my supposed views. I wrote a stinking letter back. Everything I say I mean, I told him, and I believe in everything I say. If those views about asylum seekers really had been mine, I would have defended them to the hilt. I don't make public statements and then back away from them. That just is not me. I'm a fighter, not a quitter, so would he kindly keep his bigoted views to himself?

The whole affair had taken up far too much of everyone's time. I was understandably annoyed and disappointed that my pleas on behalf of veterans and service people were in danger of getting sidelined. We had all got entrenched looking for argument rather than resolution. It was far more important that we should try to resolve these issues instead of just talking around them.

I remember talking to Ben about this. I said, 'Look, Ben, how do we move forward on this? I'd like to give Lady Brittan a call. What do you think?' There are far more talented letter-writers than me, but I felt if I could speak to her personally, I could make myself understood. Ben agreed and Lady Brittan took the call straight away, as soon as she came into the office. She very graciously said, 'Come and meet us. We'll get together a group of representative service organisations and let's talk.'

That's exactly what we did. A group of us went along to see Lady Brittan and her staff at the Community Fund's offices in London to talk about getting better access to Lottery funding. There was Combat Stress, the Royal Star & Garter Home, Gifford House, the Royal Air Force Association representing all the armed services, and one or two others. Unfortunately the Royal British Legion refused to take part, saying they didn't want to get involved in any campaign, even though I had tried to explain that it wasn't a campaign but a simple case of redressing the balance. Their response disappointed me hugely. As the leading and largest service organisation in this country, they really should have been there.

Although at the time I wasn't sure the meeting achieved anything very much, within just a few months two service organisations had secured funding of around £1 million between them, effectively doubling the amount of money the Community Fund had given to service charities in the whole of its first seven years.

At the dinner held to celebrate Weston Spirit's 15th anniversary, Lady Brittan said to me, 'That's all because of you and what you started.' So it really is worth standing up for your convictions and taking the flak, because if you believe in something strongly enough, a lot of good can come out of all the hassle. In a roundabout and very perverse way, I have the *Daily Mail* to thank for sparking the original furore because if it hadn't, my speech would not have continued to receive the attention it did and in the end we may not have got the result we did. I hope it's just the beginning of proper funding for the men and women who give up so much for their country.

18
Weston on War

BOB MONKHOUSE SUMMED IT UP nicely when he said war is not about who's right or wrong, it's about who's left. I think my views on war baffle a lot of people – I'm not anti-war but I hate war. War is what you get when the politicians fail to resolve their differences through words.

Living in the past doesn't interest me. I'm not at all keen on putting up the sandbags or swinging the old tin canteen every week because that means you're still clinging to the past, not the future. I want to enjoy my life and I want others to be able to enjoy theirs – which is why I put so much time into Weston Spirit. I can't enjoy life if I'm twisted up in hatred and bitterness. You can't afford to carry that kind of baggage with you. If you do, it will destroy you.

My interest in war is humanitarian and not at all gung-ho. That's for young men and those who have never been to war. I remember some words of President Roosevelt scribbled among the shithouse poetry on the walls of the latrines in 'D' Lines barracks at Pirbright, my army training centre. They were really old toilets, painted over many times, but Roosevelt's words always came out strong. They said, 'For those of us who have known combat, life has a flavour that the protected will never ever know.'

As I said at the beginning of this book, there's nothing victorious or glorious gained in any conflict. Among service people you've got two sets of people: the losers and the bigger losers. There are no winners. At the same time I hate the White Poppy brigade because they say people like me glorify war. How stupid can people be? They say remembrance is about glorifying war when it has nothing to do with that. Remembrance is for those who are alive; it's a day you get together collectively to remember those who didn't come back. Remembrance is for families who have lost loved ones and it reminds everybody throughout the whole world about the sacrifices being made by young men and women to maintain our freedoms. It reminds us also of all the civilians who have lost their lives in war because the innocent give their lives too – perhaps not as freely but at no less a cost. Remembrance is about recalling the human sacrifice as well as the hopes, the desires and the dreams of world peace.

'Some people call themselves pacifists and I am a pacifist,' said Tony Benn to me when I interviewed him for my radio show. 'When I made the conscious decision to join the RAF in the last war, it was as a pacifist and not as a conscientious objector, because I believe the true definition of a pacifist is somebody who is prepared to lay down his life for peace.'

Yes, war is nothing less than a tragedy – it's a tragedy that anybody has to do it. And yet for all that, I still care about the military and feel at my happiest in a military environment. Until I got injured the army was my life and when my army career was taken away from me I missed it terribly. I don't think I missed the job itself, which is hard, dirty, heavy and dangerous, but I missed the life and felt even worse because the decision was taken out of my hands. If I had stayed in the army I would have had to leave about now anyway, unless I had attained the skills or a rank that would allow me to transfer to the long-service list. I find that ludicrous. A lot of guys my age are just getting into their prime but they still have to leave because of legislation written many years ago.

I usually celebrate my own remembrance quite privately, preferring not to attend big ceremonies to remember the war dead. But one reunion I now attend every year is for Welsh Guards who served in the Falklands. It's held in Wrexham on 8 June, the day the *Sir Galahad* was bombed. The get-togethers started about ten years ago but I've only been going for the last three or four, since I first heard about them. I stay with Mark Pemberton, his wife Bella and their two lovely daughters, Sarah and Pollyanna. Rodney Wrong Charge and Cappa come too.

We first of all gather at the grave of Neil Hughes, who was in my mortar crew – '11 Hughes' as he was called, because there were so many Hugheses in the Welsh Guards it was easiest to identify him by the last two digits of his army number. There's a few of us who gather there with 11's family – Gentle Ben, Slab, Pem, Rodney, Cappa and me, Squeaky – sounds like one of those comedy sketches, doesn't it? We lay a little wreath at his grave and have a little minute's silence, then we go off to the memorial service in one of the oldest churches in Wales.

The boys in Wrexham and North Wales got together and formed a memorial association, really just to keep the service going. They hold the odd fund-raiser to raise a few bob, and bought a replica granite cross – a miniature version of the one down in the Falklands, though it's still about six feet tall – that stands as a war memorial in a prominent spot in Wrexham. The last time I went up there for the service there were maybe about 300 of us out of a possible 650. A lot of guys don't know about it still. After you finish in the army, you just bomb-burst away and not everybody gets the message. There are guys living all over – in the north of Scotland, New Zealand, South Africa, America, Australia, Ireland and Northern Ireland, the south-east of England.

After the service we wander off down to the United Services Club, where they lay on facilities and we get slowly mortalled over the next 12 hours or so. You get reacquainted with guys you may not have seen for a year or two, and some guys you haven't seen for 20. There'll be a few people you didn't get on with last time, so you try to reconcile your differences, just like in any big family. We do very little reminiscing about the Falklands; it's more about current-affairing yourself with what's been happening in people's lives, where you're at, what you've done, how your families are.

Some people there are definitely a bit antsy towards me, but I'm a big boy and have learnt to live with that. Some of the guys from the Welsh Guards and other regiments feel aggrieved at the attention I get, but it's just one of those things. You're never going to satisfy everybody. Being in the public eye has been wonderful for me and it has also allowed me to do more than just enjoy it for myself. I've worked hard for an awful lot of other people and made an awful lot possible for them. I haven't just gone out and taken selfishly for myself, giving nothing back.

I can't turn the clock back and wouldn't want to. If people don't like me because I've achieved a certain amount of public notice, then tough, I don't care. I'm not an apologist and I won't apologise for doing the best I possibly can for those people I care about. I have never sold anybody short. I have never rubbished anybody or the regiment and I never shall. If people think I've done a bad job – well, fine, tell me. At reunions, I don't let it bother me. I'm a man and if people want to get shirty with me, that's their problem, not mine.

* * *

It was through a contact re-established at the Wrexham reunion that I found myself facing my toughest-ever challenge as a motivational speaker – talking to the boys from the SAS at their annual debrief, 'the bunfight' they call it. Now, I'm used to trying to motivate people but what can you possibly say to the SAS that will fire them up any more than they already are? These guys are called in by governments around the world to train their special services and are routinely expected to perform impossible (and secret) feats for our own. And what am I? Twenty years ago I was a scrawny guy in the infantry – well, maybe not so scrawny – who served with a lot of the guys who are now in the SAS and coming to the end of their careers, distinguished careers during which they have served all over the world and covered themselves in glory.

The invitation to speak to the SAS had come through my friend Dale Loveridge, who served with me in the Welsh Guards. We played rugby together when we were in the battalion: I was a prop forward and he was a flanker behind me. After the Falklands he moved over to the SAS, where he ended up as one of five senior warrant officers.

Dale is coming to the end of his career now and he's done really well. He always was a brave lad. We'd been quite close friends and then you lose touch for a time as you move on. Our lives were going in different directions and in his job Dale didn't need any of my baggage or the weight of being around somebody who was injured. We met up again at the Wrexham reunion and he just asked me if I would come along to talk to them at the bunfight. It's always after a drink that I manage to commit myself to things that terrify me. But what the heck can you possibly say to them?

I was still pondering this question when I drove up to their spanking new barracks in Hereford one morning last December, a bit late because the Christmas traffic was horrendous, but I didn't let that throw me. I parked at the barracks and walked over to the lecture theatre with Dale, still wondering what I was going to say. It was the Commanding Officer's last day and he was looking a bit sad but very proud as he had led the SAS through some very interesting times. His wife was looking exceptionally pleased that he was finishing his time with them. The new guy was there too, very much on a high. It's such an intense job but a huge privilege to make it as boss of the SAS.

I met a lot of the guys who were milling about outside the foyer having a cigarette. I found it very relaxed there. The guys salute and call people 'sir', but they aren't as regimented as everybody else in the British armed forces. They are all very clued up, very intelligent. That's what struck me most – the amount of intelligence that exists among them all. They are ordinary guys who have harnessed all these different energies and compartmentalised everything, the aggression, the intelligence, the powers of observation, the ability to assess things quickly. You talk to them and you can almost hear them analysing what you've said. Yet they are very relaxed and incredibly generous with their time. I didn't encounter a mite of arrogance either – confidence, yes, but not arrogance.

I still didn't have a clue about what I was going to say – this genuinely was going to come from the heart and off the cuff – so I went over to the Commanding Officer and said, 'Excuse me, sir, what exactly do you want me to talk about?'

Luckily what he wanted from me coincided with the few thoughts I already had. At the end of the day, these guys are only human beings. Okay, so they are highly motivated, highly skilled, immensely tough and very good at their job, but they are not the hardest men in the world. One guy alone couldn't walk into a bar and beat up 20 others single-handed. They are not superhuman and nor are they immortal. Yet because of all the skills they have learnt and the jobs they do, they can in turn suffer high levels of stress and sometimes this shows itself in many of the different manifestations of PTSD. If they have one flaw in their make-up, it's this – that when they are feeling stressed or down, they are reluctant to talk to anybody or seek help.

Jim Davidson's close friend and bodyguard was a casualty of this reluctance to seek help. A former member of the regiment – they call themselves 'the badged blokes' – he completely lost it and threw himself out of an aeroplane, though he may also have had other psychological problems unrelated to his service days.

It's a huge tragedy. These guys don't understand the risks fully when they join, though they learn soon enough afterwards. It's almost impossible to train people to cope with the stresses and strains they will face, especially as a lot of service people never go to war. It's the last thing you want to teach a 17-year-old recruit. The SAS face more risks than anybody else and more is expected of them. Incredibly self-motivated, they must be prepared to endure greater hardships and be mentally prepared to go to the last drop of energy and sacrifice. In combat they work on the principle of not 'if' we win but 'when'.

The rewards aren't huge but the difference is that these guys actually love what they do and they're the best in the world at it. They're certainly not doing it for the money. You look at them and they talk in a very caring way about each other. 'He's so intelligent,' they'll say. 'This guy's so fit and this one is just all-round excellent.' That's how they talk about one another, it's quite strange to experience. It shows that they are all tuned in to each other and to you as well. If they recognise your strengths, then they can clearly spot your weaknesses too.

As you can imagine, I found it was a bit scary to stand up in front of these guys and talk to them for 40 minutes flat. Dale said afterwards he had no idea I'd be able to do it, certainly not without notes. That was such a confidence-booster I'm glad he said it to me afterwards. But I told them a little of my story, and some of the funny bits. Asking for help is no weakness. Opening up is a sign of strength, and post-traumatic stress is a very real disorder, one that won't just go away.

After my session was finished I watched one squadron play another at rugby. It wasn't the prettiest game of rugby I've ever seen, I must admit, not that they were especially brutal but they don't have enough time to train to keep them up to a high level. So it was all a bit scrappy and they obviously don't want to cripple each other, either, because in their job, if they're out of the loop for any length of time it can be hard to catch up. It's like in education – you've got to stay right up with it and not lose pace.

While the boys were playing rugby, a helicopter landed right next to the playing field and nobody paid it the slightest attention. I fell back immediately into my old army thought processes, like you don't smoke on a helipad, but these guys were walking past the helicopter smoking without giving it a second thought.

They're a fabulous bunch of guys really, and never at any point was I made to feel beneath them in any way, even though every single one of them had done more, seen more, achieved more in their military service than I ever had. But the fact that I had been in the military and seen what I had seen meant that they treated me with the utmost respect. It doesn't matter if you're in the military for five minutes or five years – once you've been injured in combat, they accept and respect what you've done.

I asked Dale about it afterwards. 'Simon,' he said, 'they know you've been there and done it. That's what they understand and respect.' I had gone to Hereford with a huge amount of awe and my day with them confirmed everything I had thought about the SAS. They are bright, intelligent, kind people who do a bloody scary job. And it was nice that they totally supported my views on pro-curement and all the other things I'd been saying at the Tory Party conference and elsewhere. So you understand now why I think they are such an intelligent bunch, if they all agree with what I say.

After rugby we had lunch and then, as it was the last day of the debrief, there was a drinking session, which I declined as I didn't feel it was right for me to stay any longer than I had. However welcome they had made me feel, it was close to Christmas and I felt I should get home as I'm a dad first and foremost. But I was very pleased to be invited back for a charity boxing match to raise money for SAS members who get injured, and the families of those who are injured or killed. While they get things right most of the time, the nature of their job inevitably means that things can sometimes go horribly wrong for them.

* * *

When I visited the SAS barracks, in December 2002, the US and Britain were moving closer to war with Iraq as

Bush and Blair sought to rid the country of weapons of mass destruction and unseat the regime of President Saddam Hussein, with or without United Nations approval.

Though I count myself a passionate supporter of Britain and our military, I still believe that going to war at that time was a big mistake. I had two main worries. My first concerns were – and still are – that the argument was never properly made. There's no doubt that Saddam Hussein was a lunatic dictator and cruel despot, responsible for horrendous acts of savagery within his own country. But I don't think we ever properly made the case for this war, and the argument got lost in its own power.

At the United Nations in New York, Colin Powell and Jack Straw both tried to deliver stirring speeches about the weapons of mass destruction the Iraqis were stockpiling and what they were planning to do with them, but the evidence never materialised before we went to war. We should have exercised more patience and let the UN weapons inspectors continue their search. Hans Blix said he needed more time and he thought the war shouldn't have gone ahead when it did. Until you find a crime, you can't convict somebody, nor can you convict in the absence of evidence. Tony Blair had asked us to believe him but why should we? He's a politician and we all know that politicians are continually lying to people – that's what they do for a living, they're all professional liars who tell us half-truths at best.

I think in all honesty there probably were (and probably still are) chemical and biological weapons in Iraq – we supplied some of them, after all, as did the Americans. But we should have let the UN weapons inspectors find them and order their destruction. As for the nuclear weapons capability, where were they hiding it? A nuclear power plant is colossal. You can't just tuck one away in an urban environment. They are bigger than Cardiff's new Millennium Stadium and that sticks out like the Coliseum in Rome. Nor can you just bury one under a mountain in an underground bunker. Nuclear plants rely on the free movement of materials, expertise, equipment, engineers, specialised machinery. How on earth are we to believe Saddam smuggled those undetected through the closed borders of his pariah state when we're told that spy planes today can read a newspaper from five miles up in the sky?

I also feel that going to war without the backing of the United Nations was wrong when there was no direct threat to the security of either the United States or ourselves. We were in effect invading a sovereign territory and imposing our will on somebody else. What about all the other despot states around the world who haven't ever been challenged? What about the killing fields of Cambodia, or Robert Mugabe in Zimbabwe? One could only assume that we were singling out Iraq because Saddam Hussein was sitting on one of the largest oil reserves in the world and that to my mind was not a proper reason to go to war when we did.

The conflict has clearly weakened the power of the United Nations – that has been usurped by the United States, which has virtually dismissed the UN as irrelevant. They have even said they are not going to allow the UN into the war zone. If that's the case, what relevance does the UN have any longer? To my mind, none whatsoever. I think the US attitude towards the UN is hugely problematic, but I also think that those countries who so emphatically said no to any further UN resolution caused as much damage to the UN as anybody else. By their threatened veto, France and Russia showed they had hidden agendas of their own. Possibly the only people who had no real hidden agendas were the British and the Australians, who I think also genuinely believed in what they were doing.

A weakened UN worries me because nobody is going to look on them as a credible peacekeeping force any more. Think of the discipline that has at last been established in the Balkan states, largely as a result of UN efforts. They are still experiencing some problems over there, sure, but at least they have now enjoyed a relative peace. It seems doubly farcical to hear recent calls for UN troops to patrol the streets of Northern Ireland.

As for the United States, I feel very uncomfortable at the thought of one country enforcing its will on the rest of the world and acting as the world's policeman. It seems they want to claim the right to go into any country and do whatever they like, irrespective of what the rest of the world might think. But in the end, they have only their own interests at heart.

I did at least get a chance to make public my opposition to the war on televised debates and through the press. In late January, before war had broken out, I got a phone call from *Daily Mirror* journalist Don Mackay, whom I had known for several years through his wife, actress Nicola McAuliffe. She once taught me how to read a poem by the World War I poet Woodbine Willy, for a charity show. Don calls me up every now and again when he wants to talk about military things and I trust him implicitly. If he ever tried to do anything underhand, Nicola would punch his head in – she's absolutely fantastic but fearsome and very principled, and I like that.

When Don asked me to support the *Mirror's* anti-war petition I agreed, on condition that the paper made clear two of my very special concerns: for the innocent civilians caught up in the conflict, and for our service people, who were even then preparing to head out to the Gulf. Don and I spoke a bit over the phone and we had lunch the following day in London, where I was due to record an interview with GMTV about forgiveness. I didn't know then that the *Mirror* proposed to headline my views across its front page.

That sort of attention scares me sometimes, because I'm just an ordinary guy. But then you begin to realise that even if it does nothing else, it gives you the chance to make other people think. Just after the GMTV interview I was travelling by tube when an American guy said to me, 'I liked what you had to say. You talk a lot of sense, boy.' Then he walked off. He must have sensed that at no point was I being anti-American, or anti-anything at all. I wanted most of all to be persuaded that going to war this time was right, but nothing was said to make me change my mind.

Whatever I thought about the legitimacy of the war itself, I knew that once any fighting broke out, we had to give our full support to the boys and girls involved in the conflict. They must never be placed in a situation where they come back as pariahs when every single one of them is a hero. As war was declared, my heart went out to the families who were sending their loved ones over there. I felt like just about every other person I met. These people are important – they are British. I cared about the US service people just as much, and about the innocent Iraqis who had only sticks and stones to defend themselves against our armies.

Since the war itself has ended, I continue to be asked for my comments on many different aspects of the conflict and on issues such as equipment levels. Nothing that has happened – not even the capture of Saddam Hussein – has shaken any of the statements I made earlier. As time marches on, my grave doubts and misgivings about lack of equipment for the troops and about the conflict itself have been fully borne out by many different sources.

A few months after this book was first published, the commanding officer of the Black Watch, Lt Col James Cowan, was quoted as saying that his regiment went to war under-equipped, left badly short of kit by the Ministry of Defence. Despite government assertions that the purpose of the war was to remove Saddam's weapons of mass destruction, units like the Black Watch were sent to the Gulf without enough biological and chemical protection suits to go round, and without the equipment to detect or deal with any possible decontamination.

Of course to date, no chemical or biological weapons of mass destruction have been found, and with all the revelations coming out of Iraq, it seems extremely unlikely that any ever will be. As an Iraqi said to me recently, the people who were feeding information to the Americans and to the British were clearly telling them what they wanted to hear. There couldn't be a wider gap between the apparent intelligence claims about the weapons Saddam Hussein possessed and those that he was later found to have had. As for the claim that he could deploy 'weapons of mass destruction' within 45 minutes, it now seems clear that this could only refer to conventional battlefield rockets, which Saddam was entitled to have anyway, to protect his own borders.

As cruel and as vile a man as he was, did we really need to go to war and stir up the terrorist threat that is even greater now than it was? If the judgement of this government is to be believed and trusted, then how is it that the Germans and the French and almost everybody else in the free world could see that the available evidence and intelligence were nowhere near conclusive enough to justify going to any kind of war?

I am and remain non-political and don't want to be seen to be making political capital out of any of this; my concerns are humanitarian rather than political. When we send our troops into war, they have to be correctly armed and correctly equipped so that we give them the best chance of coming home again. And the conflict must be justifiable.

It's a sad fact that a lot of good people are now retiring from the armed forces because of political interference in the way they are run. One of the most publicised resignations came from Col Tim Collins, who won fame for his inspirational eve-of-battle speech to the soldiers under his command and who was later vindicated after allegations were made against him of ill-treating Iraqi prisoners. But it's no use trying to be politically correct in a war. As a soldier, you go in as a warrior not as a boy scout; you have to take risks, it really is as simple as that. Today we see far too much interference in the way the military do their job, not least by accountants who prefer to pinch pennies rather than to provide the best equipment for the troops.

Yet despite all my misgivings over the war and its aftermath, I remain an optimist at heart. I hope and believe that things will turn out right despite the cack-handedness of people. There's a lovely statement by the great football manager Bill Shankly, that football is a simple game complicated by people who ought to know better. I believe life is a simple game complicated by people with hidden desires.

In essence, life really is very simple. It's not that difficult to live, if people would only stop complicating it. If they would only stop trying to enforce their will on other people. If they would only stop trying to do things to other people. If they would just get on with the business of living, and if politicians would just get on with the business of politics – decent politics, like trade and health and education – instead of trying to become world leaders obsessed with power. I hate the phrase 'New World Order', that vision that Tony Blair is always talking about. Every time I hear it, I think of a film with Sylvester Stallone in which a guy with a big sharp knife was always hacking people to bits. He called it the New World Order too.

In the New World Order, people are always dictating to others what they should and shouldn't do. I believe instead we can encourage people to live peacefully with each other. And because I'm the eternal optimist, I truly believe we can succeed, as long as we keep on trying.

19

A 15th-Birthday Party

'CHOICE AND CONSEQUENCES' is one of the exercises Paul Oginsky invented for Weston Spirit. It's played in a group, a bit like a party game, except the issues it tackles are those of conscience and moral choice. The rules are pretty simple. There's a bag containing hundreds of money tokens in the centre: most are for 50p but there are some £1s, a few £5 tokens and even one for £10. Going round the circle and addressing each player in turn, the youth worker reads out a task written on a card. If you agree to do it, you get to put your hand in the bag for a token, and as soon as you have three tokens, you can exchange them for real money. If you choose not to undertake a task, you have to give back any uncashed tokens and drop out of the game, though you stay in the room and still get to take part in all the discussions.

The tasks start out fairly light: 'Tell us your favourite team,' it might be, or 'Give us the name of somebody you care about.' But they get progressively harder – 'Would you slag off your favourite team for a token?' 'What about the person you said you cared about?' Suddenly there's a question that really challenges you. Some players will hand over their tokens and drop out, others will continue when they wished they hadn't. It's a way of getting people to examine their feelings and their beliefs when there's something real at stake – the chance to win real money, at a price.

Then we'll get to a point where we say, 'Here's a toy that's going to a children's hospital. You can keep your tokens and get another one – which might of course be the £10 token – but only if you stamp on this toy. That's your choice: stamp on the toy and keep the money, or save the toy for the kiddies and give us back all your tokens.' It's always a very taut moment. A lot of players have dropped out by now and the atmosphere in the room is palpable.

One time we were playing the game in a young offenders' institution. There was just one lad left in the game when we came to the toy question. You could tell a lot of the players hadn't had that great a childhood or that many toys when they were young, and they really wanted the toy to go to the hospital. But when the task was explained to the lad, he duly stamped on the toy in an act of bravado, calculated to impress. A great shock went through the room, and some of the others clearly felt that this was out of order.

We let him keep all the money he'd won, but in the debrief afterwards we asked him, 'Okay, so why did you stamp all over the toy?'

He said, 'Well, that's what I thought everybody wanted me to do.' Then he stopped and thought about what he'd done and a little while later he said, more poignantly, 'I guess that's why I'm in here, eh?'

Weston Spirit had won over at least one young person that day. It's a story about peer influence and peer pressure but one that the players must discover for themselves. You can't afford to preach at young people because that would switch them off instantly and they would simply disengage.

A lot of our programmes are really imaginative and good fun – Paul has seen to that. Most young people who come along enjoy themselves. Paul reminds me of a time when we sent the youngsters out to play hide-and-seek around the building. 'Can we wear disguise?' they asked. 'No problem,' we said. They weren't going far and we didn't think anything much could go wrong. Unfortunately one of the lads chose a balaclava as his disguise and he went off to hide in a bank. We didn't see him again until the police brought him back. Even the best-laid plans can go wrong, and it just goes to prove that for every action there's a reaction.

But over the years we've been going from strength to strength, and to the centres already open in 1998 at the year of our tenth anniversary we've added new ones in Leeds, Manchester and Nottingham, and joined forces with a strategic partner in Belfast. For Ben one of the definite high points has been creating a new vision and a new goal that says in 2007 we'll be operating from 21 centres and working with 100,000 young people in that year alone. Deciding to aim that high was quite a defining moment for us. A guy called Malcolm Hughes helped us put the plan together. He's the one who kicked us out of where we were. 'Do you want to stay on the margins and remain small,' he asked, 'or do you want to really go for it? Either way, don't go for the middle ground.' He's been a real influence, helping us set up a commercial company that generates profits for the charity without straying from our original ethos.

In PR terms, 2002 was a really great year for Weston Spirit as we had a number of good opportunities to put our story across to the public on television and in the media. The charity world is as competitive as any other and you have to rise out of the ordinary to get noticed. GMTV chose Weston Spirit as one of five charities to benefit from its 'Get Up and Give' appeal. They filmed us on the ferry across the Mersey. Bloody freezing it was – I was chilled to the marrow. John Stapleton was the presenter and there were several supporters and runners for the marathon. That same year we were delighted when BSkyB chose us as its Charity of the Year. Both BSkyB and GMTV are seen as young people's television, and that kind of branding is very important to us.

With BSkyB and the Learning & Skills Council, we've developed the hugely exciting 'Reach for the Sky on Tour' programme, which gives 14–16-year-olds a taster of some great things they can do with their lives. There are five different zones and the youngsters get to experiment with each one over a single day – drama, journalism, dance, media production and music. I took part myself one day when we were visiting a community college smack in the centre of Nottingham. I found it very worthwhile but undeniably intensive. You can't just go along for a free ride – you have to try everything. I was knackered by the end of the day. Each zone gives the young people a specific task. In the journalism zone, I remember, they took a camera out in the streets and did some vox-popping. The aim is to try to re-engage young people in the opportunities that exist all around, and to encourage them to think about things they might really like to do. A lot of young people may be stimulated by today's fast media but come unstuck when you try to sit them down to learn parrot-fashion, as most schooling still does. If you've got the passion for something more unconventional, you can begin to make it happen if you only dare to dream.

Now that Ben, Paul and I are all just hitting 40, I wonder what will happen to us over the next five years. They say you should never go into business with friends. Well, at the beginning Paul and I knew each other but we weren't what you'd call real friends. Over the years we've all three become closer and there's a greater understanding between us, but we all have our own different worlds and the way the organisation has developed, we are now all playing to our strengths. You get leadership from Ben, vision from Paul and dogged determination from me to see things through to the bitter end. If it feels right, let's get it done. That's partly how we got started, when we were little more than a good idea. Ben has a trustworthiness and financial nous I wouldn't even try to play with, but then again he once worked in a bank. Paul is definitely the fantasist and dreamer of dreams, despite spells as a Territorial Army paratrooper, an electrician and working for British Nuclear Fuels. My life in the public eye benefits Weston Spirit because the charity and I are seen to be one and the same and it helps us stand out from a lot of others competing for the same space.

A first for me was appearing on *Question Time* in the spring of 2002, along with writer and broadcaster Sandy Toksvig and a handful of the usual politicians: Alun Michael for Labour, Tory Peter Ainsworth and Helen Mary Jones of Plaid Cymru. She got me really exasperated as she was forever bouncing about, trying to score points off everybody. 'For heaven's sake,' I said, 'stop trampolining about.' That's really what it felt like, to be sat there beside her. Sandy, by contrast, was a joy to be around, straight-talking and very pleasant. She just made the whole thing bright. I tried to talk common sense, the kind of things people in the street are saying, because you speak as you know. Afterwards David Dimbleby said to me, 'Well done, you got three mentions of Weston Spirit into the programme.' I hadn't even realised I was doing it, but Ben was pleased as he reckons it helped us pass through another barrier into serious debate.

This year, 2003, is the year of our 15th birthday. To kick off the celebrations, a group of young people on one of the current programmes co-hosted a special event at the House of Commons. Three of them – Samuel Etienne, Lucy Knight and Jovan Laronde – got up and spoke to a room packed with people of every persuasion. They spoke so well and their humour came out; that was a really great day.

A few weeks later we had a fund-raising and celebratory dinner at the Landmark Hotel in Marylebone, central London. Douglas Glen, the manager, was incredibly helpful and so were his staff in making it possible. The guests included our patron, the Duke of York, Lady Brittan, Sir Richard Branson, footballer Alan Hansen, Lionel Blair and many of our most influential backers and supporters. Rory Bremner provided the entertainment and Dr David Bull of the BBC's *Watchdog* did the auction, making sure we ended up in profit. I would like to say more about the dinner but I was sick as a dog with fever. I was sweating. I was uncomfortable. I was dehydrated. I felt ill. I felt sick. I couldn't tell you what the food was and I was drinking water incessantly, that's how bad I felt. I still had to get up and make a speech. If I'd been there just for myself, I would have said, 'Sod it, I'm off to bed.' But I didn't have a choice because the night was more important than me.

Two guests I was very pleased to welcome were our new President, Lord Charles Guthrie, and his wife. Lord Guthrie was my commanding officer in the Welsh Guards. It had been Ben's idea to ask him to take over from Sir Michael Hobbs, and I thought he was perfect for the role. We had first met in Berlin in the 1970s – actually he was the first man to charge me when I joined the battalion, and he still remembers the incident, which is pretty amazing, considering how many squaddies he must have charged since.

I was only 17 and I'd got drunk with some of the older soldiers. We'd gone into the sergeants' mess after a do, looking for some food. The duty cook refused to let us have any, so one of the boys with us picked him up by his ankles and shook him, then somebody found a vat of strawberries, which was useless to me because I can't stand them, and somebody else found some bread and a bit of meat. That killed our hunger. We were sat round the back on some tank traps eating the food we'd pinched from the sergeants' mess and generally fooling around (well, in actual fact a couple of the lads were ludicrously battling with parts of the anatomy they shouldn't have) when we got arrested by the guard sergeant, Fat Pat we called him – I don't think he's changed shape in all this time. The next morning we were dragged out of our beds to go before the drill sergeant, Tony Davies (known as '22'). I remember rolling up in a pair of baggy jeans, a vest and flip-flops, still squiffy from the night before. After we'd told the sergeant what we'd done he said, 'Right, see the Commanding Officer tomorrow morning first thing.' So I was on CO's report already, and I'd only been in the battalion a few weeks. He said, 'Turn to your right, gain height and get out of my office.' We were just about to march out of the room when he called out, 'Wait there. Tell me, who won?' We laughed so much we were snorting as we went out.

The next morning on the CO's parade the guy in front of us, a corporal in Support Company, had been hauled up for fighting. He'd been playing cards in the underground storerooms and stood to lose a month's wages when he caught one of the other guys cheating and gave him one hell of a hiding. We could hear Lieutenant Colonel Guthrie going ballistic through the door. 'Corporal Brown,' he said, 'what have you got to say for yourself before I sentence you?'

'Thank you for leave to speak, sir,' said Brown. 'Had I been a cowboy I would have shot him.'

* * *

I poured my heart into setting up Weston Spirit because I didn't want to be pigeonholed, and I'm pleased to find myself constantly surprised by the way the organisation continues to develop. The last time that happened was shortly after the furore over the *Daily Mail* and my speech to the Tory Party conference, when Ben and I had got our wires uncrossed and I agreed to withdraw my resignation. 'Let's not go down that road,' Ben had said, 'but you must accept that perception is reality.'

I was sitting at home in Cardiff, about to have my evening meal when I got a telephone call from Paul. We were chatting about this and that, and then he said, 'By the way, I'm at Ben's. I'm just about to have my tea here.' 'Oh aye,' I said, 'what's that about?' Paul said, 'We're going over to Tranmere Rovers because we want to discuss buying the club and taking it over.'

I said, 'Taking over Tranmere Rovers? You what?'

He said, 'Well, Weston Spirit are going to look at the taking over and running of Tranmere Rovers.'

That set my hackles going and I knew I had to go up to find out what was going on. I jumped in my car and drove straight up to Merseyside. I was there by 8.30 p.m. and stayed the night with Lucy's mum and dad. The next morning I was in Ben's office by 9 a.m., absolutely fuming. My great worry was that if people thought we were rich enough to buy a football club (which we aren't) Weston Spirit might just as well shut up shop as a fund-raiser.

'Ben,' I said, 'you went to a meeting last night and it says on Ceefax this morning that we are buying Tranmere Rovers.'

Ben said, 'Well, that's not quite true.'

He told me a little about what was going on – how we were talking about getting involved in a supporters' trust that would bring regeneration back to the community and a future back to the club. We would never be involved in the actual running of the football side, or financially linked in any way apart from renting a property on site, which would give us an office in a focal part of the community. We would not, he assured me, be putting any money into the club but we would be lending our weight to what the supporters' trust might achieve.

'Okay,' I said, a little easier in my mind but still not quite won over to the idea. 'Do you remember what you said to me about the *Daily Mail*? How perception is reality?'

Ben looked at me and laughed. 'You got me on that one,' he said.

We'll just have to see how it develops. The way Ben talks about it is immensely exciting, but then he always did have a soft spot for Tranmere Rovers. Apart from the handful of rich clubs like my team, Manchester United, football is almost bust. Ben has a vision of taking the game back into the heart of working-class communities, where he believes its true roots lie. Weston Spirit would have a presence there, a toe in the door, able to draw young people into our many opportunities. As well as Tranmere Rovers, we're talking to a club in South Yorkshire, Barnsley, where the idea is to get a coalfield trust interested in joining forces with us. That would give us a blueprint to use with other clubs who wanted to get involved.

I'm keeping an eye on how it all develops. The only times Ben, Paul and I have fallen out have arisen over lack of communication – over the *Daily Mail* furore, for instance, and mixed messages over football. I felt happier when I learnt that they couldn't have told me any earlier, as the meeting with Tranmere was called and took place in the space of about 12 hours. Ben has assured me we're not putting any Weston Spirit money into the football ventures and that's how it should be. If anything else materialises, we'll have to revisit and review the situation.

Building up Weston Spirit over the past 15 years is something we are all immensely proud of and the fact that we have helped to make such a massive difference to thousands of young lives. We continue to grow year on year even though markets have crashed to the detriment of many other charities. The only way to deal with these problems is to get out, knock on doors and encourage people to support Weston Spirit above the competition.

The real lows you get with this kind of organisation come when you hear of one young person who just drops off, or dies, or turns to drugs. We heard of one who died in a climbing accident – that was a huge low for me – and another who turned to drugs in his twenties, which felt so wrong to me, after he'd been given the chance to do something with his life. Then there are the young people who turn their back on you or get involved in something else. When you give people the chance to take part and you watch them walking out of the door, saying, 'I'm not doing this,' that's sad. But really there are very few who don't go on to achieve the things they want from life and I suppose it's because they are so few, they're the ones who stick with you. You don't want there to be any – it just seems such a waste.

20
Moving On

IT WAS MY FRIEND David FitzGerald who suggested the title for this book. I was talking to Fitz, trying to find a punchy phrase that would encapsulate all the positive aspects of my life, when Fitz remarked, 'You said you wanted to move on, so why don't you call it *Moving On*?' Brilliant, I thought, and so simple. Why couldn't I come up with that? I'll go for it because really that's what my life has been all about. I have never stayed in the past. The past is dead, gone. You can't affect it, you can only deal with the here and now and try your best to affect the future.

I never intended to write this book. People like me normally only get to write one book of autobiography at best, and this will be my third. The publishers approached me – I hadn't thought to write another – but when you start digging about in your life it's amazing what you uncover. There's probably a whole heap of things I've done that have got lost in the amber amnesia and people I haven't mentioned even though they mean a huge amount to me – great friends like Bob and Beth Hunt from Liverpool,

Clive 'Swamp Frog' Morgan and his wife Marie from Goose Green in Wigan and a host of others. It's not that I've forgotten them, but if you try to include everybody and everything you've done you'll end up with something as fat as *War and Peace*.

I have been back to the Falklands three times now and genuinely feel that I have come to terms with what happened. I sincerely believe I can move on to other things. Although I still have to talk about the conflict in public, I don't have to live in that era and privately I'll very rarely talk about it unless I'm asked. This doesn't mean that I seek to bury my past in a box. Around my house you'll find one or two mementoes from the Falklands and my time in the military; the rest are up in the attic somewhere. There's that lump of granite from Gelligaer quarry outside, and I was delighted at the recent arrival of a garden bench made out of teak from the original *Sir Galahad*.

Behind this is a brilliant story that says something to me about survival. Through Weston Spirit, I received an email from a guy called Jeffrey Collings from Tyneside. He had a bench belonging to his father made out of the original teak from the ship. It must have been taken out of the *Sir Galahad* at a refit sometime before the ship sailed off to the South Atlantic in 1982. I'm told the Royal Navy used teak around gun emplacements and places where you don't want materials that will splinter. The wood had been stripped out of the ship and stored in the Collingses' shed. Then one day Jeff and his brother were burning the wood from an old metal-framed bench. 'Why don't we line the frame with teak from the shed?' one of them said. And so they fitted the frame with wood from the old logistics ship and the bench sat in their dad's garden for many years until after his death, when Jeff and his brother started to clear out some of their father's artefacts.

Recognising the historical importance of the bench, they said, 'Why don't we give it to somebody who understands what it means?' They instantly thought of me, and as soon as I got their email I felt it was a great honour. My sister emailed him back and I phoned up.

'Do you want it?' asked Jeffrey Collings.

'Oh, absolutely,' I said.

This bench is something I can pass on to my kids in later years if they want it and are not too bored by me and my tales. To me it tells an extraordinary story of survival because the wood must have been taken out of the ship more than 20 years ago. Teak is so tough and hard it will last another 100 years or more – the metal will probably fail before the teak rots. I like the fact that all the armed services have played a part in its story: the Royal Navy supplied the ship to the army and then the Royal Air Force got involved in bringing the bench down to me by three-day transport, wrapped around with bubble wrap in a cardboard box and strapped to a pallet because of its weight. Eventually I plan to put it in my front garden, in a little area I'm going to pave and turn into a sitting area for warm, sunny days. That's a very Welsh thing to do, sit out front and chat to your neighbours.

It seems that as I move on, reminders of the past keep coming back, but that's okay. For me, it was hugely poignant to learn that the replacement *Sir Galahad* was the first ship to deliver humanitarian aid to Iraq during the recent Gulf War. This ship has such a fantastic history, one that lives up to its fabled name (and a name that may well have been Welsh). Son of Sir Lancelot, Sir Galahad was the perfect knight who eventually found the Holy Grail. He's lucky, he knew what he was looking for – I'm still trying to discover what my holy grail is. But all these reminders I find intensely positive – the bench survived, I survived, the ship itself helps people to survive. It's as if Sir Galahad really was the perfect white knight. And even if the story has its tragic moments, it is about more than tragedy. Every phoenix is actually a success. People like Pierre, Pem, Jimmy and myself, we all came back from the burning ship and that's a success, even if we had problems or issues to deal with. The fact is, we survived and we continue to remember those who were not so lucky.

Another side to moving on, which I've talked about a lot in this book, is being ready to accept new challenges. We all need new horizons or our lives run the risk of getting stuck in a rut. I have to say that people who make assumptions about me don't really know me. Perceptions shouldn't become reality, whatever Ben and I might say to each other. Just at the moment you think you know who I am, I'll do something that will totally surprise you.

A lot of people fight against change. For me, I want change – though perhaps not in every part of my life. As far as my family is concerned, the only change I desire is to give them greater happiness and greater success. I want them to achieve things with my support, and my love and my backing. The whole point of everything I am and everything I do is to make sure they are well catered for – in this, I'm no different from any other family man. But for the rest, I like change and I'm comfortable with it.

Weston Spirit is totally about change, about throwing off your old self and exploring new universes. We see ourselves as a bit like Captain Kirk and his starship *Enterprise*, trying to boldly go where nobody has ever gone before. We're breaking into new ground and trying to experience new things for, with and because of young people. But that's exactly what I'm trying to do for the veterans of the Royal Star & Garter Home as well, and in my professional speaking and, indeed, in my whole life. People often think continuity is the most important factor. Well, there is continuity in constant change. You can find continuity and positivity in almost anything you want.

I could be wallowing in negativity right now because of what happened in the Gulf. But I'm looking up, hoping that we win the peace in a war I felt at the time we shouldn't have fought, not then at any rate, but we did and we must just accept that. Whatever problems our troops have experienced in the past with weapons and equipment supply, at least they've been brought out into the open and the old mistakes can't carry on as before. However disgraceful I find the court verdict on veterans and PTSD, and however deplorable the run-down of MoD medical and psychiatric facilities, at least the NHS has been given clear responsibilities to help psychologically damaged war veterans, and we won't let it run away from doing its duty. There is a positive side to everything. Everything has a good eventual outcome if you work at it hard enough. The problem is that too often we don't work hard enough at it, or we simply sit back and accept things as they are. It's like never thinking for yourself, never voting, always doing things because that's the way your parents did them, when it's much better taking things on board because that's how and why you want to do them, because you desire change.

Looking to the future, I see lots of new challenges coming towards me. There's a cartoon character I'm developing with Fitz and Pat Hill. Pat and I are talking about writing another thriller, and over the horizon there's the possibility of taking part in a car race from London to Sydney. The idea is to take an able-bodied and a disabled driver, so I'd be driving only half the distance. It would be great to go with a friend from the services, somebody like Rodney 'Wrong Charge', because then we'd know how to ignore each other's moods. You learn that in the military, how to ignore bad habits and just get on with it. If you have a falling out, you don't let it become personal. That's what relationships are all about, getting to know another person so well that you take no notice of their bad moods, which everybody has at some point.

Even further beyond the horizon, there's talk of making a film of my life, but as I know from past experiences, you can't guarantee something like that will ever happen. It would certainly bring my new life full circle, as it all started with another film, *Simon's War*, the first of Malcolm's documentaries. I would also like to explore working more in television and radio, on programmes not connected with the military. I enjoyed doing the voice-over commentary for *Simon's Heroes* and loved more than anything the fact that people told me they enjoyed it. Even Sir John Nott said he liked it, and it won a Royal Television Society award. When you get compliments about a programme from people in the military, you know it's not bad. When those compliments come from people who are professionally involved in the media, you know it's on its way to being quite good because they're looking out not just for subject matter but at the way content is presented.

Yes, I love all that and I enjoy working in the media. Lots of celebrities complain about the intrusiveness of the media but I don't see it that way. Without the media, none of us would be in the public eye. They help us tremendously and there has to be a quid pro quo. You have to give them something every now and again to help satisfy the voracious appetites of their editors or their programme controllers for stories. When there's something we want to put across to the public, they do us a good turn in just the same way.

As you'd expect from an ex-squaddie, I've had a lot to say in this book about war and its aftermath. So many tragedies have come out of the Falklands War and all the conflicts since – the people who have taken their own lives, the people who've died and the families who've been left in turmoil and torment. Out of all these conflicts, different individuals have risen to the fore, making the best out of their experiences and good luck to them.

Some people think that the price I and many of my colleagues paid was far too high but I don't see it that way, I genuinely don't. I see what happened to me as just another hurdle to jump. Of course, I didn't see it quite like that in the beginning. If I had only had in my youth the wit and wisdom that comes with experience I would be a millionaire by now. But riches are not necessarily what you have in the bank. I'm not sad or upset at what happened to me. Yes, in all honesty, if you asked me whether I would prefer not to have been injured, I'd be a fool to say I'm glad it happened. But as it did happen, I can only say that I'm glad I survived.

I've been very fortunate to have been surrounded by a number of wonderful characters who have added so much to my life. People could say that Carlos took a lot away from my life, but I would say he added a huge amount to it. Whatever the trials and tribulations of my injuries have been, they created a character that almost definitely would not have existed had I not been injured.

I know it has been incredibly hard for a lot of people – my family, my friends, Carl, Bobby, all the people who supported me through the worst of it, the chip-shop owner in Nelson and Franco, the café owner, who both used to send up goodies for me. I was in hospital and the village used to send get-well cards signed by just about everybody. Without all those people fighting my corner, always there to support and encourage me, I couldn't have turned myself around. There were times when I was terribly antisocial, foolish and ignorant. It wasn't deliberate. It wasn't the real me, it was something over which I had no control. I'm just so lucky to have survived and to have been surrounded by all those people.

Carlos and Graciela started the change in me, setting me off on a different path, but I had been supported for the ten years before I met Carlos by people like my surgeon, Colonel (now Brigadier) Bruce McDermott, the nurses and all the support staff at the hospital and the rehabilitation centre. There are far too many for me to thank them all individually, much as I'd like to.

Among the people who have really made a difference to me, Malcolm started the ball rolling. Without his dedicated support and excellence, I don't think I would have been anything because it would never have happened. Malcolm was the catalyst that helped create the Simon Weston of today. He passed me on to Geoff, who was a guiding light for many years and gave me the straight talking I needed to stop me becoming a complete and utter prat. He gave me guidance when I needed it, never peeled any eggs with me. I've been around people like that for a long time – Keith Cullen was another one – and I really appreciate it.

In later years, since I married Lucy, her mum and dad and their friends have been fantastic people and tremendously supportive. Frank and Julie have welcomed me into their family and that really makes a big difference; it could have been very uncomfortable for them, but they never made it so.

Lucy is without doubt the final piece in the jigsaw of my personal life, who added those even more recent pieces, our three great kids. Yet none of this would have been possible without Lofty and my Mam, whose support and love have been immeasurable. They made me who I am. They helped create the person who was fortunate enough to meet and fall in love with Lucy. They helped to fashion the person Lucy fell in love with. They made all this possible because they're the ones who really nurtured me back to health and life.

There's something very rewarding about my life, for me. Whether it is for others, I don't know. But for me it is good and the future looks rosy even if I have no idea precisely what next year or the year after will hold. They will certainly contain lots of new departures and possibly some more of the old things, but done in a different way. My life is irregular, constantly going back and changing and evolving into something new, again and again. A lot of the time I'm content just to see what happens. If you don't take a gamble on yourself, who else can you gamble on?

It's got to be an educated gamble, all the same. I'm not a hard man. I'm not a good-looking man. I'm not the funniest guy in the world, or the wittiest. But I do have certain talents – to speak, to project, to inspire, to connect, to encourage, to motivate – and if I'm going to get anywhere in life, I've got to use all those things to communicate as best I can. And really I'm so very happy with the way things have turned out. I'm so very lucky that things are the way they are, and that I'll be able to move forward for the rest of my life with a smile on my face, even this face that comes from my arse, as Lucy won't let me say any more. You only have to take one look at me to know that my chops will be forever grinning.